FAMOUS LAST WORDS:

"I Will Survive"

Christi Golden-Clark

ISBN: 978-1-63684-602-6   (Paperback Edition)
ISBN: 978-1-63684-603-3   (Hardcover Edition)
ISBN: 978-1-63684-601-9   (E-book Edition)

Some characters and events in this book are fictitious. Any similarity to real persons, living or dead, is coincidental and not intended by the author.

Book Ordering Information

Phone Number: 315 288-7939 ext. 1000 or 347-901-4920
Email: info@globalsummithouse.com
Global Summit House
www.globalsummithouse.com

Printed in the United States of America

CONTENTS

DEDICATION

I am dedicating this second book, as I did my first book, to my extraordinary granddaughter, Savanna Marie Hamlin, more affectionately known as Savanna Miracle. My goal for this second book is to show the reader the look of domestic violence up close and personal, to show how domestic violence can change a person and their life forever, to help Overcomers of Domestic Violence, and also to use the proceeds to help Savanna to meet her medical and physical needs—which are many.

On July 14, 1997 Savanna, nine years old then, was riding with me, Megan, her younger sister, her, Uncle Kevin and Aunt Chandi, in my minivan. In the blink of an eye, she went from laughing with the other three kids to lying on a hot, asphalt pavement of a parking lot. The blood-curdling screams from the kids, "Savanna fell out!"—made me stop. There she was, lifeless. I called 911, then her parents.

"911. What is your emergency?" the dispatcher asked.

I immediately told her, "I think I just killed my granddaughter. She fell out of my van and is lying on the hot asphalt lifeless. Send an ambulance right away, please hurry."

The ambulance came, but she was dead on arrival to the hospital.

Right behind the ambulance was the news crew from WLOS. Now it was turning into a three-ring circus. Police demanded

I get out of the van, but I explained I was on crutches, had no sense of balance and could not stand for long. They told me to stay in my van. They detained me for four long hours. I wanted to go to the hospital to see Savanna.

With one bad decision, she was gone. My mistake was leaving the sliding door open, even though I was moving slowly and in a parking lot. You never know when tragedy will strike. I prayed to God like I had never prayed before. She was in a coma for several weeks, but God was in control. He allowed her to come back to her mother, Annemarie, my oldest daughter, her dad, Tony, and little sister, Megan. Because of this horrific accident, I have made it my life's mission to help with Savanna whenever and wherever I can. The doctors said she would not make it, but God saw differently. I am happy to say, Savanna celebrated her thirty-second birthday in 2020. Savanna and I have gone through similar tragic events in our lives, and yet she is positive and uplifting. She is an inspiration to so many. She loves to meet people; she knows no stranger. She is smart, funny, and caring, but she can show her temper when needed. I look at her and have to think that what happened to me is nothing compared to what she has had to endure. Like the saying goes, "Walk a mile in my shoes." She and I went through her tragedy together. I feel so blessed that God gave Savanna back to us, as she was DOA on the way to the hospital. I owe Savanna everything and hope this book can help to get the things she needs. You are the Eighth Wonder of the World in my eyes. I love you, Savanna Miracle!

I would also like to dedicate my second book to my grandsons, TJ Hamlin and Kyle Logan-Lee Shope. I like to think they both take after me, with a typically German, blond-haired, blue-eyed look, and they're both very smart. TJ is Savanna's younger brother and has grown into such a fine young man. He is talented in sports and academics at school, making excellent grades. He has been taking all Honor classes since his freshman year and graduated June 11, 2016 with Honors. I am hoping he will continue on the path toward playing professional baseball. His two uncles, Vic and Kevin, also were extremely talented in sports, but never pursued professional sports after high school. TJ is gifted in many ways. He is kind, caring, thoughtful and smart. He plans on going to college to become an electrical engineer and taking over his dad's business of Tony Hamlin Construction, to make sure he has a bright future ahead of him. He even owns a 1974 Greenwood two of a kind Corvette free and clear. Not bad for a seventeen-year-old kid just fresh out of high school. I love you, TJ.

Kyle is my little man. I raised him from the time he was born until eight months old while his mother worked. After that, he spent every weekend at my house until Chris's birthday in 2012. He loved most going to Sunday School. He had many little friends there. He loved any church activities, including Vacation Bible School. When he wasn't at church he loved watching VHS tapes that I had bought for his mother when she was his age, like the *"Land Before Time"* series, the Walt Disney movies, and all the super hero movies. He could entertain himself for hours or interact with me while playing with his "Hot Wheel" cars and buildings. He enjoyed getting on my bed and using the remote to lift the head and feet, so I could read to him. He is such a smart little boy. He quickly learned his prayers—one before he ate and the other before he went to sleep. You will always have a special place in my heart. I love you, Kyle.

Lastly, I would like to dedicate this second book to my birth mother, Annemarie, the woman who gave me life. I started to look for my real mother at the age of 16. I didn't get very far since information was scarce back then. In the 1970s, I went to my neighbor, Mr. Fengler, who was also from Germany. He tried to help by writing letters to places like the hospital and police stations, because residents had to register every time they moved. He was not able to find her.

Luckily, I kept in touch with my cousin, Kathy, who was also adopted from Germany by my adopted dad's brother. She put me in touch with Leonie Boehmer, who did only German, Swedish and Austrian adoptions. In the late 1990s she took my information, which was not much, and started a search. I had my German birth certificate, which had my mother's name, my date of birth, city of birth and registration number. It took a couple of years talking back and forth, but she found a woman, not in Germany, but here in the states, with the same unusually-spelled name. She found, what I thought was quite a bit of information, and gave me an address. It took me a while to get the courage to write, but write I did, three pages' worth. My letter started out by saying very boldly, *I think you are my mother*. I got a phone call a short time later. It was my mother.

All the information turned out to be correct. The phone call lasted quite a long time with many questions from each of us. We made arrangements for her to come to Asheville from just before Halloween until after Thanksgiving. I got her a dozen roses, a small, black and white TV with a VHS player built in and many "old" movies she loved from the 40s and 50s. She shared Barbie Dolls with hand-made outfits and pictures. I was still skeptical, but when she showed me three pictures of me, I knew she was my mother, because I had the other two in the set of five. My dream had come true. Now I had someone to love me and I now knew who I looked like and found out there were no medical problems in my background. I also found out my dad's name. I immediately started a search for him. I did get some information from the US Government, but it was too late. He was deceased, but at least I now knew both sides of my family. I have three half-sisters on my mother's side and two half-sisters and two half-brothers on my dad's side. Thanks Mama, I love you.

I can't forget my beautiful and talented daughter, Annemarie, who helped me with both books. She is an amazing daughter, wife, mother, grandmother, and aunt. She was born out of less than favorable circumstances, but God has shown favorably on her and is truly an amazing woman. A strong Christian and an even stronger advocate for Savanna and Traumatic Brain Injury, she speaks for those who are not heard. She is a mama Tiger with her cubs. I don't know how I deserved her, but I am honored to be called her mother.

Annemarie, I love you so much.

PREFACE

I wrote this second book for all the women who have been hurt in some way, shape or form; the ones who are fighters and survivors, and even the ones who have lost their lives. This is for the ones who have been physically assaulted, used, mentally and physically, or sexually abused. There is no greater betrayal than that of the one who told you he loved you and yet hurts you. *Famous Last Words: "I Will Survive,"* tells in raw terms and descriptions what the abuser can do to us. There is no sugar coating or telling politely what horrible things we have endured. Today women have choices, safe havens and laws to protect them, unlike the 60s and 70s, but even in today's times, too many women are still dying at the hands of their abusers. In 1999 Cherica Adams was murdered by a hit man hired by her boyfriend, now ex- NFL Panthers player, Rae Carruth in Charlotte, NC. Another tragic death was Shelby Wilkie, on January 1, 2012, when her husband burned her body to ashes in Hendersonville, NC. She was an employee of the popular radio station Mix Radio 96.5. A twist on domestic violence was the shooting death of WLOS employee, Tim Fry, shot by his girlfriend in December of 2015 in Arden, NC. Being aware and educated means being forearmed. We must also be willing to make change happen. We must be strong and dedicated to our decisions. We must never take any abuse from anyone.

This is for all the women who are true survivors. Stand tall, be proud and don't forget, you are worth something to someone. Remember, you have always been loved by and seen as beautiful in the eyes of God.

I didn't think about it before, but I also want to address the abusers. I have wondered over the years just why you feel the need to be hurtful, shaming, and physically cruel to the one who you are supposed to love and care for. Why do you act out on these bursts of anger? Why do you feel you are right and we are wrong? Why do you not seek help when you know you are being an abuser? How do you live with yourself after being a big bully and striking out? Do you have no self-control? Is this what was taught to you as a child? If you have children, do you want them to grow up to be just like you? Do you know you cannot own another person? How would you feel if the tables were turned and we abused you? Would you like it or would you want the violence stopped? If you know you are abusing someone, then get professional help! Make a change!

Walk a mile in our shoes and I believe things would be very different. The abuse stops here and now. We, as a society, need to eradicate domestic violence from every corner of the world. Make love, not war. Give peace a chance. There is a thin line between love and hate. Give way to the downtrodden and broken hearted. Keep your obsession, anger, temper and jealousy in check. Domestic Violence stops now! Are you with me?

ACKNOWLEDGMENT

Annemarie, my oldest and most cherished daughter. Once again, helping me on book Two has been amazing. You have improved and learned so much, that you will have no problem when you help Savanna write her story. With me writing the basic lines and you tweaking words or lines, we make a phenomenal pair. It was hard for me to revisit some of the horrific events I had to endure, but you helped me get through the anger and the tears. I salute you for living your life honestly, caring, sharing and being an inspiration to so many people. I'm glad you got to know your dad, Victor Robert Golden, Jr. the good and the bad, through this book. He is missing out on a wonderful daughter, but that was his choice. You are a tower of strength. God is so proud of you, your choices and your accomplishments. Savanna is a true testimony of your love. Never change!

Mitzi, my dear friend from then and now. Once again you came through with information to add to my second book. Thanks for being there when I needed you. Your memories and descriptions added to the realness of the moment. Without you visiting me, while all the tubes and machines were hooked up to me, I would never be able to describe the sad scene. Even though I was in a coma, I felt your presence t and the warmth of your love and concern. You definitely aided in my recuperation and healing. I'm so glad we've remained friends all these years. Here's to 48 more. God Bless You and Yours!

James Leo Hemauer, thank you so much for allowing me to use your authentic photos of the infamous circular bed we both experienced, aiding in our recuperation. *On July 1, 1970, I awoke early to go to work on a farm just east of Plymouth, Wisconsin Going to "BAB" for a swim was the unanimous decision. I landed in 2-3 feet of water, hitting bottom headfirst. The impact was so violent it crushed the third and fourth vertebrae in my neck and severely damaging my spinal cord. I was paralyzed instantly, unable to move my arms or legs. Unknown to me, I had just become a C 3-4 quadriplegic. I had sustained a traumatic spinal cord injury. My life would never be the same.* To read more go to: http://www. public.asu.edu/~gimpy/The_Injury.htm. God bless you, James!

Kathy Gurzenski, thank you so very much for putting Leonie Boehmer and me together. It is strange how you found her in Albuquerque, New Mexico. Since we are cousins by adoption, she worked on both of our adoptions to find our biological mothers in Germany. I am so sad your mom died six years before you found her, but I am very fortunate to find my mother (who will be 92 in 2017) still alive and living right here in the states. I am honored to have you as my cousin and that we have kept in touch with each other throughout these many years. I never want to lose touch with each other. I love you, Cuz.

Emmett Armstrong, respected Detroit Police Officer with the Tactical Mobile Unit since 1967, during the Detroit 1967 Riots, was a wonderful consultant giving me accurate information. He told me the real procedures of what happened the day I was shot, giving me the color and make of the cars used, lingo used in that era and much other pertinent and invaluable information. He and his assigned partner, Ralph Craig, were the first to arrive on the scene of the shooting. Though he did not remember every detail, he did say that after leaving my scene he had eight or nine more shootings to go to that day. His mind and memory was incredibly sharp and accurate. He gave me invaluable information. He retired in 2001.

I salute you, officer Emmett Armstrong.

Again, I want to thank my copyeditor, Mirra Price, who has worked with the language in the book to make it convey more clearly my intention. She, a former English teacher and Harvard graduate, has painstakingly honed the contents to make this book better and more inviting to read. She has diligently worked on my two books and brought them to the polished and finished condition they are in. I definitely would recommend her to anyone who needs a topnotch copyeditor. Her services are well worth the money and more than reasonable.

You may contact her at info@mirraedits.com.

Once again, I would like to thank Evelyn Reilly for restoring the photo used for the front cover by removing the spots in the background and hat. She also scanned the interior photos so they could be blown up to fit a half and a full page of the book. She is talented in many aspects of restoration and graphics. If you are in need of this type of work, you may contact Evelyn at evelynreilly@gmail.com.

I must thank Mi Vosburg Kell for her services as my proofreader, finding those pesky little errors and missing words or letters. Thanks for your idea for the end of the book concerning what I am up to today. So many people have asked that exact question and now I have an answer. Mi is the now retired internet proofreader of Drs. Foster and Smith for eleven years. Just as important is that she is a dear classmate of mine from Dearborn High School. Thank you, Mi.

I cannot forget to thank all the police officers, phone receptionists, clerks and all other employees of the Detroit Police Department and Dearborn Police Department for all the help in gathering information to make the facts accurate regarding phone calls, emails and reports sent via US mail about dates, policies, laws, copies of reports and other information. My sincere gratitude and thank you to all, and especially to TMU officer, Emmett Armstrong, Mrs. T. Jackson, John Struman, and Ken Grod.

In Memory

My adopted parents
My adopted brother, Tony
Coleman Cobb
Jim (Papaw), Carolyn (Meme) Hamlin
MaKenna Faith Fore
Victor Robert Golden, Sr.
Anne, Glenn Lake
Richard Montanbault
George Lawrence DeAngelis
Patrick Joseph Neenan
Kathy Budai
Brian Zarbaugh
Brian Docherty
Terry Petersen
Albert "Bootie" Sabaugh
Jimmy Radoff
Det/Sgt. William Rushing
Judy Willyard Temple
Chris Stepchuck Bayoff Cain
Dennis Mitchell
Vic Hedges
Blake Bradley
Norman Robinson
David P. Bianco
Pat Stolte Lawrence
Jim Brock 3-31-68 Gia Dinh, Vietnam
James Hath 9-5-68 Quang Ngai, Vietnam
Larry Gambotto 9-13-68 Quang Duc, Vietnam
Tom Gentinne 5-12-69 Pleiku, Vietnam
Larry Shortridge
Annie May Golden
To All My DHS Classmates of 1965

CHAPTER 1

Another Shooting in Detroit

*2714 2nd Ave. Detroit, Michigan, scene of the attempted murder
by my husband, Victor Robert Golden, Jr.*

"Shots fired! Shots fired! He shot her! He shot her! Oh God, there's so much blood! She's not moving. I think she's dead. Oh God hurry. I think she's dead. 2714 Second Avenue. Oh God, please hurry!"

"Calm down, calm down," the operator on the other end of the phone said. "I'll connect you to the Detroit police immediately."

The operator connected the panicked caller to the Beaubien precinct.

"I have the Detroit police on the line, go ahead caller," the operator said.

A call came through to the main Detroit police, First Precinct, at 1300 Beaubien.

"Dispatch, First Precinct, what is your emergency?" the dispatcher asked.

"Oh God, come quick! He shot her! He shot her! There's so much blood. I think she's dead. Oh God, please hurry!" the caller screamed.

"What's your location?" the dispatcher asked.

"2714 Second Avenue.: It's the apartment building at the corner of Second and Cass. Just hurry!"

"Is the shooter still there?"

"No, yes, I don't know," the caller said in a very panicked voice.

"Hold the line while I send some cars."

"I need a TMU to 2714 Second at Cass. We have shots fired and one victim down. The shooter may still be in the vicinity," the dispatcher announced over the radio. "OK, we have two cars on the way. Please stay inside of your apartment to be safe."

After getting off the phone, the dispatcher called the local ambulance service. "We need an ambulance to 2714 Second at

Cass. A shooting victim. I don't have any more information at this time."

A car from the Tactical Mobile Unit (TMU), Officers Emmett Armstrong and Ralph Craig, were immediately dispatched to 2714 Second Avenue. They had their sirens blasting and their roof-top blue lights, or double bubbles as they were referred to, flashing as they raced to the scene until they came closer to the scene, then they shut off their lights and sirens, as not to alert the shooter.

Detroit Police Tactical Mobile Unit car
Emmett Armstrong and Ralph Craig

Regular Detroit Police patrol car

Officers James Brown and Curtis Bell were in the immediate area, so they responded also to help the TMU officers. They were informed that this was a shooting, so they would need to be looking for at least one gunman. Showing up first, Armstrong and Craig screeched to a halt in front of the building, while just a couple of minutes behind, Brown and Bell drove into the side parking lot, slammed on their brakes and hopped out to cover the rear of the apartment building.

"No way is he getting away," Officer Armstrong said to his partner.

"Clear in the back. We'll stay back here if anyone shows!" Brown yelled.

You could hear the dispatcher over the radios as he was trying to verify that the officers had made it to the scene and to find out if they needed anymore back up while talking to the officers on their Motorola Prep Radios. These radios were portable, but big and cumbersome, almost a foot long. Though big, they were an important piece of equipment for communicating between dispatch and officers.

Officer Emmett Armstrong, being a TMU, always arrived first on the scene and this scene was no different. He had his gun drawn as soon as he exited his car and slowly approached the apartment building. Slowly, looking in all directions, he climbed the cement steps to the front door. He carefully opened the door to check for anyone on the other side. His partner, Officer Ralph Craig, was right behind him. The body of a young girl was lying in a pool of blood. He looked for signs of life; the chest rising, some kind of sign of the girl still breathing. She was breathing, but just barely. He immediately got on his Motorola radio and called for an ambulance.

"I need an ambulance at 2714 Second Avenue at Cass right away. We have a young girl, a shooting victim. She's losing a lot of blood," Officer Armstrong said.

Then looking back at the girl again, he said, "Hey young lady, don't give up just yet. The ambulance is on the way and will be here in just a minute."

Seeing that the victim was still alive, they immediately started knocking on apartment doors looking for the gunman.

I felt the presence of God. I knew I was dying, but I felt such a serene calm, a feeling of peace. I couldn't move, open my eyes or speak, but I was able to rattle off the Lord's Prayer in my head and that in itself gave me the hope I needed to get to Heaven. I was so thankful for my Christian upbringing. It was all in God's hands now.

"You take the right side and I'll take the left side," Officer Armstrong said to Officer Craig.

Craig stepped around the girl, so as not to disturb the crime scene, and Armstrong knocked on the first door on the left, #102. No answer. Before he could knock on the next door, the door opened, but was chained.

"Anyone know who the girl is?" Officer Armstrong asked the person in apartment #104, peeking out of their chained door.

"Yeah, she lives at the end of the hall on the left, in apartment #108. I heard two shots fired. I think the guy is still in her apartment, some skinny, white dude in a brown coat," the tenant answered.

"Did you see or hear anything else?" Armstrong asked.

"No, just the one white dude standing over the girl's body and holding the gun like he was gonna shoot her again, only he didn't."

"Thanks, you've been helpful, but shut your door and keep it shut until it's safe," then Armstrong, taking his Motorola, alerted the other officers at the scene that they were looking for a white, skinny dude with a brown coat on. Since this went over the radio to other cars, also, any white, skinny or slender males with a brown coat on would be apprehended in the vicinity of the crime scene.

Officer Craig had knocked on apartment door numbers 101, 103, and 105, but with no answers.

Officer Armstrong went to the next apartment, #106, and knocked on the door.

"Detroit Police, anyone home? We need to talk to you," Officer Armstrong asked.

The door opened just a crack and a girl answered saying, "I heard the gun shots, two, I think. We just moved here and we don't really know anyone. My boyfriend is here. You want to talk to him?"

"Yes, he may know something," Armstrong said, but no sooner did he say 'yes', then a guy came to the door and said, "We didn't see anything, sorry, we can't help you," and closed the door.

By this time Craig had been to all four apartments on the right, but with none of the tenants being home, or at least not answering their doors. Officer Armstrong now only had one more apartment to go to, the victim's apartment, #108. Armstrong got on his Motorola radio and asked if officers Brown or Bell, who were still at the rear of the building and covering the sides, if they heard or saw anything.

They replied, "No one is back here. We still have it covered. We will wait for the all clear."

Officer Armstrong knocked on the door of the last apartment on the left, #108. This was the victim's apartment, according to another tenant. Armstrong had his gun drawn, leaning against the wall, as he knocked, not knowing if the suspect was hiding inside.

"Detroit Police. We got you surrounded. Open the door slowly and come out with your hands up," Armstrong said in a loud, deep voice.

From the inside of the apartment a female's voice said, "Don't shoot! Don't shoot! It's just me. Did you get him? Is she dead? Oh God, please help."

The door knob quickly turned, and the sound of locks being unlocked were heard. The door then opened as a slender, young lady stood there in her nightgown.

Officer Armstrong asked, "Who are you and what is your name?"

"I'm Peggy, Christi's friend. We work together. Where is she?"

"An ambulance is on the way to get her. Is anyone else in the apartment?"

"No," Peggy replied. "It's just me now. They were arguing at the door. I heard a gunshot, then she took off running and he followed after her. I heard another gunshot, so I jumped up, ran to the door to shut and lock it. Please tell me she is still alive."

Officer Armstrong said, "Go back inside and lock the door. Don't open the door and wait for the detectives. They will need to ask you a few questions."

Just then Peggy looked down the hall to her right and could see a body lying on the floor.

"Oh God. He killed her, didn't he?" she said.

"Ma'am, just go back inside where you will be safe. We haven't apprehended a suspect yet," Officer Armstrong replied.

As she turned and went back into the apartment, Officer Armstrong went back towards the front of the apartment building. As he walked down the long, narrow hallway, he noticed a set of stairs on the left, going down into what appeared to be a basement. While Officer Craig was checking all the upstairs apartments. Officer Armstrong cautiously went into the basement looking for the suspect.

After checking out the entire basement and finding no one, he gave the all clear to the other three officers. Officer Craig also gave an all clear for the upper apartments.

Another report of shots fired in Detroit came across the radio, so Officers Armstrong and Craig had to leave. Officers Brown and Bell came around to the front and stayed with the victim until the ambulance and detectives arrived.

Within moments, an unmarked police car arrived on the scene of the shooting. They were Det./Sgt. William Rushing and Det./Sgt. Robert Williams, both of the Detroit police. They had had their portable flashing red light on top of their car on, but no siren. Det./Sgt. Rushing, a seasoned detective and with the Detroit police since 1949, parked in the front of the building. He and Williams hopped out and went directly into the apartment building to officers Bell and Brown.

Det./Sgt. Rushing asked Officers Bell and Brown, "What do we have here?"

"We were unable to locate a gunman. The apartment building has been cleared. The victim's name is Christi Golden. She lives in apartment #108. She and her husband, who doesn't live here, were arguing in her doorway. He shot her at close range and then again as she was attempting to escape, her roommate told Officer Armstrong. Armstrong and Craig knocked on every door, looking for the gunman and questioning the tenants. An ambulance has been dispatched. That's all I know as of now," said patrolman, Curtis Bell.

"You said the victim is from apartment #108 and she has a roommate who saw who did this? Is the roommate there now?"

"Yes, Officer Armstrong told her to stay in her apartment and wait for the detectives."

"All right. We will go and question the witness," said Det./Sgt. Rushing.

A small crowd had gathered outside in the street and across the street and it was getting bigger by the minute. Officers Bell and Brown had their hands full with watching for the shooter and keeping the crowd back.

"Run! Move! Get out of the way!" the first ambulance attendant yelled as he and his partner tried to push their way through the crowd to make their way to the victim who had just been shot. They had showed up within three to four minutes after the police had arrived.

The call came in at just after 10:00 a.m. on December 18, 1969. The caller said, "Shots fired at 2714 Second Avenue and Cass, Apartment #108. One victim down!"

Oh man, there's so much blood! the first attendant thought.

"OK, at the count of three, let's flip her over and then lift her up onto the stretcher. One, two, three!" the second attendant yelled.

They picked up the stretcher, raced out the front door of the apartment building and down the front stairs. One attendant tripped on the cement steps, but he managed to catch his balance.

Overnight there had been only a light dusting of snow, nothing of any significance. There was no visible snow on the surrounding rooftops. The sky was gray, no sun beaming down, just an abundance of clouds. The trees and bushes looked naked because of the absence of any green, lush leaves and there were no flowers in bloom. The frozen ground was lifeless, just like the body of the young girl they were carrying. The dead brown grass was peeking through the tiny bit of snow that had fallen on the surface. It seemed as though all vegetation was dead to the world. They passed all the red and blue flashing lights from the police cars, shoved the stretcher into the ambulance, then jumped in and slammed the doors, so as not to waste any precious seconds.

The siren screamed at the traffic jam blocking the ambulance's way. The lights were flashing as the ambulance raced to Detroit General Hospital, running through red light after red light.

The first attendant placed a handful of cloths on the chest wound, applying direct pressure to try to stop the bleeding. The other attached an oxygen mask over the shooting victim's nose and mouth. He started an IV to keep her from becoming dehydrated, and took her vital signs. They had little information to go on except what the officer had told them. Since it was the middle of winter, he put a blanket around her, avoiding all the tubes, and covering her light-blue nightgown, which was soaked in blood.

"Her name is Christi Golden. She looks between sixteen and eighteen years old. It appears that the victim has two gunshot wounds. The first bullet seems to have entered into her chest, just missing the heart, and another bullet has entered in through her back. The front entrance wound looks as though it may have entered into her lung. Come on little lady, hang in there, don't give up. You have to fight, come on, don't give up," the first attendant said.

"Her breathing is very shallow and I'm having a hard time finding a pulse. Her blood pressure is 30/20," the second attendant said, as they continued on to the hospital. "We've lost the readings. She's stopped breathing!" the second attendant yelled.

The first attendant commanded, "Start CPR, and don't stop!" while still holding steady pressure on her chest. "We're not going to lose her. Come on man; we're not going to lose this one. She deserves to live. She's too young to die. Come on, keep it up," he said, with much determination in his voice as his partner performed CPR on the victim. "We're almost to Detroit General. Keep her alive!" he said, trying to stay optimistic.

"Hang on; we're turning the corner fast. We're almost there. Doctors are waiting for this little lady. God has to step in now to save this one," the second attendant said.

The ambulance screeched to a halt, with doctors and interns waiting with a gurney to take the patient out of the ambulance and rush her to the emergency room.

Meanwhile, back at the apartment building, Det./Sgt. Rushing and Det./Sgt. Williams went to the victim's apartment to speak with her roommate who had witnessed the shooting.

The detectives knocked on the door.

From within the apartment, a female voice answered very cautiously, "Who is it?"

"I'm Det./Sgt. Rushing, and with me is my partner Det./Sgt. Williams. We would like to speak to you about the shooting."

She quickly opened the door and let the detectives in.

"Do you mind if we sit down?" Det./Sgt. Rushing asked.

"Sure, I'll grab a couple of kitchen chairs," Peggy answered.

"Thank you. What can you tell us about what happened?" Det/Sgt Rushing asked.

"Well, it all started around eight o'clock this morning. Her husband, Vic, came over, banging on the door. When she opened the door to let him in, well she didn't actually let him in, he forced his way in. In the beginning, they were talking quietly; he was being nice. Something about maybe it was his birthday or something and he wanted them to be with him."

"He wanted who to be with him? You said he said he wanted 'them' to be with him." Det./Sgt. Rushing asked.

"Oh, they have a baby, a little boy. My mom babysits him. His name is Little Vic. He's a year-and-a half old."

"Do you live here with the victim? Are you her roommate?"

"No, I don't live here. We only work together and we were working today at the same place so she asked if I wanted to spend the night since I lived so far from work and we would go in to work together. I had no idea he was showing up here today."

"Oh, I see. Do you know what her husband's full name is?"

"All I know is Vic Golden. Her name is Christi Golden. The longer they talked the louder he got. He started demanding she pack up all her stuff and go back with him. When she refused, he started shoving her around."

"What do you mean shoving her around?" Det./Sgt. Rushing asked.

"Well, he shoved her over by the closet and demanded she get her clothes packed up. I was pretending to be asleep because I didn't want to get in the middle of it. I would open one eye and peak every now and again. She stood her ground, though. She was determined not to leave with him. She told me he was always hitting, pushing, pulling on her, but she would say she could handle him. The funny thing is, she always said they would get back together again. She really loved him, but why I'll never understand. I would never like a guy who was so possessive like him and hit me."

"Can you give us a description of him?"

"He's kind of thin, maybe 130 or 140 pounds maybe, I guess. Maybe around 5'10" or so. His hair wasn't real blond, more like a dirty blond. He combs it in a waterfall."

"Do you recall what he was wearing?"

"Yeah, he was wearing a brown coat. Well, I don't know if you would call it a coat. It wasn't long like a coat, it was shorter, but not as short as a jacket, but it was definitely brown. Is she going to be ok?"

"I'm not sure of her condition. They have taken her to the hospital, probably Detroit General. From the large amount of blood on the floor, I don't think she is doing very well. Do you know where he lives?"

"I don't know his exact address, but I do know he is from Dearborn just like her. She mentioned one time that he was living with his mother. Christi said his mom hated her. Vic was her baby and she didn't like the fact that Vic fell in love with and married Christi."

Det./Sgt. Williams interrupted, "Can you hold on, I am having a hard time keeping up with writing all this down."

"Sorry. Let's slow down just a little. Ok, you said her husband mentioned something about it being his birthday. Do you think his birthday is today?"

"I don't really know. They argued for a couple of hours."

"Well, today is December 18ᵗʰ. His birthday could possibly be today. Do you know how old he is or how old your friend is?"

"Not really. We've only known each other for four months. We met at work. She did mention he was younger than her, though. I remember she made the comment about she always attracted the younger guys."

"Do you know if he came alone or was anyone with him?"

"No, I only saw him."

"Do you know how he got here? Did he walk or drive?"

"I'm not sure. I assume he drove, though."

"Do you know what kind of car he drives?"

"He drives a gold Chevy Malibu with a black vinyl top."

"Do you know what year it is?"

"Nope," Peggy answered.

"Do you know or did you see the tag number on the car?"

"No"

"So, did you actually hear any gunshots?"

"Yeah."

"How many did you hear?"

"Two."

"Did you actually see him shoot her?"

"Yes, once at the door inside the apartment and then he stepped into the hallway, aimed and fired again, so I saw him shoot her twice."

"You said he shot her once while they were standing and arguing in the doorway here, is that correct?"

Det./Sgt. Rushing got up and walked towards the door, looking around for the casing to the bullet on the odd chance they might have been ejected.

"Yeah. I was lying here in the Murphy Bed so I could see all of him. They kept arguing. They started getting louder and louder. She kept telling him to leave and they could talk later. She kept telling him she was tired. We just got home from work around 5 a.m. She kept saying she would talk to him later after she got some sleep, but he kept demanding that she was going to leave with him. All of a sudden, without any warning, he pulled out a gun and just shot her. I don't even think she knew she had been shot right away because she was still talking for a few seconds. Then suddenly, she started screaming, telling me to get out, and then she took off down the hallway."

"Did they wrestle for the gun? Did your friend try to grab it or anything?"

"No. She must not have known he had a gun, let alone know she'd been shot. He took it out and fired it so quickly, she couldn't have known. Like I said, she even talked for a few more seconds before she looked down and noticed all the blood. That's when I think she realized she had been shot. It was right after I heard him say, *'If I can't have you, no one else can,'* and then that's when he shot her the first time."

"What exactly was she screaming?"

"She was screaming 'I've been shot!'. Get up! Get up, Peggy! He shot me!"

"And what did you do?" Det/Sgt Rushing asked.

Peggy said, "Well, after she started running down the hall, he ran to the door, stepped into the hallway and just fired again. Then he started to walk down towards her. I jumped out of bed and looked out the door. I saw her lying near the front door and he was still walking towards her. She was bleeding a lot. I freaked and slammed the door, locked all three locks and called the cops and told them she needed an ambulance."

"Do you think you can identify Mr. Golden?"

"Oh yeah, I have seen him several times at our work."

"I think we have enough information for now, but please do not leave Wayne County in case we need to talk to you again. Please give Det/Sgt Williams your name, address and phone number, so we can reach you. Thank you. You have been very helpful," Det/Sgt Rushing said very politely.

"Is she gonna make it?

"I don't know. It's in God's hands now."

With that said, Det/Sgt William Rushing and Det/Sgt Robert Williams were ready to head back to Beaubien to fill out all their paperwork. As they were leaving the building, a man approached them.

The man asked, "Who is going to clean up all this blood?"

"And who are you?" Det/Sgt Rushing asked the man.

"I'm the manager of the building. I guess she won't be getting her deposit back because I'll have to use it to clean up all this blood. Blood is hard to get out of carpeting, you know. I may even have to replace the carpet," he answered.

"You're all heart. Get out of my way. Stay out of our crime scene and if I see you messing with my crime scene, I'll have you arrested for obstruction of justice and tampering with evidence and whatever else I can think of, got it?" Det/Sgt Williams said sarcastically and with biting anger.

Back at the station, Det/Sgt Rushing announced, "I need to call the PA (prosecuting attorney) for a warrant for a Victor Golden in Dearborn." Speaking to Williams, "Can you give me all you can find on a Victor Golden and Christi Golden?

Anything; address, birthdate, vehicles they own, work place, anything you can give me. This may be a long night."

"I'll put all my notes in my report," Det/Sgt Robert Williams said, wanting this case to be solved.

After hours of working on the Golden case, Rushing yelled, "Well, it's about time. We are looking for a Victor Robert Golden, DOB 12-18-49, twenty years old today just like we thought, lives with his mother, Annie Golden, at 3841 Merrick, in Dearborn. He doesn't own a car, but the victim does, Christi Golden, a 1968 Chevy Malibu and I'll bet its gold with a black vinyl top. The Prosecutor's office is not open now, but first thing tomorrow morning, December 19, we'll have us a warrant and we'll pick this guy up and hear what he has to say."

The next morning, Det/Sgt Rushing went to the PA's office and got a felony warrant for Victor Robert Golden living at 3841 Merrick in Dearborn. The charge was *"assault with intent to kill with force and arms, in and upon the above complainant with a certain dangerous weapon, to-wit, a .32 caliber revolver in a dangerously wickedly and with malice aforethought, did make an assault with intent to kill and murder contrary to Sec. 750,83, C. L. 1948."* He called from their office to the Dearborn police and asked them to have a car meet them at the house. He picked up his partner, Det/Sgt Williams to go to Dearborn and arrest their suspect, Victor Robert Golden, for the heinous crime of attempted murder.

Vic's mother's house at 3841 Merrick
Dearborn, Michigan

1968 Chevrolet Chevelle Malibu Classic

One pair of Dearborn police officers and one pair of detectives from Detroit arrived and parked in front of the house at 3841 Merrick, Dearborn.

"Well look what's in the driveway, a gold Chevy Malibu with a black vinyl top just like our witness said. I know we are at the right place now. Let's go get him," Rushing said to Williams.

One Dearborn officer and Det/Sgt Rushing went to the front door and the other Dearborn officer and Det/Sgt Williams went to the back in case the suspect thought of escaping. Det/Sgt Rushing and the Dearborn officer both knocked on the front door, announcing their presence and that they were there to serve a felony warrant on Victor Robert Golden.

"Detroit Police and Dearborn Police. We have a warrant for a Victor Robert Golden," both officers announced while knocking on the front door.

The officers waited for a minute, but no one answered.

Rushing said to the Dearborn officer, "I'll bet he's here. That is the victim's car that our witness told us he was driving. We may have to use force to enter."

"Come out with your hands up," the Dearborn officer said loudly with his gun drawn.

"Victor Robert Golden, come out or we will kick in the door," Det/Sgt Rushing yelled, also with his gun drawn.

A guy came to the door dressed in a pair of pants and a white T-shirt with a pack of cigarettes rolled up in his right short shirt-sleeve. He looked like he had just been woken up from a sound sleep.

"What the hell you banging on my door for?" he asked.

"Are you Victor Robert Golden?" Det/Sgt Rushing asked.

"Yeah, so what's it to you?" the guy answered, obviously in no mood to hold a conversation.

Rushing replied, "You are under arrest on the charge of **assault with intent to kill and murder**. Come out with your hands up."

"Oh, hell no," was his answer and Vic attempted to slam the door, but Rushing caught the door before it closed.

Det/Sgt Rushing forced open the door and grabbed Vic by his T-shirt, pulled him out of the house and put him down on the front porch, face down. He pulled his handcuffs out and proceeded to put Vic's hands behind his back and handcuffed him securely.

Det/Sgt Rushing yelled to Williams and the other Dearborn police officer around back, "We got him. He's in cuffs. Let's take this tough guy in."

Williams and the second Dearborn officer came around to the front. Both Rushing and Williams had ahold of an arm and escorted Vic to the Detroit unmarked police car.

Vic started to protest, yelling, "Hey man, you got the wrong guy. I didn't do anything."

Rushing pushed Vic's head down to get him into the car and shut the door, which automatically locked.

Rushing asked the Dearborn police, "Will one of you come with me and my partner and the other stay with the prisoner? We need to go back into the house to see if we can locate the gun used in the shooting and any other possible evidence to link him to this case."

Many neighbors had their doors open to see what was going on.

One neighbor came over and said, "There is always trouble at that house. The way he talks to his mother, shameful, just shameful and how he treated that poor little wife he had, terrible, just no respect. What did he do this time?"

"Nothing ma'am, just go back into your house. We have this under control," Rushing answered.

"It must be bad if you had to send four officers out," the neighbor replied.

"Have a good day, ma'am."

Rushing, Williams and one of the Dearborn officers went back into the house with their warrant to look for the weapon that was used to shoot the victim. They searched the house; first the living room, then the dining room, kitchen, bathroom and then the back bedrooms. Looking in the rear left bedroom they found what they were looking for, a .32 caliber revolver with two bullets missing.

"Williams said to Rushing with a smile on his face, "I think we found our weapon. He took out his handkerchief to pick up the gun. Bag it and tag it and let's go. Some criminals are not very smart. Who hides a gun in a record case?"

This was their lucky day. Not only had they found the gun used in the shooting, but in the closet, they found a brown coat they believed he wore while committing the crime. Rushing and Williams drove Vic to the first precinct at 1300 Beaubein and took him directly to the interrogation room. The coat and gun was taken to the evidence room for processing.

Det/Sgt William Rushing was a white Detroit detective, about five feet ten and between 150-175 pounds, physically in good shape, dressed in a suit and tie and polished shoes.

"I'm going to start off by saying, we have eye witnesses who saw the whole thing up close and personal and several people put you at the scene. So, with that said, why did you try to kill you wife?" Det/Sgt Rushing asked Vic.

"Who says I shot my wife? Who says I even have a wife?" Vic asked.

"Who said you shot your wife? I never said you shot your wife, I only said you tried to kill your wife." Rushing said.

"Yes, you did. Well, I didn't shoot her or stab her or anything else," Vic quickly replied.

"Oh, you want to play games. Well tough guy, I got all night, but I really want to go home to my wife and kids. So, once again, why did you try to kill your wife by shooting her? Christi is your wife, right? You're a lucky guy to have such a pretty wife, so why would you want to hurt her?"

"All I wanted was to spend my birthday with my wife and kid. Was that too much to ask? After all, she belongs to me," Vic replied.

"So...you did try to kill her then, all because she didn't want to spend your birthday with you," Rushing said.

"I think she has a damn boyfriend that drives a blue GTX. Maybe he shot her. Have you ever thought of that?"

"Like I told you in the beginning, we have a witness who saw you shoot your wife, so let's cut the crap and get to the truth. So, why did you shoot her? Whose gun did you use and where is it now?"

"I don't know," Vic answered.

"Let's not play games. We have the gun and it won't be long before we get the fingerprints off of it and find out who it is registered to. It is registered, isn't it? Funny, the gun we found in your bedroom also has two bullets missing, just like your wife had two bullets pumped into her. So, why did you need a gun? You live in Dearborn, hardly a high crime area. You have neighbors who look out for you, as we witnessed today."

"OK, so I shot her. I didn't mean to. She really pissed me off. She wouldn't come with me. It was my birthday. Is that too much to ask? She belongs to me and she didn't need to be with that guy with the GTX and she didn't need to be around that whore who was at her apartment. Man, don't you understand? She's my wife, she's mine.

Det/Sgt Williams entered the room. He was a big, muscular, black Detroit detective, standing a little over six-foot-tall and easily near two hundred pounds, well-built and physically in shape, also dressed in a suit and tie.

He said to Vic, "You know, smart-ass, if she dies, you'll be looking at a murder charge, so you better pray she makes it. If she dies, we won't need anyone signing a complaint or pressing charges and you'll fry."

"Who the hell are you?" Vic asked

"I'm your worst nightmare, punk. Sit your ass down and you better try listening. This here detective is being nice, putting up with your crap, but I'm not him, so sit your ass down, shut up and listen. You'll have an arraignment, then a bail bond hearing, so now until then you're going to jail, compliments of the city of Detroit. Enjoy your stay and this ain't Dearborn."

"I didn't do anything and I'm not admitting to anything, so you can get the hell out," Vic yelled.

"You already admitted to shooting your wife and we have witnesses that saw you shoot her. Without warning, Williams got in Vic's face and banged on the table with his fists saying,

"What, are you stupid or just acting like it? We have an air tight case against you, but a confession is only icing on the cake," Det/Sgt Williams said to Vic, getting short tempered now.

"I don't need to listen to you stupid Detroit cops. You think you're bad, but you ain't. Need I remind you about the '67 riots. I rode right through the middle of that shit and I'm still here to tell about it, yeah, this white boy and my wife was with me. So, what do you say to that?" Vic asked.

"We got that under control just like I'm going to get this under control."

"Yeah, and it took you a week to do it," Vic answered very sarcastically.

"Listen up, you belligerent punk. You wouldn't last a week in Detroit, you little white boy from Dearborn. You can't even be a man. You got to beat up and shoot your woman. Yeah, you a real man alright."

Pointing to Rushing, Williams said, "Ask my partner to step outside for a minute and I'll show you who is bad and who ain't."

"You can't do that, I have rights," Vic said, noticeably shaken.

"Rights, you want to talk about rights? Where was your wife's rights when you gunned her down? She had a right to feel safe and she had the right to keep away from the likes of you. You seem to forget who is sitting in jail and who is fighting for her life. If it was up to me, you'd be hanging right now, no trial, no jury, just hung, like the old days. Where were her rights? You stole those rights from her. She's dying and you're still breathing. I don't see that as fair, do you?" Williams said.

"Hey man, get me out of here. This guy is crazy or nuts or something. He can't threaten me like that, can he?" Vic asked, looking at Det/Sgt Rushing.

Rushing replied, "I think you should cut your losses. We have you dead to rights with witnesses, the gun, fingerprints, your coat and your wife. You better pray she makes it is all I can say."

After hours of interrogation, Vic was finger-printed, had his mug shot taken and officially booked.

The next morning, December 20th, Vic was taken for his arraignment and bond hearing. The judge determined the amount of bail money that had to be posted in order to secure a release from jail was $50,000. December 20th was also the date of another special day. It was four years to the day that I had first met Vic at Blazo's on Michigan Avenue.

His mother was successful in coming up with the money needed to get her son released.

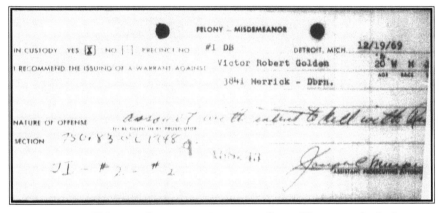

12-19-69 Witness list, eye witness, police officers and victim.

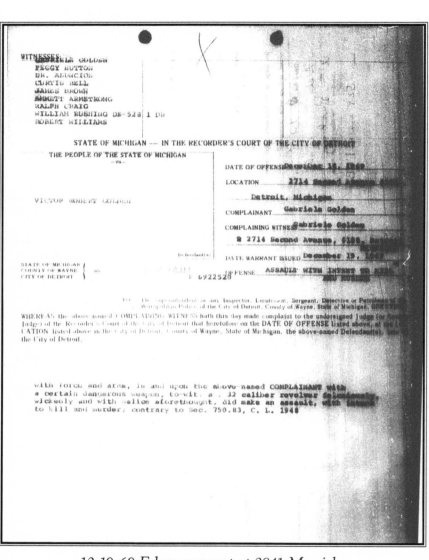

12-19-69 Felony warrant at 3841 Merrick,
for assault with intent to kill with revolver

30

Detroit Police Department

Detroit, Mich. December 19, 1969 19

The People of the State of Michigan
vs
Victor Robert Golden

IN THE RECORDER'S COURT

Defendant | Offense for which Defendant is held to Recorder's Court

E. BURKE MONTGOMERY, Esq.
Clerk of Recorder's Court

Dear Sir — The names and residences of the witnesses for the people in the above entitled cause are as follows:

NAMES		RESIDENCES
Gabriele Golden	Mrs. Complaining Witness	2714 Second #108
Peggy Hutton	Ms.	601 Brockton Madison Hts.
Dr. Asuncion	M.D.	Det. Gen. Hosp.
Curtis Bell	Patr.	#1 Prect.
James Brown	Patr.	#1 Prect.
Emmett Armstrong	Patr.	T.M.U.
Ralph Craig	Patr.	T.M.U.
William Rushing dec.	D/Sgt.	#1 DB
Robert Williams	D/Sgt.	#1 DB

Respectfully,

Det. Sgt. William Rushing, DB 528

Det. Sgt. Robert Williams, DB
#1 DB

Badge No. | Precinct No.

3-6-70 ...with force and arms, in and upon, the above named
complainant with a certain dangerous weapon,
to wit, a .32 caliber revolver feloniously, wickedly
and with malice and forethought, did make an
assault with intent to kill and murder.
Court papers for attempted murder for
Victor Robert Golden, Jr.

31

STATE OF MICHIGAN — IN THE RECORDER'S COURT OF THE CITY OF DETROIT

THE PEOPLE OF THE STATE OF MICHIGAN

– vs –

DATE OF OFFENSE_____

LOCATION_____

Detroit, Michigan

VICTOR ROBERT GOLDEN

COMPLAINANT_____

COMPLAINING WITNESS_____

@ 2714 Second Avenue, _____

(Defendant(s))

DATE WARRANT ISSUED_____

STATE OF MICHIGAN
COUNTY OF WAYNE
CITY OF DETROIT

INFORMATION

P 6923820

OFFENSE ASSAULT WITH _____ TO _____

IN THE NAME OF THE PEOPLE OF THE STATE OF MICHIGAN, WILLIAM L. CAHALAN, Prosecuting Attorney in and for the said County of Wayne, State of Michigan, who prosecutes for and on behalf of the People of the State of Michigan, comes now here in said Court in the current term thereof, and gives the said Court to understand and be informed that the above named Defendant(s), late of the said City of Detroit, heretofore on or about the DATE OF OFFENSE set forth above, at the LOCATION set forth above, in the City of Detroit, County of Wayne, State of Michigan

with force and arms, in and upon the above-named COMPLAINANT with a certain dangerous weapon, to-wit: a .32 caliber revolver feloniously, wickedly and with malice aforethought, did make an assault, with intent to kill and murder; contrary to Sec. 750.83, C. L. 1948

FILED

MAR 6 1970

E. BURKE MONTGOMERY

PER_____

and against the peace and dignity of the People of the State of Michigan

Dated by

William L. Cahalan
Prosecuting Attorney

To: DEFENSE COUNSEL: Please take notice that the People intend to use in evidence in said prosecution the following confessions and admissions obtained from defendant(s) by law enforcing officers and persons acting in concert with such officers

CONFESSION BY

ADMISSION BY

Defendant (Oral)

DATE 12/18/69

DATE

No. A

WILLIAM L. CAHALAN, Prosecuting Attorney
300 Police Headquarters Bldg., Detroit, Mich.

4-13-70 Prosecutor recommends acceptance of
guilty plea to felonious assault, signed by Vic's attorney.
Prosecutor recommends accepting plea of guilty

Date _____ 4-23-70 _____ Case No, _____ 158243 _____

People vs. _____ Victor Goode _____

Charge _____ Assault w/ intent _____

1. No reduced pleas _____

2. To be dismissed _____

3. Adjournment requested (plea or other) _____ *Shuttex*

   to date _____ A Fage _____ recommends acceptance of

4. _____

   (Assistant Prosecuting Attorney)

   plea of guilty to _____ Felonous Assault

   _____, which is an

    (a) included offense - Sec. ✓_____

    (b) added count - Sec. _____

    (c) maximum penalty - Sec. 4/yrs

5. I have been informed that the prosecutor will recommend the

   above mentioned plea. (Signed) (1) Wm Rushing

        (Officer in Charge)

I, _____, being the

defendant in the above entitled cause, having been arraigned therein

on the charge of _____

_____

and having had opportunity to consult with counsel do hereby

voluntarily offer plead guilty to _____

I realize that my lawyer discussed this matter with the Prosecutor's

office, and he did so at my direction. If a count is to be added

it is done at my request and with my full compliance; and I waive

any preliminary hearings I may be entitled to.

    (Signed) _____

          (Defendant)

    (Signed) _____ John Cloh _____

          (Attorney for Defendant)

4-24-70 Recorder's Court, Vic signs guilty to Felonous Assault
(premeditated attempted murder)

33

STATE OF MICHIGAN
In the Recorder's Court for the City of Detroit

THE PEOPLE

vs.

_____
Defendant

No. _A 158843_

Offense: _____

At a session of the Recorder's Court for the City of Detroit held in said city on the ___24___

day of _____ A.D. 19___

PRESENT Hon. _____
Judge of Recorder's Court

_____, being the defendant in the above entitled cause, having been arraigned therein on the charge of _____ and having had opportunity to consult with counsel, do hereby in open Court voluntarily waive and relinquish my right to a trial by jury and elect to be tried by a judge of the above named Court in which this cause is pending.

I fully understand that under the laws of this state I have a constitutional right to a trial by jury.

(Signed) _____

I have advised the above named defendant of his constitutional right to a trial by jury.

(Signed) _____
Attorney for defendant

The above named defendant signed his name to the foregoing waiver of trial by jury in my presence on the above recited date.

_____

5-22-70 Vic seek psychiatric help, support wife and child, no gambling.

CHAPTER 2

The Awakening

One doctor yelled, "OR #2 is ready for her! Hurry, we're losing her! I don't feel a pulse. Get the paddles now!" A nurse got the paddles ready as an intern tore my nightgown down the front.

"She's flat lining. Hurry, give me the paddles!" Dr. Asuncion yelled. "Clear!" as he zapped me. Nothing. "Clear!" he said, zapping me once more. "Again, clear" he said. Third time was a charm. Then he smiled because he saw my heart rate on the monitor.

I was then quickly taken to X-ray to find the exact location of the two bullets, and then back to the operating room where they transferred me from the gurney onto the operating table. I was found to have a collapsed lung; I was drowning in my own blood. I was lucky the first bullet hit my lung and not my heart. They inserted a breathing tube down my throat which they connected to the respirator machine. I was also connected to a machine to monitor my vital signs. My blood was typed and cross-matched immediately; a bag of life-sustaining blood was placed on the bag hanger and released to flow. The bag of glucose and water, which was attached to my IV, was hung next to the bag of blood. I had lost two to three pints of blood out of approximately eight in my body while lying at the feet of my assailant.

Dr. Asuncion operated on my left lung where the bullet had made a gaping hole by making an incision through my left side. He inserted a chest tube into my lung to drain the blood out. After several hours of touch-and-go surgery, he finally finished. Success!

"We lost her there for a minute, but we got her back with the help of God, some great nurses, interns, and her own will to live. Now that's what I call teamwork. Next time, let's not cut it so close. I don't like to sweat," Dr. Asuncion said, smiling calmly, addressing all the people in the operating room. From the operating room, I was taken directly to the ICU (Intensive Care Unit). Now it was all up to God.

"Let's get her to ICU. Now we play the waiting game to see when she wakes up. Comas are a funny thing. Sometimes you're out for hours, sometimes days or weeks and worst-case scenario, for years, but I don't think that's the case here. She should wake up in minimal time.

Where's her family?" Dr. Asuncion asked an intern.

"I don't think anyone is here with her. The attendants said they didn't have much information on her other than her name, Christi Golden, and she is approximately 18 years old. Her roommate didn't know of any family, other than her husband, and he's the one they think shot her," a nurse told Dr. Asuncion.

"Well, I guess someone will be calling and looking for her."

I had slipped into a coma for four days, but thankfully woke up because I still needed to have my spine operated on.

The x-rays showed that the first bullet tore through my lung, making a gaping hole. It then spiraled downward, broke my two floating ribs and lodged in my abdomen. The second bullet had fragmented severely in my spine at T-11. Machines and tubes were everywhere.

Since I was shot, I could not have been taken to a better hospital because Detroit General Hospital specialized in trauma and emergency situations, especially gunshot victims. History of DGH is unique, also. Ronald L. Krome, M.D., graduated from the Wayne State Surgery residency in 1969 and was assigned staff-oversight responsibility for the DGH emergency room. The American College of Emergency Physicians (ACEP) was also incorporated in 1969.

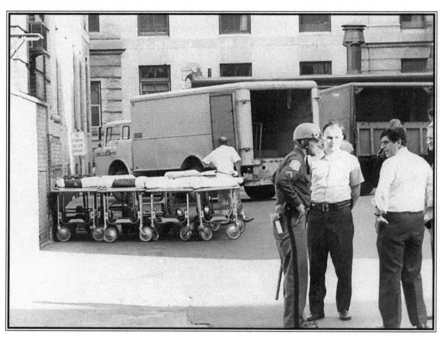

1967 Detroit General Hospital emergency/rear entrance

1970 Detroit General Hospital front entrance

Unbeknownst to me, Mitzi had come to visit me on December 19th, the day after I was shot. Mitzi was my best friend at work; she also had told me to go home with her the night before the shooting. If only I had listened to her, I would be walking today. She came to the floor where the ICU was located, but did not enter. She stopped a nurse and asked what my condition was and if they knew if I was going to make a complete recovery. She also inquired if she knew when I was going to wake up.

When she saw me lying in the hospital bed with all of those tubes and machines that I was hooked up to, she broke down and cried. She asked the first nurse if she could talk to my doctor to find out what damage the bullets had done. That nurse told her that no information could be given out to anyone about my condition and no one was to talk to my doctor about anything. Being just like me, headstrong and determined, she refused to take no for an answer. She waited just outside the ICU, watching for that first nurse to leave and the next one to come in. She then approached the next nurse to see if she could get any further information about me.

The second nurse, being much more cordial, explained to Mitzi about all the tubes and machines I was hooked up to. She told Mitzi about the first surgery on my lung and about the second surgery I would need on my spine. She also explained that the outcome looked good and that they were hopeful that I was going to live. However, it didn't look as promising that I would ever be able to walk again or live independently, but the first thing I needed to do was wake up from being in a coma. With that information, she decided to approach me to talk to me.

She said to me while sobbing, "Christi, I'm so sorry. I wish this never would have happened. I don't even know if you can hear me, but I've been told people in comas can still hear, so I hope you can hear me. I told you to come home with me, but you are so damn stubborn. I told you I had a feeling something bad was going to happen. Why didn't you listen to me when I told you I had a bad feeling?"

"You think you're so tough, but you're not as tough as you think—and this proves it. I knew when I saw your husband in the bar the night before, something was not right with him. He was so angry, so enraged. I could tell he loved you so much, and yet he wanted to kill you for not leaving with him right then and there. And I told you I heard him tell you, *'If I can't have you, no one else can'* either. I guess he meant it, because here you are fighting for your life."

"Come on, Christi, you gotta fight with all you got. You are a fighter and a survivor. You gotta make it. You are like a big sister to me and I don't want to lose you. It's me, Little One, talking to you. So many people from both bars are pulling for you. Some of them are here right now, giving blood for you. Come on, wake up. Show me those big, green, cat eyes. Please wake up. If you stop fighting and give up, then your husband will have won. But also, if you give up then who is going to watch over me and who am I going to joke around with at work, dancing on the tables and all the stupid things we did together? Besides, I still need you to drive me home after work."

Mitzi was desperately trying to lighten things up as she continued, "Listen Christi, if not for me, then you have to fight to live for your son, your baby boy, who needs you. You said to me more than once you didn't want your husband or his mother raising him, so don't give up. Wake up for Little Vic, your son. I'm sorry, but I can't keep it together, so I am going to leave for now before I break down completely, but I'll be back. I love you, big sis. You better be alive, awake, and making plans for you and your son the next time I see you, is all I can say," Mitzi said to me, trying to hold back the flood of tears.

I could hear her every word, but I couldn't move or talk back. *Was this real or was I only dreaming?* Everything was dark, black, billowing swirls of clouds, like I was sleeping, but yet I could hear the voices. I tried to open my eyes, but to no avail. I could see white noise every time she spoke. *Why couldn't I wake up?* I tried to move, to reach out to Mitzi, but I couldn't. I wanted to let Mitzi know I could hear her, and I wanted to let her know I was fighting for my life. I hadn't lost my will to live. I had the best reason ever to live—and that was my son.

In four days from the time I got shot, December 22nd, I finally woke up. I looked around and just knew I had made it to Heaven. Everything was white; all the surroundings, and all the people's clothes. I imagined the people in heaven would be wearing toga type clothes like in Jesus' day, not long blazers, pants, plain dresses and hats all in white. But it didn't matter. I made it to heaven.

Oh, thank you, God, I thought.

I tried to get up, but couldn't. I didn't understand. In Heaven, you are made whole again. *Maybe this is not Heaven, but Hell. If this is Hell, it's not hot like I pictured it in my mind. No flames, no one with pitch forks. So, where was I?* All of a sudden, without warning, I was in pain. That convinced me I was in Hell because Hell is all about pain and suffering.

"Oh, God, please forgive me. Please let me into your Heaven with you. I am so sorry for all the times I ran away from home and caused my parents anguish. And I'm sorry for stealing from stores when I was a teenager in junior high, and I'm sorry for telling any lies, and I'm sorry for taking my mom's Caddy during church service, and for not taking care of my younger brother, Tony, and I'm sorry for skipping school that one day, and oh, God please forgive me for everything I have ever done wrong. I can't take this pain," I silently said to God very sincerely as I desperately wanted and needed forgiveness.

Since I was awake now, they moved me out of the ICU and to a ward with eleven other female patients.

Tears were streaming down my face when I heard, "Are you Miss Golden? I am Det/Sgt Rushing, and this is Det/Sgt Williams. Today is December 22, 1969. We were here the day you were admitted and also yesterday, but you were still unconscious. We would like to talk to you about who shot you. We were able to obtain a warrant to arrest your husband; however, his mother had come up with the money he needed to bond out. We need for you to press charges or his attorney may try to have the case dismissed, and that is why we're here. A court date will be scheduled soon. We were looking at a homicide, but we're glad you made it. I guess you scared a lot of people. You've got quite a few friends here giving blood for you. You must have a guardian angel watching over you, little lady. Do you feel up to talking to us or would you rather us come back later or tomorrow?" Det/Sgt Rushing asked.

Right now I was in so much pain I didn't want to talk to anyone. I just wanted something to take this pain away. If I had to endure this pain, I wished I would've died.

"I can't take it anymore. Help me," I tried to say, but my words were not audible due to the fact I had a breathing tube down my throat.

I started crying again.

The detective said, "We'll come back tomorrow. Hopefully by then, they will have removed the breathing tube and we'll be able to better understand you. You take care and try to feel better.

CHAPTER 3

The Closing

It was two days after Christmas and a strange man approached me while I was lying in bed.

"Are you Christi Golden? My name is Nick Richards. I'm here to close on your house you purchased in October, 1969," he said.

I couldn't believe what I was hearing. There I was, dying in a hospital and they wanted to close on a loan I applied for back in October. *If that don't beat all. Well, if they are that dumb to allow someone who was dying in the hospital to complete the loan and finish closing on the house, while being confined to a hospital bed, then I'll do it.* I had no use of my legs. I had no job, and hence, I had no income. Roger Ward Babson (entrepreneur, 1875-1967) once said, *"The successful man is the one who had the chance and took it."* *This may be my chance,* I thought. I had bought the house in an all brick neighborhood where the elected mayor of Detroit, Roman Gribbs, lived. It was a three bedroom, all brick, one-and-half story house with one full bath, kitchen, dining room, living room with a natural wood burning fireplace, a finished full basement, a screened-in back porch, and a one-and-a-half car garage with a fenced in back yard.

My first house, the Detroit house

I had bought it in hopes that Vic and I would sort out our problems and we would become a family of three again. I certainly was making very good money between the two jobs I had. I was bringing home as much as fifteen hundred dollars a week, which was a lot of money for 1969. I saved every penny I made with the exception of food, rent and gas for my boss 1969 Plymouth Road Runner, and of course, for babysitters. Now, here I was with half a body, closing on a house I would never live in.

Someone once said, "Real estate is the best investment one can ever make." So now I'll see if they were right.

"Where do I sign?" I asked the loan officer.

"Right here, Mrs. Golden," he replied. He pointed to the line where it said, "Buyer".

"Do I get a copy?" I asked.

"You certainly do. Please remember to press hard because you are signing in triplicate. Now all you have to do is date it, December 27, 1969, and that will complete the transaction," he told me.

"Can you get in touch with my real estate agent?" I asked the loan officer.

"I'm not sure, but I'll see what I can do. Signed, sealed and delivered. You should receive the papers in the mail in about ten to fourteen days after they have been recorded at the Wayne County Building. Here's my card in case you need to get in touch with me. If I can be of further assistance, please let me know. Congratulations on the purchase of your new home. I hope you enjoy it, Mrs. Golden," he said.

He extended his hand, smiled, and then shook my hand. I could not believe what had just transpired. I wonder if anyone has ever closed on a house while they were dying in the hospital. I couldn't believe the bank would even consider allowing anyone to close on a house under those circumstances. No matter, I just bought myself a house. I was now officially a homeowner. That did sound pretty cool. This only gave me more determination to get better and get out of that place. In the meantime, I had to figure out a way to make my house payment or I would lose my house as quickly as I had bought it. I hoped Mr. Richards was able to get a hold of my real estate agent, so that he could find me a renter, and quick, who would make the payments until I knew how my situation was going to play out. That sure didn't take long, maybe an hour or so. Wow, the owner of a house at the age of twenty-two. Not bad, not bad at all.

Christmas had come and gone. On Christmas Day, I had been in the hospital for exactly one week, seven days. I had given Vic his presents early. One of the presents I got him was the expensive coat he wore when he came to my apartment and shot me. I felt bad I couldn't be with my son, Little Vic, so I could have given him his presents and watched the excitement on his little face while he was opening his presents.

It was extremely depressing to be laid up and unable to move. I never dreamed of starting the new year of 1970 in the hospital, or of owning a house, or for that matter, never walking again. That was a lot to take in. It was a lot for my mind to process. How could Vic do such a horrible thing like shooting me? No matter how much I hated a person, I could never, ever, ever take their life. I hated my daddy for how rotten he treated me, beating me all the time, but I would never shoot him. I could never shoot Vic's mother, even though I totally hated and resented her. No matter what Vic had done to me, I could never shoot him. Especially, since he always told me how much he loved me. You don't shoot someone you love. In fact, no man has the right to shoot another human being. That is up to God to decide when a person must die. God obviously had other plans for me because two bullets couldn't kill me.

"Thank you, Lord Jesus," I said out loud.

New Year's Eve arrived and a lot of my friends from work came by to say hello and wished me a 'Happy New Year' and a speedy recovery. Everyone was dressed so nice.

Mitzi looked especially nice in her beautiful red dress. With her red nails and lipstick, it really set off her beautiful, blonde hair. She sure looked different from how she normally looked at work. Diane and Kathy looked nice in their beautiful party dresses with all the accessories and Ron and Frank looked so handsome in their rarely worn suits. They all came by to see me before they went out to party to bring in the New Year, 1970.

Mitzi was most definitely my best friend at work. In my opinion, I thought she was cute and bubbly, the darling of the bar scene. I would say beautiful, but I think of beautiful as women like Sophia Loren, Elizabeth Taylor and definitely Marilyn Monroe. We always competed in fun against each other for who was the best dancer, who could carry the most drinks, which she always won, and who got the most tips. But outside of work, she was just like me; she was a mother to a little boy she adored.

I liked Diane, who was also a good friend and co-worker of mine. Kathy, well... we also were co-workers, but I always felt she was a little jealous of me. Jealous of what, I wasn't sure, but it seemed like she always needed to compete against me. I'm not sure if I was right, but I just got that feeling. Ron was the head manager of the Red Umbrella. He looked out for me when I was at work. He even threw out a paying customer once because he slapped me on my derriere, or in plain English, my ass. He also gave me the idea to tell the bartender to use just plain OJ when making me a screwdriver, bought and paid for by one of the paying customers. I didn't drink, nor did I smoke.

It was great to see my friends, but really depressing when they all left my bedside. Then I had nothing but time to think of what a crummy life I had to look forward to, or ways to end it all.

Yes, suicide had entered my mind more than once, but each time I thought about it, I looked over at my neighbor in the bed next to me. I think I figured out why she was not taking her pills; she was hoarding them in a plan to commit suicide. It got to the point where I watched her all the time. I felt so sorry for her, this little, elderly, colored lady. Only one young woman came to visit her, which was the hospital librarian. So many times, I wanted to say something to somebody, but she made it very clear it was none of my business. All I could do was watch and wait to see what was going to happen. I think she gave me the idea unconsciously, because I was starting to hoard my pain pills, too. Then I would start to think of Little Vic and how I could not leave him behind to be raised by Vic and his awful mother.

I was coming back from physical therapy, PT, as they called it. There were two men waiting for me in suits, I didn't have to wait to find out who they were or what they wanted.

"I'm Det/Sgt William Rushing and he is Det/Sgt Robert Williams; remember us? We're here to talk to you about the shooting. We've been here before, but we keep missing you. We have identified the weapon as a thirty-two (.32) caliber revolver, which is registered to one Annie May Golden. I assume that is your husband's mother?" Det/Sgt Rushing asked me.

I thought to myself, *if she lives in Dearborn then why does she need a gun? It's not like they live in Detroit, which is known as the Murder Capital of the World.*

"We are charging your husband, Victor Robert Golden, Jr. with *"attempted murder with malice and forethought did make an assault with the intent to commit murder and do great bodily harm with a .32 caliber revolver."* He was apprehended the next day at his mother's house and was taken to the Detroit Jail. We would like you to sign this complaint. Had you died, we wouldn't need your signature, because he would've been charged with murder. I understand you are lucky to be alive, young lady. So, we are here for you to sign this official complaint. We are going ahead and pressing charges and setting a trial date." Det/Sgt Rushing said.

"I can't," I said, as I started to cower.

"What do you mean you can't? The man tried to kill you; do you not want him to serve his time for his crime? You better think long and hard on this one, Missy. The man deserves to rot in prison. This was premeditated attempted murder. He meant to kill you, to end your life forever. Do you not understand the ramifications of his actions? Ma'am, if you were my little girl, believe me, he'd be under the jail, no trial needed. He deserves to be punished. He didn't shoot you in the head, did he?" Det/Sgt Williams asked with a sarcastic tone in his voice and was getting a bit short tempered because of my refusal.

"No," I answered.

"Well then think about what you are doing," he said to me very sternly.

I could tell Det/Sgt Williams was really mad at me, but he didn't understand. He didn't know Vic like I did. He didn't know how violent Vic got with his mood swings. He acted like he was just plain nuts. He didn't know how Vic abused me in the past. He didn't know Vic's temper. He didn't know that he was the kind, if he went to prison, he would finish the job when he got out. And he would get out, in four short years, since I didn't die. He would probably get out early for good behavior, because Vic could put on a good act just to get what he wanted. The police couldn't guarantee my safety or the safety of my little boy, the only family I had in the whole, wide, world now.

"I *am* thinking, and that is why I can't do or say anything against Vic. You will never know the fear Vic has instilled in me. I know firsthand because I've had to live with him and his uncontrollable temper. I want to live to see my little boy grow up. I am too afraid that Vic will come back and finish the job the next time, and there will be a next time, and I won't be so lucky, I'll be dead." I told Det/Sgt Williams.

"Why didn't you leave him?" Det/Sgt Rushing asked me.

"I did. Why do you think I was at the apartment? I lived there because I left him," I answered Det/Sgt Rushing, hoping he would understand.

"Ma'am, the best thing you can do is be in court as the complaining witness for the prosecutor's office and have him put in prison as long as the law will allow. This will keep him from hurting you, or maybe some other unsuspecting woman," Det/Sgt Williams said.

"Then what? Live in fear while he's in prison, waiting for him to get out? No thanks. I want to end this here and now before he does kill me. He is very possessive. He can charm the socks right off of you. He's a Dr. Jekyll and Mr. Hyde, and you never know when the Jekyll will come out. His whole family is nuts," I tried to explain to Det/Sgt Williams.

"All the more reason to put him away for good, or at least a good, long time," Det/Sgt Williams said to me.

"I believe Annie May Golden, his mother, brainwashed him against me and deliberately let him know where that gun was being kept. She probably bought the gun, knowing with enough antagonizing; he would snap and go after me with the gun. She is that kind of sadistic person who would do that to get me out of her son's life. I'm sure she didn't come right out and tell Vic to shoot me, but I'm sure she told him something like: "Chris is whoring around on you. Are you going to let her get away with that? She has taken your son and ruined your life. Stand up for yourself. Be a man. Put her in her place and get your son back." I can see her saying those things. I guess I just need to hear from Vic's lips how he got the gun and why he shot me. Not going with him on his birthday is just too trivial of a reason to shoot someone. Something or someone triggered him to act like a killer, a glorified hit man," I told Det/Sgt Williams.

"She said all that?" he asked.

"Well, I don't know, but I'm sure she said things like that to my husband. I'm sure she poisoned his mind against me. I believe she drove him to shooting me. I blame her for half of all this. She never had a gun in her house before, or at least she never told anyone. And why did she even need a gun? She lived in Dearborn, for God's sakes, hardly a high crime city, not like Detroit. She had a dog there and also had a roommate with a kid. So, she was never alone. My husband and his sister also lived with her. So, as far as I'm concerned, she had no reason to own a gun.

"OK, you make some good arguments."

"Are you getting the picture yet? I can't press charges because I can't jeopardize my life or the life of my little boy. I owe it to him to protect him. I'd like to press charges on her! Is that possible?"

Det/Sgt Rushing., in a very serious tone of voice, said to me, "No, I'm afraid that is not possible, but I understand what you are saying," takes a breath and then continues,

"I'd just like to see all these bastards; the ones who beat up, abuse, and especially the ones who kill women, never see the light of day. You're sure I can't change your mind?" Det/Sgt Williams said.

"I'm sure."

"You know; I have a daughter just about your age. She is the most precious thing to me. I wish you the best, but if you ever change your mind, let me know," Det/Sgt Rushing interjected.

"Come on. We've got reports to file. We have to go. Remember to contact us if you change your mind," Det/Sgt Williams reminded me.

"I hope everything turns out all right."

Det/Sgt Rushing touched my lower leg and then looked at me, as if to say, *"Hang in there."* He turned around, pulled the curtain back, walked to the entrance of the ward and then both detectives disappeared around the corner.

Now I had to deal with my conscience. *Was I making the right decision? Should I have pressed charges against Vic? Should I have stood my ground? Was I really that afraid?* All my life, I was never afraid of anyone or anything. Even when Vic hit me, I hit him back, but somehow this was different. Maybe it was because I had a baby to think about. It was not just me anymore. I had to protect Little Vic at all costs. I wished I had never met Vic. No, that's not true because then I wouldn't have my precious son. Little Vic meant the world to me. I would lay down my life for him. On the other hand, I didn't want to take away Little Vic's father. A child needed two parents, two nurturing parents. I wasn't sure. I wished someone would give me the right answer or let me know what I should have done.

I cried out loud, "Oh Mommy, please help me and tell me what to do!"

Tears welled up in my eyes so much, it seemed like a curtain of rain was blinding me.

Simone Elkeles said, *"There is a thin line between love and hate. Maybe you are confusing your emotions."*

No truer words were ever said. She was right on the money. What a great quote. I thought to myself, *Am I confusing my emotions? Could I still love Vic? No, that was too absurd. How could I love him after he tried to kill me? Was Vic still in love with me, in some twisted way?* All I knew was that I was confused. Here I was, lying in a hospital bed with the wounds of the aftermath of Vic's rage. What I realized, but didn't understand, was this tragic event happened on Thursday, December 18, 1969, which was Vic's twentieth birthday. *Why did Vic pick his own birthday to carry out such a horrible, evil, and tragic plan?* Birthdays are supposed to be such happy occasions, but this birthday was anything, but happy! *How could two people tear each other apart so badly?* Vic ruined three lives that fateful day; his, mine, and our son's. Things would never be the same, not ever! How could one person be so controlling over another and then try to kill them? I didn't understand it.

Marriage is like a garden; it must have the proper amount of rain and sunshine to flourish. You must also have the proper tools to plant, prune and clear out strangling weeds, so the garden can grow. So, with marriage, you have to work at it to keep it alive. There must be happy with sad, good with the bad, and you must have the proper tools to fix things when they go wrong. I didn't think Vic and I had the proper tools to fix things.

I grew up in a family where the man was dominant and sometimes violent. Vic came from a broken home where the mother would over-indulge her son and would never give him up to another woman, namely, me.

As long as Vic remained under his mother's influence, he would never be able to breathe. He would never be able to be his own person, to be independent. He would never experience real love and joy, family togetherness, real happiness and most of all, the blessings God has always wanted for all of us. Lying in a hospital bed gave me time to think and reflect. What if I would have done this instead of that, or not done that or done things differently? How would it have all turned out? There were many things I would have changed in my life. Then there were things I would have done exactly the same.

One thing was certain in my mind—his mother was the root of all evil, or should I say, to most all of our problems. She was divorced from the man whom she obviously never wanted to give up. Funny thing is, I never, ever heard her tell Vic or Vickie "I love you", nor did I ever see her kiss either of them. She always seemed like a very cold person to me. I, on the other hand, was the total opposite, I was always telling Vic and Little Vic I loved them and I kissed both of them a lot. I was a very affectionate type of person. I loved hugging, kissing, and holding hands, Vic's arm around me, all the little signs that told someone you loved them.

Yes, being in a hospital, gave me a lot of time for soul searching and reflecting on my life. With 1969 closing, and this chapter of my life closing, I had to start to try to build a new life. My life was forever changed in the blink of an eye. Vic did the deed and I will pay with my life, for the rest of my life. Was it fair? No! But then life was not always fair. I found out first hand that God is the final closer! Only He will decide when the final chapter of my life will close permanently. Fighting against all odds, even two bullets couldn't stop me. That told me in no uncertain terms that God had other plans for me and I needed to go forward, full steam ahead. No closure for me.

CHAPTER 4

The Circular Bed

I f I had to be in the hospital, then January, 1970 was the perfect month. I had been in the hospital for two weeks now. Not much was happening in the dead of winter, at least not for me. The only thing I could think of was snow skiing, but I never learned to snow ski, so I didn't miss it. I had learned to ice skate, which I did miss and also going tobogganing. I would get woken up at 6:00 a.m.; take pills and then lay in my bed doing nothing except watching my favorite programs on my little TV set. This was my routine. Thank goodness for my TV, or I would have been bored out of my mind. The pain hadn't gone away and my legs would start shaking for no apparent reason.

"What is going on? Take the pain away!" I screamed.

I screamed so loudly that I'm sure they heard me on that whole floor of the hospital where I was. It took a long time for a nurse to come.

"Can I help you? What do you need?" my nurse, Angela, asked.

"I need this pain to stop; I can't take it any longer. I can't feel my legs, yet they hurt and so does my chest," I told her.

"I'll check your chart to see when last you were given some pain meds," she answered.

"Why are my legs shaking so bad?"

"They are called spasms. I'll ask your doctor about getting you a prescription to calm the spasms. Anything else I can get you?"

"Not right now, thanks."

All I did was lie there. The doctor forgot to tell me, but there is something attached to the inside of my private part. I felt like I had to go pee really badly, but I couldn't go.

I yelled again for a nurse, "I need help. I need to use the bed pan and I still need pain medicine."

Why does it take so long to get someone's attention? I thought. When a nurse finally came, I asked why it took so long for her to get to me.

"We're short staffed and the nurses' assistants are on strike," she told me.

"So, what does that mean?" I asked her, being puzzled about a strike by the nurses' aides.

"It means we can't get to each patient immediately. We get there as quick as we can," she informed me.

"I still need to use the bed pan and I still need some pain medicine," I told her, in a bit more urgent tone of voice.

While the nurses' aides were on strike, I received really bad care; as far as being moved, or changed, or being able to use the bed pan. I had to use a catheter in order to eliminate my urine, but I still needed to use the bed pan for my bowels. When I asked for the bed pan, once again, I was told by the nurse they could not help me because it was not their job, but the job of the nurses' aides. Well, that did me no good. I had no control and ended up lying in my own shit, feces, or diarrhea, whatever you wanted to call it. It was three days before anyone changed me or my bed. I didn't know it at the time, but I ended up with severe bed sores because I had no feeling from the waist down. I did feel pain in my legs, though.

"The strike should be ending soon and we will have many more staffers back to work," a nurse informed me.

"Well, you should make some kind of arrangements for patient care. This is ridiculous."

The nurses wouldn't do the jobs of aides, which was also ridiculous. I didn't have any feeling from the waist down, so I didn't know if something was hurting or being injured. That's why I have these bed sores on my rear end and because I didn't feel the pressure, especially while lying in my own crap for three days. *That was really great care. I hurt so badly, that I just can't take it anymore. It's too much for me. Please give me something, anything,* I thought to myself.

"My legs are shaking and I can't feel anything below my waist," I said.

"You are what is called a paraplegic. It means you are paralyzed from the waist down and don't have use of your legs. The young girl across from you is only twelve years old and broke her neck diving into a pool. She is now considered a quadriplegic. She has no use of her body from her neck down," my nurse, Angela sadly told me.

"I'm sorry about the young girl. At least I had a life until the age of twenty-two," I said.

"Yes, you never miss anything until you lose it," she replied.

I was feeling sorry for myself until I heard about the twelve-year-old little girl. Now, I felt bad for her. At least I could move all of my upper body; my arms, hands, and head.

Angela then told me I would be put on the circular bed. She said it was to get me off my butt since I had developed some bed sores.

"Oh great, bed sores, that is just what I needed," I said.

"Someone will be up in just a minute to get you. They will take you to the physical therapy room. That's where they keep the circular bed. I think you'll like it. You'll feel much better when they flip you over and off your bottom," Angela said to me.

She was right. In a matter of a few minutes a big, jolly, colored lady came to get me.

"Are you Mrs. Golden?" she asked.

"Yes," I answered and then asked her, "What is your name?"

"My name is Minnie. They call me Skinny Minnie. The name fits, don't you think?" she said, and then laughed.

I looked back at her and couldn't help, but start laughing too.

"Well, Honey, I'm going to take you on the ride of your life. You are going to the circular bed and that is a trip in itself," she told me very excitedly.

"What do you mean?"

"Just wait and see, Honey"

She rolled me down the hall, into the elevator and went down to the physical therapy floor. She rolled me out of the elevator and down to the end of the hall and turned left into the PT room. There it was. It was a huge Ferris wheel, with a bed mounted smack dab in the center of the spinning wheel. Actually, it looked like a gigantic hamster treadmill with a bed in the middle. The bed sandwiched you between two boards. The top board was identical to the bottom except it had a hole cut out of it for your face, so that you could breathe when flipped onto your stomach. When it rotated, you ended up flipping onto your stomach, placing you face down in the hole.

"How does it work?" I asked.

"The bed rotates inside the huge circular bars. It's for patients with spinal injuries, who can't be moved, patients in traction, or with severe burns, and patients with severe skin conditions."

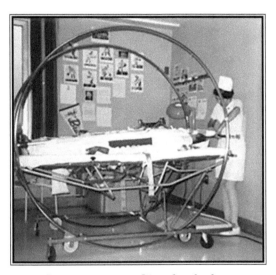

January, 1970 Circular bed--1

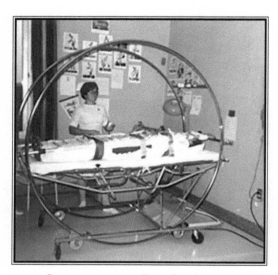

January, 1970 Circular bed--2

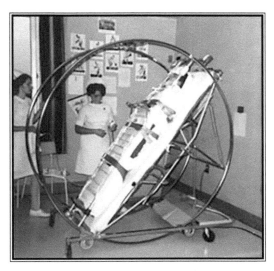

January, 1970 Circular bed--3

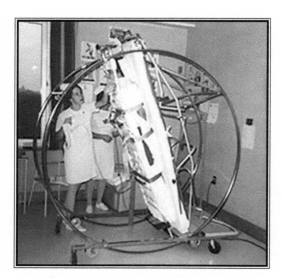

January, 1970 Circular bed--4

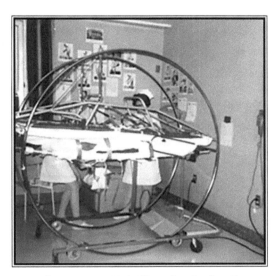

January, 1970 Circular bed—5

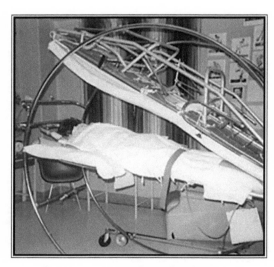

January, 1970 Circular bed-- 6

"I guess that qualifies me," I replied.

"Can I get some help over here? I have Mrs. Golden here needing to use the circular bed," Minnie announced to everyone in the room.

A man, who was helping another patient walking in the parallel bars, said, "Hold on and I'll help you. Let me get my patient back to her wheelchair."

"You got to hurry because I don't have all day," Minnie said in a kidding way.

"How long do I have to stay on that bed?" I asked her.

"We'll see how long you can tolerate it for your first time."

"Will it make me sick?"

"No, it shouldn't, but it sure will make your little behind feel a lot better," she interjected.

Staring at that monstrosity, I was beginning to get a bad feeling, even before being put on it.

"OK, what do you need and what can I help you with?" the man asked.

She said, "I need you to help me put Mrs. Golden on the bed. We'll transfer her on the count of three. One, two, three."

And over I went onto the circular bed. It felt comfortable enough.

"Thank you, John," she said.

"You're more than welcome," he replied back to Minnie.

Minnie put a sheet over me and then strapped me in. I wondered why I needed straps. I guessed that I would soon find out. The bed started moving and literally turned me upside down.

"I'm getting sick," I said to Minnie.

"What kind of sick? Throw up sick or light headed sick?"

"Both!"

There was a hole for my face to fit in. All of a sudden, I threw up, and I felt dizzy too. I stayed on the circular bed for only a short time, maybe a few minutes.

"That went well, don't you think?" she asked me.

"Not so well," I replied.

"You'll get used to it. You probably haven't been on your stomach for a while, have you?"

"No, I have only been on my back."

John and Minnie got me turned back again and they proceeded to get me off the circular bed and onto the gurney. The next day, when I was on the circular bed, I didn't throw up much, but still got dizzy. The following day I didn't throw up and felt hardly dizzy at all. Well, just a little.

I picked a great time to be in this hospital. The nurse's aides went on strike and the nurses would not do the jobs the nurse's aides were required to do. I guess it was beneath them or they thought they were too good. I didn't know what their deal was. I knew how I got the bed sores. I lay in my own shit because the nurses wouldn't give me the bed pan to use, so I went in my bed. Then they wouldn't change my bed, so I lay in the shit for three days before someone did change my bed. Ain't that a crock? They have gloves to use, so I don't know what the big deal was. If they would have given me the bed pan in the first place, I never would have made a mess, never mind the embarrassment I felt. Somehow, I made it through that ordeal. My heels were getting pressure sores on them too, but my nurse did put a pillow under my feet, so it would keep my heels from resting on the bed. That got pretty painful. And my feet would turn in and I developed drop foot. I had developed all kinds of new problems, all stemming from my immobility due to my spinal cord injury.

I thought to myself and then said out loud, "Thanks Vic, thanks a lot!"

Though I was enduring all this physical pain, I continued to have flashbacks of Vic and his psychotic family. Annie was not an affectionate type of woman. I had never seen her kiss or hug Vic or Vickie. I never heard her say to either of them, "I love you." She over-indulged them, and aware or not, she dominated their lives. She also picked her favorite, Vic, while Vickie was always pushed to the side. Vickie was not the pretty little girl that all mothers dream of having. She had no drive to accomplish anything in her life. Both of her children were failures in love. Both children, though they were twins, were as different as night and day. Vic was the good looking one, the one who had a lot of friends and many girlfriends. On the other hand, Vickie was more of an introvert and had more visible mental problems and no boyfriends. Anything could set her off. She would tell a story that would be extremely exaggerated and yet she really believed what she said. I see great similarities between Vic and Vickie, too.

I wish I had known this from the start. He had deep-seated, emotional problems, which he kept hidden, but the signs were there. I just didn't see them, or didn't want to see them. Thinking back, it was all so visible; the little squirrel shot and killed in his mother's living room, the cats he hung and set on fire from the clothesline I was told about, the fights he had with his sister, the drinking, the physical abuse I suffered at his hands. All these were some kind of psychotic episodes. A cold chill traveled down my spine just thinking about all these horrible events. I am no psychiatrist, but I now saw the damage a person like that caused around them. It was like a volcano erupting and it destroyed all things in its path with no pity; no remorse, just destruction; and devastation lasting a long time, sometimes forever.

"Mrs. Golden, are you all right? It's time to take your meds," my nurse, Angela, informed me.

Thankfully interrupting my thoughts, I answered, "I'm glad you're here. I was really getting sad and depressed about my life. I hope you have some pain meds for me because my legs are shaking again and yet I can't feel them. What are they giving me for my leg shakes anyway?"

"You're getting five mg of Valium. What color is the pill?" the nurse asked.

"Yellow," I told her.

"Yes, that is five milligrams. I can ask your doctor to up the dose to ten milligrams if he thinks that would be better for you. Maybe a stronger dose will help your leg spasms? Your doctor is making his rounds now and when he gets here, you can ask him yourself," Angela said.

The nurse finished with me, turned, and walked over to give the little, old, colored lady her meds.

I couldn't help, but notice that every time the nurse gave the colored lady to my left,

her pills, she would continue to spit them out and put them in her drawer beside her bed. I wondered why she always did that. Did she think she knew more than the doctor or did she not want to take them, so she would die? I decided to ask her one day why she always spit her pills out. She told me very matter-of-factly to mind my own business. I never saw anyone coming to visit her. I wondered about her family or if she even had a family. Did she have any friends? Did anyone even know she was here in the hospital? Surely there was someone who cared about her—a son, a daughter, a husband, brother, sister, parents, some kind of relative. Sure, I didn't have family who came to visit me since my father disowned me, but at least I had friends and co-workers who have come to visit. I decided to get my courage up and asked her.

"My name is Christi, what's yours?" I asked.

I waited for her to answer, but no answer came.

Again, I asked, "What's your name?" and again, I got no response.

After several attempts, I gave up and closed my eyes to take a nap.

Then all of a sudden, I heard her say very softly, "Earlene."

I opened my eyes and turned my head towards her and said, "I'm sorry if I'm bothering you, but I just thought you might want someone to talk to. It's really boring in here and I have noticed you haven't had any visitors since I've been here. Do you have any kids? I have a little boy, he's 21 months old."

"I have a daughter. Her name is Raylene. I named her after her father, Ray. She lives far away, in Texas. We haven't spoken in a long time. She has two boys, Richie and Lionel. I still picture them as little boys. They were five and six years old when I last saw them. I'm sure they have grown into fine, young men. They are now around 18 or 20. They looked so much like their grandfather, Ray. He passed away five years ago. I do miss him. Our daughter married a man whom we didn't approve of. He was not good to her or the boys. It breaks my heart that my own grandsons don't know me. I wish they could visit me. I wish I could see them one last time. The doctors say I don't have long to live, and I'm in so much pain, I'm not sure how much more I can take," she explained.

"I'm so sorry to hear that. I haven't seen or heard from my daddy for four years now. He disowned me because of my husband. Can I ask you a question?"

"Well… what is it?"

"Why do you keep spitting out your pills and putting them in your drawer?"

I paused for an answer.

"Are you hearing me, Earlene? Earlene?" I asked her, trying to find out a little about her and her family.

"I'm tired and need to get some rest, dearie," Earline said, and closed her eyes.

Okay, that was a start. At least I was able to get her to begin talking with me. I took my pills, or at least acted like I did. I had started to horde my pills too, just like Earlene next to me. Would I really be able to commit suicide? I didn't know, but if I decided to, I would have the pills at my disposal.

I had been in the hospital for several weeks now, but it felt like an eternity. The longest I had ever been in a hospital was six days, when I gave birth to my son—my first born, the love of my life, the apple of my eye, my whole world. The doctor finally came to see me.

He asked the same questions as he always did, "How are you today? Are you having any changes in your feeling or movement?"

And my answer was always the same emphatic, "No."

"We are making arrangements with the Detroit Rehabilitation Hospital to transfer you, so you can start some rigorous physical therapy. In the meantime, we'll keep you on the current meds and physical therapy you are on now. Do you have any questions?" he asked.

"No. Well, yes. Why do my legs shake and yet I don't feel them?"

"You can't feel them or move voluntarily because there is a loss of connection in your spinal cord and the nerves cannot send the message to your brain. The message to move is not being transmitted to the brain because the bullet fragments bruised the spinal cord and caused a block, so it cannot carry any messages to your brain," he informed me.

"Was my spinal cord cut?"

"No, the cord was not severed, but it was severely bruised, since the bullet fragmented."

"So, what does that mean?"

"That means you probably won't walk again. You'll be lucky to transfer from a bed to a wheelchair, but anything is possible, so keep a positive attitude. You're a pretty, young lady, so try to smile more often."

Smile? I thought to myself, *what have I got to smile about?* I've just been told I'll never walk again. The only thing keeping me alive is the thoughts of my precious baby boy. If I didn't have him, I'd already have checked out and ended it.

"Why is all of this happening to me?" I cried out.

God must really be punishing me for all the wrong things I've done in my lifetime. Maybe God was saving me from myself. Maybe he was getting me out of the fast lane and allowing me to reflect on all the bad choices I have made along the way.

Gandhi once said, "I object to violence because when it appears to do good, the good is only temporary. The evil it does is permanent."

75

Gandhi must have been talking about me in that statement, in no uncertain terms! I saw evil the moment Vic forced his way into my apartment. I was so thankful Kathy did not get shot and I'm absolutely sure she felt the same. Dinner time was nearing and I was hungry. I couldn't wait.

Too often, though, the food was not edible. Here it comes. Mystery meat that looked like dog food; no, wait, dog food in a can looked better than this and probably tasted better, too. Then there was watered down mashed potatoes. Didn't they know rationing ended in the 1940s? Ah, a mound of green stuff that was totally unidentifiable, and for dessert, a cookie. No wonder people talk so negatively about hospital food. This is a classic example of garbage. I would have to be force fed before any of that ended up in my stomach.

The nurse told me, "You weighed only 80 something pounds when you were admitted. You are only teetering at 90 pounds now, so you not eating is not helping your weight problem."

"Oh well, the joys of eating hospital cuisine, unmatched and unrivaled by anything else," I said. Dinner trays were all collected. Now we were able to have some free time, which was usually spent lying in bed, looking at all the patients or watching the doctors, nurses, and visitors pass by the door of this ward. I guess it beat counting the tiles in the ceiling. It was really boring and I was ready to move to the Detroit Rehabilitation Hospital. I was really looking forward to the transfer. I turned on my little television set and decided to watch my favorite programs, or fall asleep, whichever came first.

CHAPTER 5

The Suicide

Finally, February had arrived. 1970 was moving along quickly. I had been in the hospital for over two months now. I had not been outside in the fresh air since before I got shot. I knew it was winter because it was February. I was sure it was cold outside. I wondered how much snow we had gotten. It was really odd how much we took for granted in life. All of a sudden, I found myself lying there thinking about all of the things I could no longer do for myself. The smallest things were not possible for me to do without help. I thought, *how was I going to manage taking care of myself and my son when I leave here?* All I knew were these four walls in this hospital ward and I was beginning to go crazy.

I had been going to physical therapy and I felt stronger than when I was first admitted. I was determined to get my independence back. I was not going to continue to live like this, with needing someone to do everything for me. I wondered if any of my friends were going to still be my friends, now that I couldn't walk or drive. My friends were not going to want to take care of me if we go out somewhere. Again, I thought, *how was I going to get through this?* I missed my son; I missed my friends, and I missed my mom and daddy. I hardly saw anyone anymore. Everyone must have gone back to working, hanging out with their friends, cruising and enjoying life. I guess life goes on except when you're in a hospital. Here, time seemed to stand still.

I had broken the silent curtain with my neighbor in the bed next to me. Her name was Earlene. She had a daughter named Raylene and two grandsons, Richie and Lionel. Unfortunately, they had not spoken for a long time. I heard and felt the pain in her voice when she spoke of her daughter and grandsons. I wondered what happened that had kept them apart all this time. I wondered if her daughter knew how brokenhearted she was, and I wondered if she even cared. I hoped that she and her daughter would work things out before something happened to Earlene. I knew she would be devastated if she died without seeing her daughter and grandsons at least one last time. I knew she would want to hold them close and tell them how much she loved them. I just couldn't imagine what happened. After getting to know her, I couldn't imagine her having a mean bone in her frail, petite, little body. Her voice was so soft and gentle.

Thinking about Earlene and her daughter was making me think about my own mom now. I knew what happened between us, though. My daddy disowned me for marrying Vic. Looking back, I knew that my daddy could see something I couldn't about Vic. They say love is blind and since I loved Vic, I couldn't see it. My daddy, on the other hand, didn't love Vic, so he could see right through him. I had lost my family because of Vic. I wondered if Raylene's husband was the reason they no longer spoke.

I felt such an emotional attachment to this little lady. There had to be a reason we met. Is it because we had more in common with each other than what we thought? Was I supposed to be doing something to help her? I was trying to be her friend. I wanted to talk about the happy times that we both had had in our lives. We needed each other because right now it looked like each other was all we had.

I still watched her and saw what she was doing with her pills. She had told me in no uncertain terms to butt out, but I felt I needed to watch over her, anyway. She was really a sweet, little, old lady who didn't feel she had anything to live for. She must have had a mountain of pills in her drawer by now. I wished I could have walked over there and took the pills and disposed of them, so she wouldn't do anything stupid like off herself. Of course, if she decided to terminate her life, she was in the right place to get help. I wished I could have done more for her.

She was a hard nut to crack, but I finally found the gentleness inside. She kept a lot of things to herself. I still wondered where her family and friends were, or why the people from her church hadn't been here. I'm sure she went to church somewhere. Most elderly people attended church. I just found it so strange that she had not had any visitors at all, not even one. Maybe no one knew she was even here. *What could she be planning?* I thought. It just didn't make any sense to me. She was so lonely. Surely there must be someone out there who was missing her.

I wondered if she was afraid or at peace with the thought of dying. I knew the feeling of the shadow of death standing over me, standing at death's door, and it was more than terrifying to me. I was not ready to die. But then again, I was young. Older people seemed to be closer to God and they were looking forward to the day they meet their Maker. Earlene seemed to be hanging in there. I didn't know if she had a will to live now, or she still wanted to die. It seemed as though she really missed her husband and if he was in Heaven, I was sure that's where she wanted to be, also. She told me that he was the one and only love of her life, and that they married at a young age, and had always been together until the day he died.

She looked pretty old to me, so if her husband had been dead almost five years now, and she had grandsons who were between eighteen and twenty years old, then that would mean they had been together for a really long time. I could not imagine being alone after being with someone for so many years. Now, it all seemed to be making sense to me. I would bet that she was planning on taking her pills that she has been hoarding in her nightstand drawer all at once, so that she could go and be reunited with her husband in Heaven. My heart was breaking at the thought of that. I didn't really know her, but yet I felt like I knew her very well. I almost envied the long life she and her husband had shared together. That was something I had always longed for.

I always looked forward to celebrating my 50th Golden Wedding Anniversary with Vic. I knew now that day would never be a reality. Now that I was in this wheelchair, I probably would never find that special someone who would love me unconditionally and who wanted to marry me and live happily ever after. Vic had totally ruined all my hopes and dreams. He had sentenced me to a life of misery. *I was now a freak of nature. Who made him judge and jury, anyway?* I thought. It wasn't up to him what happened to me and yet, here I was, both my body and my life in shambles. I wondered how much planning went into the scheme to get rid of me. Remembering back when Vic was shooting at my little squirrel, he missed hitting him. And then on that fateful morning, Vic took two shots, two perfect shots to do the absolute most collateral damage. He must have practiced for that moment a lot. No one could be that lucky to get not one, but two perfect shots off. That took some skill, talent, planning and real guts. He had all this planned, premeditated for my demise. I blamed his mother for having the gun in the first place. If she never had the gun, he would have never found one. I was sure of that. I was not excusing him, but rather spreading the blame around. He truly was a monster. I hoped he burned in Hell.

"Burn, baby, burn. Burn for all eternity," I yelled, because I was going to suffer for a lifetime, but I hoped and prayed, not for all eternity. I thought, *God forgive me for feeling this way.* I was so angry, and it was this anger and hatred that was consuming me and was making me a very bitter person. I also blamed myself for not seeing all this darkness. Vic had had major episodes of violence toward me, and I just refused to see it. How I wished I could turn back the hands of time. How I longed to be 16 years old again and be with my first true love, Ronnie Turner. Life was so good then!

I didn't know how Earlene was holding on. She hardly complained about anything except when you tried to get in her business. She was a very private person. She didn't care much about passing the time. I had tried to talk to her about off the wall stuff like cooking. I told her I could not cook. She liked to talk a little about knitting, which was foreign to me.

I told her we should sneak out and go to a night club and dance the night away. Her eyes lit up when I suggested that.

Earlene said to me, "You know, that reminds me of when Ray and I first met. World War II had just started. It was 1939, the year I turned 17. I was working at the local PX when I noticed this handsome young man in his uniform just standing there like he was lost. I was not shy at all, so I walked over to him and asked if I could help him. He said he was looking for razors and shaving cream. I told him to look no further, to just follow me. I started to walk towards the aisle where the razors were when I wondered if he needed a brush for the shaving cream which was in the aisle we were passing. As I stopped to turn around, which he was not expecting, he ran right into me. He must have been walking on my heels. As we bumped into each other, he looked straight into my eyes and told me that I had the most beautiful, brown eyes he had ever seen. He asked me if he had died and gone to Heaven because I had the face of an angel. I absolutely melted and even blushed a bit. I had to pull myself together. I needed to find him what he was looking for, so he could be on his way. We gathered his things and I led him to where he needed to pay for his items. He thanked me kindly and told me good-bye and that my kindness made his day. All I did was think about him the rest of the day and all through the night. I went into work the next morning and you would never guess who came in."

"Let me guess—Ray?" I asked her.

"Oh, you're a smart little cookie. Yes, as I looked up, there he was, walking towards me. He came up to me and asked if I could help him find some shaving cream and razors. I laughed at him. He said he couldn't think of anything else to say and that he had gotten tongue tied. He planned on giving me this long, sweet speech, but when he was finally standing in front of me, he forgot everything he was going to say. All he could think of was yesterday and the shaving cream and razors. We talked for just a few minutes and I told him I would be finished with work at 7 o'clock that evening and that, if he would like, he could walk me home. He said he would see me at 7 o'clock on the dot. As he was walking out he turned back and said, "By the way, my name is Ray and what would your name be?" I answered back, 'My name is Earlene.' He then said, 'OK, I will see you soon, Earlene.'

"When 7 o'clock arrived I walked outside, and there he was. I pointed him in the direction of where I lived and we started walking. He very politely asked if he could perhaps hold my hand. Although my hands were probably sweaty, I accepted. We made conversation all the way to my house. I felt like I had known him all my life. I never wanted him to let go of my hand, but eventually we reached my home. He walked me up to the front door and asked if I would be interested if he could be courting me. I accepted and then he slowly lifted my hand up to his lips and kissed it ever so tenderly. He was such a gentleman. It was from that day forward we were inseparable. It wasn't long after that he asked me to marry him and once again, I said yes! I was not letting him get away from me."

"While he was state-side, we spent most nights going to blues bars and he would play his sax. We would spend our time just dancing the night away and listening to him playing his saxophone. The war was beginning and he had received his orders. They called this war World War II and it looked like it would be really bad, worse than World War I. We decided to get married right away. He would be leaving the next day to go overseas. I kept the house and waited for him to come home to me. Every day I would pray for God to keep him safe and make sure he came home."

"I took a job at one of the factories to help out with the war efforts. He was gone for two long years before God brought him back safe and sound. Shortly after he returned home, I found out I was pregnant. We were both over the moon. Nine months later I gave birth to a beautiful little girl. We decided to name her after the both of us. We combined Ray with Earlene and that's how we came up with the name Raylene. I think he might have wanted a boy, but once he held her, he said that he wouldn't trade her for anything in the world. Raylene turned out to be the apple of his eye, a real daddy's little girl. That was until she met her husband, but enough about that."

"After Raylene left home, Ray and I decided to enjoy each other's company once again. We started going to blues bars again. We went to the Graystone Ballroom a few times. It was built in 1922; we cut up the rug doing the Charleston and Lindy Hop with the big bands, and later Motown took over. Such wonderful music could only come from Detroit. Did you know Barry Gordy, Jr. once owned the Graystone? I believe he bought it in 1963. So many singers were there, Marvin Gaye, Mary Wells, the Marvelettes, Temptations, Smokey Robinson and so many others. We especially liked going to the Vanity Ballroom for dancing and they say the Vanity is the most beautiful dance rendezvous. It is on the corner of East Jefferson and Newport in East Detroit. We also went to the Grande Ballroom built in 1928 on Grand River Avenue and Joy Road for the west side."

"It went from big bands in the thirties and forties to hippie type venues in the sixties. My daughter went to some of those concerts like Cream, The Who, Pink Floyd, Steve Miller Band

and so many more. So many big-name bands played there. The Eastown Theatre, located on the east side on Harper Ave. and Van Dyke, was another place we went. It was built in 1931 as a movie theater for talkies and later housed big bands, and in the 60s and 70s the biggest Rock names played there. Our daughter, Raylene saw Bob Seger, Ted Nugent, Alice Cooper, REO Speedwagon, Kinks, Yes, Steppenwolf, Procol Harum and so many more. It seemed she went each week for different groups. We were a family who loved music, all kinds of music. My Ray could still play the sax like nobody's business. I sure do miss him."

*1931 Eastown Theatre on Detroit's east side, Harper near Van Dyke.
Went from movies to famous live Rock bands*

1940s Vanity Ballroom
for dancing-Swing Era and later Rock and Roll Venues

How cool was that, I thought. I told her I sang in the junior choir at my church and at the Confetti Lounge on Pelham St. in Dearborn Heights. She told me she loved going to her church. She said it was a true gospel church where they taught from the Bible and sang old fashioned hymns, but she loved hearing the blues way back in the 30s and 40s. She said she absolutely loved Billie Holiday. Her two favorite songs were "God Bless This Child" and "All of Me". When she wanted to "cut up the rug" she said she loved listening to the Andrews Sisters (Laverne, Maxene, and Patty). She said her favorites were "Boogie Woogie Bugle Boy" and "Oh, Johnny, Oh, Johnny, Oh!". She got teary eyed on me when she was telling me about one of the last memories she had of her and Ray. It was when they got to see the Supremes and the Andrews Sisters together in 1966. They sang each other's songs. She kind of chuckled at that. She said it was kind of like the colored folk and the white folk uniting through music, and that she never thought she would live to see that happen.

Earlene said, "Martin Luther King, Jr. was a blessing to America. He helped to change the way people think about one another, and he helped bring the white folk and the colored folk together. I really thought highly of that man."

She also told me about the good old days; about the dances, the gangsters here in Detroit, the glitzy clothes she wore and raising her daughter. Her husband worked as a dishwasher for the Hilton Hotel and played the saxophone in some of the dance halls in Detroit. She was a seamstress and a cleaning lady for a white lady in Grosse Point. They both worked hard during the week, but she loved the blues bars on the weekends and taking her daughter to the park. She told me about segregation and how she had to say, "Yes, ma'am" and "No, ma'am" to all the white folk and, about riding in the back of the buses. She was like a talking book about black history.

"Do you want to see a picture of me and my husband in my blues bar outfit?" she asked me.

"Sure, where is it?"

"It's in my purse in the bottom of my cabinet. Can you call the nurse?"

"Sure, when she comes back in here I'll tell the nurse to get you your purse."

In a few minutes, a nurse came in to see about one of the other patients, and I got her attention.

"Will you get Miss Earlene's purse out of her cabinet down there for her, please, before you leave the ward again?" I asked the nurse.

"I need to get my wallet out, so I can find my pictures of me and Ray, my husband," Earlene said.

The nurse got her purse and handed it to her. She carefully took the things out of her purse until she found her wallet. It wasn't really a wallet, but a bragging book of sorts.

"Will you give these to my friend next to me?" she asked the nurse.

The nurse handed me the pictures. The top picture was one I thought was her in her younger years.

I turned it around to show her the one I was looking at, exclaiming, "Wow, you were really a knock out!"

She stared at me for a moment and answered, "That's actually my daughter the last time I saw her and the boys. Everyone tells me that she looks just like me and that we could pass as twin sisters."

I then noticed a tear rolling down her cheek. The next picture was the same girl with two boys. I assumed these were her grandsons and her daughter, but I thought I would ask her, anyway.

She replied, "Yes dear, that is my daughter, Raylene with her two boys, Richie and Lionel. They were five and six at the time."

I continued looking through the pictures. She was really pretty. She kind of looked like Diana Ross. One picture was of her in a beautiful dress, mid-calf length, cap sleeves, teeny waistline and A-line for twirling while dancing and the coolest hat worn tilted to the side with netting. She definitely was a knock out and Ray was handsome in his pin-striped suit and his hat that he wore dipped below one eye. She told me a story about each picture.

1940s Swing Era fashion for men in pinstriped suit and hat

"That is a young Jimmy Hoffa. He was an American Union Leader. Hoffa was involved with the International Brotherhood of Teamsters Union as an organizer from 1932 and currently still is. He started serving as the Unions General President from 1958 and he still is President. I remember when that picture was taken. He had just been voted in as the new leader of the Teamsters Union. We were in downtown Detroit, near the river, where I saw him giving a speech. He was young, but gained much power rather quickly. He started out as President of the Local 299. Then in 1952, he was already vice-president of the national Teamsters IBT Union. He helped grow and develop the labor union and it actually became the largest union in the whole country. It's too bad he turned corrupt, sentenced to prison for 13 years for jury tampering, bribery and fraud in 1964. I heard it was then he got involved with the mob.

That is a picture I took of President Eisenhower when he came to Detroit and gave a speech at Cadillac Square on October 29, 1954. He talked about the Exit Numbering System for our highways.

"There is a picture of Henry Ford with a new 1937 Ford Coupe," she informed me. "I really admired that fellow. He has brought a lot of work to Detroit with the assembly lines. It made life a lot better for a lot of folks when he invented the first automobile. You know, we owned a1937 Ford Coupe 15 years before we bought our Studebaker. You know he's from here, just outside Detroit. He was born on a big prosperous farm which is now called Dearborn. He worked in some factories in Detroit. He loved tinkering with engines and mechanical things."

I couldn't believe how much she knew about Dearborn. I lived in Dearborn most of my life and I didn't even know that.

"I like those cars because they were driven by the gangsters," I told her.

"I'm glad you liked the pictures. They are all I have left of Ray and the good times I remember," she said.

"I loved your pictures. You are a regular talking history book."

"I'm getting tired, so I think I'll take a little nap before dinner. You should probably do the same. A person needs their rest."

With that said, she closed her eyes. I decided to do the same. I was thinking about the cars she mentioned. I couldn't get to sleep, but I did lay there with my eyes closed and pondered my thoughts.

I liked the looks of the 30s and 40s cars. I called them gangster cars, though I loved the 50s cars like the '57 Chevy or the '58 T-Bird and even the 1958 Corvette. She told me she still had her husband's 1952 Studebaker in their garage. No one drove it anymore since her husband died. Taking out these pictures turned out to be a good thing because she had turned into a regular little chatterbox. At least it took her mind off her husband not being with her anymore or her daughter not being there with her, or how she was missing her grandsons.

We really seemed to enjoy each other's company. We had found out we sure had a lot in common, though we were generations apart. We had become very close over the last month or so. I sure was glad she started talking to me. It sure had helped pass the time for me. I really enjoyed hearing all of her stories; they really made me miss my own mom.

I had not spoken to her since before my wedding shower that was given to me by Jean Fox in August of '67, after we were already married. I wondered what she was doing right now. I wondered if she knew Vic had shot me and I had been in the hospital for a couple of months now. I didn't know of any of my friends that knew her or how to contact her. I never really spoke about her since my daddy disowned me after I married Vic. I'll bet if she knew, she would be here for me, even if it was against my daddy's wishes. I was too afraid to call her for fear of my daddy answering the phone. I wished I could get up the courage to call her. I wondered how she was doing. She was diagnosed with breast cancer. She had to have a mastectomy done on her right side, but I didn't know if it had spread. She sure didn't deserve to have cancer. I have been told that is a horrible disease to deal with.

I started to think about Ronnie Turner; *what would life be like if I would have married him?* Life would be so good right now and I would still be walking. I would not have two bullets in me. Ronnie never hurt me, ever. But I couldn't change the past, so I would have to deal with the future. I just couldn't see much of a future then I seemed to fall into these bouts of sadness or started having a private pity party for myself. I was pitiful, though. I was no good to anyone anymore. *I am useless, unloved and unlovable. I am a freak of nature.* I wondered what the doctors or even my friends would think if I told them how I really felt inside. I feel so worthless. I thought that Vic was thinking I may walk again. If that was true, he may want me back, but maybe not. He can be really heartless and if I never walked again, he would kick me to the curb. He could be so cold. He should be doing everything in his power to make me feel better. He should be trying to make my life better, since he is the one who took my life away as I once knew it. *What happened to our wedding vows of "for better or worse?* I'll bet the one vow he had intended on keeping was the one that said, "Until death do us part." He had no right and he really didn't have any reason to hurt me like this. I could never imagine in a million years that Vic would ever shoot me. *Stop thinking,* I thought.

It was nearing the end of February. I had really been trying to keep my spirits up by counting down the days until my baby's second birthday. There were only eleven more days left until the big day. Things had really changed since I had the dream of what a big party I would have for Little Vic. Now I was not sure how his birthday was going to turn out. I had always dreamed of giving him a huge birthday party with lots of kids, and lots of balloons. All of our friends and family would have been there with their children. All the little kids would have been playing— lots of laughing, games being played, and tons of presents for my baby to open. He would have been the luckiest little boy in the world. I would have bought him a Sesame Street cake with all the characters on it. He absolutely adored Sesame Street. It was his favorite television show. I couldn't wait to take a million pictures of him digging into the cake and getting it all over his little hands and face. My camera would be ready for every precious and unforgettable moment. If I had it my way and we had the money, I would have had a pony as the main event for all the children to enjoy and ride on. We would have the house and yard decorated in a western theme; all the children would dress up as cowboys and cowgirls. As I was growing up, I remembered some of the kids in my neighborhood had a real pony that all of the children got to ride at their birthday parties. Since that day, I had always dreamed of having children and how I would throw them a huge birthday party, including a live pony.

My son was my world, the light of my life. He deserved only the best that life had to offer and I was going to make sure he got it, at least that was my plan—up until the day Vic shot me. I now have had to live my life day by day under the care, control, and supervision of doctors and nurses. At this point in time, I no longer had the ability to physically take care of myself. I was treated like I was incapable of making any decisions about my life. I could not walk nor do anything physically independent. My brain worked just fine though, after all, I wasn't shot in the head. All my lack of independence and inability to do things for myself was not due to anything I did, but what Vic did to me. Why then was I the one suffering the consequences of what he did? I didn't understand it. I was the one feeling like everyone around me was using this disability against me. Arrangements had already been made for me to go to Vic's mother's house to celebrate my son's birthday. Although I was excited to finally be able to see and hold my son and be reunited with him, I was upset that no one consulted with me to find out if I would agree to the arrangements the hospital made with Vic and his mother. No one asked me if I could find a ride to their house for a brief off campus visit for a few hours. No one asked me if I had anything in particular that I wanted for my son to have for his birthday. I was glad I already had Christmas presents bought for Little Vic. I would at least have those to give to my son. I hoped they were somewhere at Vic's house since I was told Vic cleaned out my apartment. Just seeing my little man would be enough to make me happy.

I was so comfortable lying on my bed with my eyes closed and thinking mostly happy thoughts. After all, Earlene said she was going to take a nap and that I should get some rest, too.

All of a sudden, my thoughts were abruptly interrupted and I heard very loudly over the PA system, "Code blue, code blue."

Suddenly and quickly, several nurses and aides came running into the ward and I heard them yelling, "Hurry, hurry, call Dr. Kessler now! Get the paddles."

What was up with all this noise and commotion? I thought to myself. Then, all of a sudden Earlene's curtain around her bed was pulled closed.

"What is going on? Is Earlene OK?" I asked an attendant.

They didn't answer me. Then it dawned on me, those damn pills. She took all those pills. Why didn't I watch her? That slick little lady. She told me I should also get some rest. Rest, my ass. She didn't want me to see her take those damn pills and kill herself. I guess she wanted privacy when she decided to leave this world and join her husband and meet her Maker in that big Beyond in the sky. She played me really good. Played me like a grand piano. I saw five people around her bed. I heard them counting and then hitting her with those paddles to try to restart her heart.

I heard, "Clear!" He said again, "Clear" and zapped her again.

Then they shocked her again. She was not responding. They tried again. No response; she's still flat lined.

The next thing I heard was the doctor's voice saying, "Call it, 6:38 pm time of death."

I thought, *That's it? Call it? That's awful. Someone just died and no one is upset or crying? Do these people not have any feelings?*

I felt like I just lost a close friend. Tears started streaming down my face uncontrollably. I thought again, Was *it too late? Should I tell them about her stash of pills she had or should I just mind my own business like she always told me? I don't guess it matters now. She's gone.* If I would only have told them about all those pills in her drawer, she would still be alive and here with us. For some reason, I was feeling somehow responsible. I should have been watching her. Although I hoped he got to Heaven with her hubby, I have heard that if you commit suicide, then you go to Hell because that is a sin. I will miss her. She was a sweet old lady and I really liked her. Too bad her daughter and grandsons never came to see her before she died. That definitely was a wakeup call for me. I was getting rid of my pills. I didn't want to die. I wanted to live.

CHAPTER 6

Physical Therapy and Drivers Training

I wish Vic really knew what he had done. He deeply hurt the one person who loved him the most. I didn't think he really knew just how much I truly loved him. I would have done anything for him. All he had to do was treat me good. Instead he chose to hurt me, abuse me, and misuse me. I loved him so much. I was literally head over heels in love with him. All he had to do was to choose me instead of his mother and love me. That was not asking too much from him, was it?

Being so isolated in the hospital allowed me to think, but sometimes I believe I thought too much. I thought of what could have been and not what was. The reality was that my life was ruined, and I have so many years ahead of me if I lived for a normal lifetime. But then again, there was nothing normal about me or my life. Right from the beginning it had been wrong. Too many things have happened to me for one person to bear. I thought Vic would be the one thing in my life that would be good for me, but he had proven to be the worst kind of wrong. I could not stop thinking about Vic and how he tried to end my life. How could you do that to someone whom you loved? I didn't understand it. *Please, someone help me understand what happened and why.* Vic had hurt me so badly I was actually thinking seriously about killing myself. The doctors may have been able to heal my body, but there was no one who could heal my heart and soul. I needed to get out from under the spell Vic had over me. Why did I still have these heartfelt feelings about Vic? Why couldn't I have listened to my daddy or my friends when they told me Vic was no good, and especially no good for me, that I could do so much better than him? Now look at me.

My life was in shambles, in ruins, damaged beyond repair. My body would never be the same again and it would only get worse with time and age. My life was changed forever in the blink of an eye and for what? I had questions and Vic had answers, but he refused to talk to me. I needed answers. My little boy seemed to be the only good thing in my life. *Please, God, take my mind off the bad and negatives and let me look to some good and positives.*

Susan B. Anthony once said, "A woman must not depend on the protection of a man. She must learn to protect herself."

Where was that advice when I needed it? If I knew then what I know now, this tragedy would have never happened.

It had been a long time coming, but with the arrival of March, 1970, so came my transfer to the Detroit Rehabilitation Institute. I was transported in a van to my new residence. The fresh air was exhilarating. This was my first time out in the cool, crisp, fresh air. I was actually put in a room and not a ward. I decided to work my tail off, so maybe I would make some kind of progress on the road to recovery. They really meant business here. My first day was a real work out. The first thing they did was have me stand in the parallel bars to build the strength in my legs and arms. Then they gave me dumbbell weights to make my arms stronger to help carry the weight of the rest of my body.

March 6th was a nice surprise for me. It was my baby boy's second birthday and I was allowed to go to Annie's house to see him.

Vic picked me up and drove me back to his mother's house, so I could spend some time with Little Vic. I felt very uncomfortable sitting next to Vic, but I never said a word and felt it was worth it if I could see my son. I didn't know who was the worst to ride with, Vic or his mother. We arrived at Annie's house and Vic carried me into the house. I dreaded seeing his mother as much as I dreaded seeing Vic, but I made the best of it for my little boy. We took a few pictures of this momentous occasion. You could tell I was not at ease. You could tell by my body language, which spoke volumes, I was not wanting Vic to kiss me. I had my hands in my pockets, not around his neck and I did not initiate the kissing. My son was a different matter. I kissed his little face all over. I was so happy to see him again. Little Vic opened his presentsimap:// christi4christ%40charter%2Enet@mobile.charter.net:143/ fetch%3EUID%3E/Sent%3E2562 - msocom 1 , blew out his two candles, and had cake and ice cream. I was gone for the whole afternoon. Vic surprised me by actually acting like my husband today. He waited on me by getting me a piece of cake with some ice cream. He sure was making an effort to be nice to me, but I was still skeptical. Would this last? Probably not, but I decided to enjoy it while it lasted. The pictures we took looked like we were happy. He was kissing me, but for some reason I did not reciprocate with a kiss or by even putting my arms around him. I just was not sure of him. I had gotten all dressed up, fixed my hair and looked my best for the two men in my life, namely Vic and Little Vic. I will admit, my emotions were all over the place. I hated Vic for what he had done by shooting me, but I longed for us to be a real family too. I was gone for the better part of the day, but all good things must come to an end and so did my son's birthday.

3-6-70 Little Vic's 2nd birthday, Vic kissing me.

The next day I was back to the same grind. Their goal was to get me up and walking on crutches. I would ultimately go from being in a wheelchair, to using a walker, to using Loftstrand crutches. The Loftstrand crutches were the kind that people with Polio used. They were better than the underarm kind, since they did not break down the tissues of the underarms. From day one, they had me on three times per day rotation to go to the Physical Therapy room. My arms were weak, and my legs were like jelly. I had drop foot in both feet, pressure sores on my bottom and on the back of my left heel. My left heel cord and both leg muscles were very tight. My spine was also weak, so I couldn't hold myself up in an upright, sitting position. I was like a rag doll. This place was amazing, though. There was no wasting time here. You either wanted to get well or at least better yourself or you went home. I was one of the ones who wanted to get better, much better. I worked my butt off and changed my attitude to a positive one. Up until now, my therapist had been focusing on building strength in my arms and legs.

Today my therapist, Kevin, said to me, "Christi, I have some good news. We are going to try something new. I think you are going to like it."

"If it's gonna help me to walk again, then I'm ready. What are we waiting for? Let's get started," I told Kevin.

"First, we have to get you out of the wheelchair and onto the mat and second, do you like music?" Kevin asked.

"I love music," I answered.

"What kind of music do you like and we'll find a radio station that has it."

"I like oldies from the fifties and sixties and anything but hard Rock. Love the Temptations, Jackson 5, Osmonds, and of course, the Bee Gees."

"I'll find a station that has soft rock. How about WKNR, Keener Radio? It always has great songs on it.

Who is your favorite DJ? Mine is Mort Crowley and Gary Stevens," Kevin announced.

"Mine are Tom Ryan, Dick Purtan and J. Michael Wilson."

When Kevin turned on the radio, the song, "Green-Eyed Lady," by Sugarloaf was playing and "The Thrill Is Gone," by B.B. King followed.

Kevin whispered, "They are singing your song about those big, green eyes of yours."

"You're funny, Kevin, but thanks, anyway," I said.

The mat was like a big table on a solid wood foundation, about eighteen inches off the ground, with a smooth, vinyl, padded top, and large enough for two people to easily move around on.

"Watch me, Kevin. I have been working really hard on my transfers. I can almost go from my chair to another surface all by myself. My arms are getting pretty strong. Just stand here next to me, but don't touch me unless you see me start to fall. I want to see if I can do it all by myself."

I took a deep breath and made sure my brakes were locked. I silently counted to three and lifted myself up out of my wheelchair, pivoted my body and successfully sat my bottom down onto the edge of the mat.

"Very good, Christi, I'm impressed. You have been working very hard, I see. I'm going to hop up and get behind you, so that I can pull you back, so that you will be sitting with your back against the wall. I don't want you to have to worry about your balance. What we are going to do today is start stretching out your tendons, muscles and heel cords. They have gotten very tight and need to be stretched back out before they get so tight that they require surgery to be lengthened.

"Just give me a minute, so I can go get our newfangled contraption we call the pulley board, for lack of a better name. I'll be right back. Don't go anywhere," he said with a chuckle.

As I sat there on the mat, leaning against the wall, I looked around the room at all the other patients. I still had not been able to accept my disability. I kept thinking, *this was all a bad dream*, but then a voice snapped me out of it.

Kevin said, "OK, I got it. What do you think, Christi? Are you ready to ride?"

"What is that thing and what does it do?" I asked.

"Like I said, we call it the pulley board. It was invented by one of the employees here. You sit on the board with your back up against the backrest. Then I am going to strap your legs down, so your knees won't pop up. I am going to then slide the footrest up against your feet. There is a pulley system that works the footrests, so you can control the amount of stretch you get. I want you to stretch as much and as long as you can tolerate. No pain, no gain. You move the pulleys with these bicycle-looking pedals. The more you pedal them forward, the more stretch you get behind your heels and calves. If you peddle backwards, it will release the amount of stretch you get. Now, the actual board you are sitting against moves, also. We can control the amount of stretch you get when it starts tilting you forward. Your legs will be getting stretched out, especially behind your knees while the footrests stretch out your heel cords which is causing the drop foot that you have in both of your feet. Your left foot seems to be worse than your right foot. In any case, let's try it out and see what you think."

Kevin helped me onto the board and handed me the pulleys, so that I could control the footrests. Kevin stood to the right of me turning the knob which he said controlled the backrest. It would tilt my upper body forward. He wasn't kidding. I could feel the stretching in all the tendons behind my knees. I was feeling the stretch in places I didn't even know I had feeling. I knew I had to keep these tendons stretched, so that I would be able to bend my knees. If they got too tight and unable to bend, it might stop me from being able to walk correctly. He told me to tell him when I couldn't stand the, stretching any longer. I was going to endure as much pain as I could. I was determined to walk again and the sooner the better. This thing was ingenious.

The stretching was rough going, though. I pushed myself really hard and made progress every day. I was able to put weights on my legs. As soon as I was able to walk the full length of the parallel bars and back again, they started me on a walker. I mastered the walker and I graduated to the Loftstrand crutches. The doctors were truly amazed at my progress, especially when I was told I'd never walk again. They told me it was my own self-determination and nothing else that would give me the ability to walk, even if it was with some kind of assistance. I knew different. Kevin told me I had a lot of tenacity, and you know what? He was right. I knew God was helping me to overcome this trauma. It said in Galatians 6:9, "And let us not grow weary of doing good, for in due season we will reap, if we do not give up." I knew God was with me while I was lying in my pool of blood, and still today he had not forsaken me. I gave all the credit to Him for my constant and astonishing progress. Thank you, God, again.

To help with my left leg, my doctor ordered me a full leg brace. This enabled me to put full weight on my left leg and use it as a sort of peg leg to be able to walk. I was told not to expect to walk like normal because I had no sense of balance. That would be my downfall to walking normally. That full leg brace must have weighed ten pounds all by itself. I had very weak ankles and my ankles would bend into the steel brace. That hurt very much. I figured out if I put something thick and soft between my ankle and the bar, that would solve the problem of the pain. I used a rolled-up sock for padding. The full leg brace had straps which buckled at my thigh and mid-calf, and then two locks slid over the right and left bar at the knee to lock the knee in place. When I sat, I had to slide the locks up to unlock it in order to bend my knee. The whole brace was attached to an all leather shoe, which was uncomfortable, not to mention ugly. All in all, I hated the full leg brace because it was downright ugly, but I wore it because it made it possible for me to walk. I guess always looking your best in public and then modeling made me feel really self-conscious of my looks. This was not a good look on me. It was definitely the ugly look. I was proud of myself, though, for all the progress I had made there. This beat the heck out of only being able to transfer from a bed to a wheelchair and back again. I was on the road to getting my independence back.

I not only learned to walk again, but I also decided to learn to drive again, even if it killed me. I had to drive. They had a sort of drivers training here also, for those who were potential drivers, and I knew I was one. "Sign me up!" I told them. They told me I had to be able to master the crutches and then I would be eligible for the drivers training. That only made me more determined. It was now the third week in March.

I was anxiously awaiting the news that I was at the top of the list for the drivers training course.

I was in the patients' dining hall when a man approached me. He looked to be around forty years old, with brown hair. He had hazel eyes and wore glasses. He was about 5'10" tall with an average build.

"Hello. Are you Christi Golden? My name is Mr. Wallen and I am the teacher for the drivers training program. I have been informed that you are next on my list. I've come to ask you if you would be available this afternoon for your first lesson?" he asked.

I was ecstatic with what I just heard.

"Of course, I am available! I have been waiting to hear those words since the day I arrived here. We can go now if you would like," I said to him.

"Hold on there. Not so fast. I have to get the car ready for you. I've come to look over your chart. Give me about half an hour to make sure the car has gas and everything. Please do me a favor and make sure you finish your lunch. I'll see you down there shortly."

I was so super stoked. My wish was finally coming true. Independence, here I come! I waited about twenty minutes and then I was on my way.

"Here I am. I'm ready when you're ready," I informed Mr. Wallen.

"You sure didn't waste any time getting down here. The first thing we need to see is how you are able to transfer from your wheelchair to the driver's seat. Do you need any help?"

"Not at all. I know I can do this! I have been working very hard in therapy. I have gotten really good with my transfers. This should be a piece of cake for me."

My transfer was a thing of beauty. A normal person couldn't have done any better. I couldn't believe I used the word normal, so that made me abnormal, yep, a freak of nature. I had to quit thinking negatively.

Mr. Wallen walked around to the passenger side and got in. He asked me to move my right foot and apply the brake. Then he asked me to take my foot off the brake and give the car some gas, as if I was driving it. Now, since I was a little nervous having Mr. Wallen watching me, my right leg went into a small spasm. Luckily, I was able to stop it almost immediately. I told him that it was because I was so nervous. He asked me to act like I was driving. He had me use my turn signals, check my rear-view mirror and look over my shoulder. I didn't have any trouble doing any of that. We focused on moving my right leg from the gas to the brake pedal and back again. We did this many times to see if the spasms would reoccur and if so, how often. Today I only had one spasm and I knew it was only because I was nervous.

Mr. Wallen told me, "I have looked over your chart and now while observing you, I see no reason for any type of special hand controls. I believe with more practice moving your right leg back and forth that in a couple of days you will be able to actually drive through the training course."

"I told you I could do it. You know I used to race at the Detroit Dragway and up and down Telegraph and other roads, so surely, I would think I could drive this tiny training course without any problems. I intend on being your best driving student."

For the next two days, when I wasn't in PT, I practiced moving my right leg back and forth. I wanted to be sure my right leg would not fail me. I felt competent enough to actually drive. The two days went by rather quickly.

"Well, Christi, are you ready to get behind the wheel and actually drive?" Mr. Wallen asked me.

"Are you kidding me, I've been ready. I've been practicing with my right leg to move back and forth, like my foot was on the gas and then I hit the brake."

"Well then let's go and take me for a ride. Where would you like to drive to? How about New York or LA or Washington, DC? You name the place. Here are the keys. Go to the car and get in, OK."

I practically flew to the car waiting for me. It was a 1967 Chevy Impala, burgundy with black interior, automatic on the column, probably a 283. I got in without any trouble in my transfer. Mr. Wallen moved my wheelchair out of my way. He then went to the passenger side and got in.

"Put the key in the ignition and start it up. Stay within the white lines, just like the regular roads and stop at all the stop signs. Then we'll try to parallel park, too."

"I can do this, no problem."

I started the car up, put it in drive and started to move. I was nervous just like when I was fifteen years old and getting my driver's permit. I did really well. I stayed in the lines, stopped at all the stop signs, used my signal, looked over my shoulder, all the things a good driver did. He even let me turn on the radio. The song playing was "Turn Back the Hands of Time" by Tyrone Davis, and then I forgot I was training to drive again and started to sing along with "We've Only Just Begun" by the Carpenters. I felt so natural, so normal, driving again. It was second nature to me. I guess once you learn to drive, you don't forget it.

"I think you have done exceptionally well today. No mistakes and good habits. Pull the car to the curb and we'll get out where we started from; I'll see you tomorrow again, same time, same place."

"I'll be ready with bells on."

Every day I went to PT (physical therapy) and worked on my strength building in my arms and legs, and I practiced driving for the rest of the week. I passed the driver's training program with flying colors and continued to go to PT.

I stayed at the Detroit Rehab Hospital for the whole month of March; finally, in April I was released to go home, wherever that was going to be. I had two requirements to fulfill before I would be discharged. One was that I had to urinate on my own, without the catheter, and the other was I had to see the hospital's social worker before I would be able to be released somewhere.

CHAPTER 7

Kept a Prisoner

pril 1, 1970. It was April Fool's Day, too. It was a
beautiful spring day. The sun was shining and the
flowers were blooming. The birds were serenading
their mates. It was even more beautiful to me because I was
being released from the Detroit Rehabilitation Hospital. I
had been here for a whole month and made quite remarkable
progress. I had improved from being bedridden to transferring
from the bed into a wheelchair, to walking with a standard
walker, walking between the parallel bars, and walking with
Loftstrand crutches. A nurse came and removed the catheter
and left a bedpan to see if I could urinate on my own. A little
later, after having the catheter out, I actually did go pee all by
myself. I was very proud of myself, in fact I was ecstatic. To
someone who had normal use of their bladder, it would be no
big deal, but to me it was a feat beyond words. It was a huge
accomplishment. I was so glad to get that thing out because it
gave me strange, sexual urges and several bladder infections,
which I didn't like.

All that was keeping me from leaving was making arrangements with some social worker. I was sure they would be able to help me find a place for my son and me. It didn't matter to me if it was a house or apartment, just as long as we were together. There were always lots of places to rent. I didn't even care in what city we would be moving to, as long as it was not a dangerous neighborhood. How hard would that be?

I waited for my belongings to be brought to me. I was so excited I couldn't even eat breakfast. Finally, a man came with a brown paper bag. He was a tall, white man, slender in stature, walking towards me.

"Are you Mrs. Christi Golden?" he asked.

"Yes, I am Christi Golden, and I'm getting out of here today," I answered.

"These are your personal belongings. Please sign here."

"OK."

"Thank you and I hope you make a speedy recovery, ma'am."

Just as soon as he had appeared, he had vanished. I opened the bag. I couldn't believe my eyes. There was my beautiful, baby-blue, baby-doll nightgown, soaked in dried blood. Why would they give this back to me? Wouldn't they know I would have no use for this? It brought back a flood of memories of the instant I was shot, not once, but twice. I didn't need this as a reminder. Along with my nightgown were my panties, also full of dried blood. I called a nurse and asked her to discard the whole bag.

"Would you throw this bag away for me, and when is the social worker supposed to come to talk to me?" I asked her.

"She should be here soon. Just be patient. She'll be here," she answered.

About an hour later, a slender, black woman approached me and asked, "Are you Mrs. Golden?"

"Yes, I am Mrs. Golden," I answered.

"I am Mrs. McKinley, the social worker for the hospital. We have made arrangements for you to be released into your mother-in-law's care," she told me, with no emotion in her voice.

"What? Are you crazy? Her son tried to kill me. Why do you think I'm here? I'm not here for a vacation, that's for sure," I told her in a very fearful, but bold voice.

"We have to go by the law and since you are married, you are legally your husband's responsibility. It would make a difference if you were independent, but you are not. You have no way of taking care of yourself. You don't have insurance to pay for an assisted facility. We have no choice, but to send you back home with your family," she stated.

"And if I don't want to go?"

"You can't stay here. You don't have a choice. I'm sorry. Your mother-in-law should be here soon. She'll have to sign some papers and then you can be released to go home," this unfeeling, uncaring woman told me.

"I guess you fooled me. I thought I was going somewhere of my own, not back to the house of horrors and the mother-in-law from Hell!" What a sad April Fools' joke on me.

A little after 4:00 pm, there she was, the woman from Hell. I wanted to scream for help, but what good would that do? I couldn't believe it. How could they do this to me? Don't they know they are signing my death sentence, especially with Vic in the same house with me? The only good thing I could see in this whole situation was I would be reunited with my son, my sweet, little boy.

115

She came over to my bed and said, "Here, I brought you some clothes."

I couldn't answer her back with a 'thank you' or anything else. I just stared at her in disbelief. I called a nurse to help me get dressed. She brought me a mismatched outfit. I'm sure she did that on purpose, to make me look stupid. I guess she forgot I got shot in the lung and the spine, not in the head. After getting dressed, the nurse helped me into the wheelchair, pushing me out of the ward, down the hall, into the elevator, and then down to the main floor to the front doors.

"Thank you so much." I told the nurse.

Annie opened the car door. The nurse helped me transfer into the front seat. Lucky for me, Annie got rid of her little red 1962 Falcon and bought a 1966 Ford Fairlane. There was more room to get in. It was the longest 45-minute drive I had ever taken. The whole trip was in dead silence. Not one word was spoken. I felt so uncomfortable. I would have rather been with a whole car full of Porcupines than to be with Vic's mother. We finally got to her house and there was Vic, standing on the front porch. He walked to the car, opened the passenger side door, and picked me up. He brought me into the house and sat me on the couch. He got a wheelchair and then sat me in the wheelchair. Why did they have a wheelchair in the first place, unless they both knew I was coming here after being released from the hospital? He didn't utter a word. They must have known about this ahead of time since they had a wheelchair in the house. He left me in the middle of the living room.

Annie told me Vic's room was all made up for me. Well, here I was, in the den of inequity. How bad could it get? I didn't even want to think about that. I was fearful, afraid for my life.

I rolled myself into the bedroom. I had brought my little black and white, nine-inch television with me and asked Vic to put it on the dresser and plug it in. I got it as a gift while I was at Detroit General Hospital. After placing my television on the dresser, plugging it in and fixing the rabbit ears, Vic left. I could hear the door slam and the car start up.

I was so glad I worked as hard as I did to regain some strength while I was in rehab. My arms were stronger. I would need them to protect myself because they were all I had now. I was forced, against my will, to live back at Vic's mother's house. I was not able to care for myself at this point. Who was the idiot that wanted to place me back at the house of the mentally and criminally insane? This was a real hell hole. I stood no chance of independence. I was given no chance to advance in my physical therapy program. I would be trapped and kept a prisoner.

Annie had fixed up Vic's bedroom for me to stay in while Vic stayed in the bedroom across from me where Little Vic's crib was. There was so much tension in this house that you could cut it with a knife. I never felt more like a stranger than I did now.

"Where is my son?" I asked Annie.

"He's in the other bedroom sleeping," she answered.

I rolled myself out of Vic's bedroom and opened the door to the other bedroom. There was my little angel. I rolled over to his crib. I just sat there and watched him as he slept.

All of a sudden, he woke up and said, "Mommy, mommy. I want mommy."

It did my heart so much good just to see him. He was holding his little hands out to me for me to pick him up. I couldn't get Little Vic out, so I asked Annie to take him out of his crib. She picked him up and placed him on my lap. I hugged

117

him so tight I was afraid I'd squish him. I missed him so much. I only saw him, while I was in the hospital, when Kathy still had him because she would bring him to see me. When Vic got him, I never saw him again while I was in the hospital. I was so glad he didn't forget me.

"Mommy, mommy," he kept saying and he hugged me ever so tightly.

I thought to myself, *this little boy is the one thing Vic and I did right.* He was so beautiful and looked just like his daddy. He was my blond-haired, blue-eyed, little man. I took him into my room and played with him.

"Are you hungry?" I asked Little Vic.

"Me hungry," he answered back.

I asked Annie to bring me something for my son to eat. She brought me a jar of baby food. Little Vic turned two years old a month ago. They were still feeding him Gerber baby food. He ate the whole jar of Turkey and Rice. Annie came in my room and grabbed Little Vic from me.

I told her, "I'm not done playing with him."

"He needs his rest," she said.

"He just got up from sleeping just a little while ago."

"You need your rest. You can see him tomorrow," she told me, like she knew what was best for me and my son.

"I'm not tired."

"Vic should be home soon. You should be in your room," she told me, like she was warning me to beware of what may happen if Vic saw me.

"I don't care where Vic is. I want my son!" I yelled at her.

"You can see him tomorrow." She turned and left my room with my son in her arms. I was not happy with how my son was being treated. He needed to be around people, especially his parents. Babies need socialization, and my son was no exception. He was in his crib far too much and too long. This care, or lack of it, could cause him to regress in his behavior and things I have taught him, like potty training. This was just a glimpse of what was to come and it didn't look pretty. I could see this would be an uphill battle in this battle of wits, and my son would be the pawn. I could tell she put Little Vic back in his crib because he started to cry. He cried until he cried himself to sleep. I felt so helpless. I had a quiet, sleepless night. There was too much on my mind.

I woke up the next morning and found Vic sleeping on the couch. Annie had already gone to work. I was going to make Little Vic and me something to eat. I got dressed and got in my wheelchair and quietly rolled into the kitchen. I couldn't get into the refrigerator. *Great*, I thought. I'd have to wait until Vic woke up. I didn't dare wake him up or no telling what would happen. I went back into my room and turned on the television. Little Vic must have still been asleep because I didn't hear a sound out of him. I waited until he woke up.

Finally, I heard my little boy cry. I went into his bedroom and there he was, standing up in his crib. I tried to get him out, but I couldn't. Just because I couldn't get him out didn't mean I had to leave him. I played with him and softly sang songs to him. I repeated nursery rhymes, which he especially liked. I had Little Vic potty trained at twenty months old, which was last December, just before I was shot. He did so well. He always knew when he had to go and would tell me, so I could clap my hands to show praise when he finished. I figured he must need to go potty soon. How would I get him out? I wasn't sure. I sure hoped Vic would wake up soon. I didn't want my son to regress in his potty training, so I had to figure out a way for me to get him out of his crib.

He was a very talented little boy. At four months old, he had pulled himself up on the side rail of his crib. At six months old, he was already walking up and down in his bed holding onto the rail. He walked independently at ten months, off the bottle at ten months and completely potty trained at twenty months. With all these early accomplishments, I knew my son would be something special, very talented in many things. I knew he would be a super star.

There had to be a way for me to get my son out of his crib. What would it take to get him out? If I sat right next to his crib and if he got his little leg over the rail, I could pull him over and onto my lap. I told him to get his foot on the top of the rail. He tried, and then tried again. He couldn't get it over. He tried again, but still no luck. We must have been trying for an hour and then, he got his foot on the top of the rail. I took his one leg and then his shoulders and helped get them over the rail, and then I pulled him all the way over.

"Hooray, now that's great! I knew we both could do it. Good for you, Little Vic," I said to my son.

He was so proud. It was a game to him, but it was a real accomplishment for me. I took him to the bathroom, so he could go potty and then took him to my room. A short while later, I heard Vic getting up and I asked him to get some food, so I could feed Little Vic. We both ate and then played in my room for a while until it was time for his afternoon nap. He slept for a couple of hours and when he woke up; we played with his trucks and did our learning time. I taught him his colors, numbers and how to count. He loved his "See 'N Say" toys. They taught him numbers, time, letters, names, and sounds. This was the basic routine.

May, 1970 arrived and with the month of May came warmer weather and flowers. Vic or his mother had hired a young, 16-year-old, Hispanic, eight-weeks pregnant girl named Maria, to be a live-in babysitter. She proved to be incompetent, and did not last very long. I didn't see Maria much because she was either in the basement or I was in my room. She was the babysitter, but I took care of my son as much as she did, and as best as I could.

It was a nice, warm, sunny day in May. I had been forced to live with Vic and his mother since my discharge from the Detroit Rehabilitation Institute in April. They wouldn't keep me any longer because I had plateaued in my progress. I had made very rapid progress until I hit that plateau. I didn't want to leave, but I had no choice. I was not happy with this situation, but I could do nothing about it. I still felt like a prisoner here, always being watched, always pushed around and told what I could or couldn't do. Like settlers in a virgin territory ravaged the land, so too, Vic ravaged my body. He left me sore and in pain from the brutal and abusive sexual assaults knowing I could never fight him back. Well, this day was going to be different. I told Maria I wanted to go outside to get some fresh air and I wanted to take my son with me.

She said, "Mr. Golden told me not to let you go out."

"And is Mr. Golden my boss?" I asked.

"No, ma'am," Maria answered, not being sure of me.

I said to Maria, "Then I suggest you get my son dressed, so I can take him out."

"Yes, ma'am, but I don't want to get in no trouble," she told me, looking a bit afraid.

"You'll be in trouble if you don't take me out," I said, having to act bossy and in charge or she wouldn't take me seriously.

I felt a little sorry for her and her situation. There she was, sixteen years old, pregnant, not married and working for some white family that probably didn't pay her minimum wage. But today I could not worry about her or her problems, because I had my own problems and agenda. I was going to make a break for it and get the hell out of Dodge, or at least this hell hole. I was tired of being kept a prisoner; picked up and moved like a piece of furniture, ordered around and sexually used for Vic's pleasure. I had no life here. My son was all that was keeping me going. I was already in my wheelchair and waiting for Maria to get Little Vic in some play clothes.

"Your little boy is ready."

Maria took us both out to the front porch. I told Little Vic to stay on the porch until Maria got me down the steps onto the sidewalk. She took me down the three cement steps backwards in the wheelchair, step by step.

When I got on the sidewalk, I told Maria, "Hold Little Vic's hand down the steps, so he doesn't fall."

When Little Vic reached the last step, he ran to me and wanted to ride on my lap. I picked my son up and off we went. I went down the front walk and turned right first onto the public sidewalk. I went down a short distance and then turned around and came back. I had to do this, so as not to make Maria suspicious.

I did the same maneuver again and when I came back I said to Maria, "Please go in the house and get me my white sweater."

When she was in the house, out of sight, I made my getaway. I had Little Vic on my lap and was pushing those big wheelchair wheels as fast as I could go. I went past the immediate neighbors on Merrick, turned left around the corner onto Carlisle and left around the corner again, so now I was on Hipp Street, on the other side of the block.

I remembered Larry Anthony lived on this street, so I went to his house at 3846 Hipp first, but no one was home, so I continued down the street. I believed if any of the Anthonys would have been home they would have helped me, especially Larry. Larry and I had always been great friends and I know he cared about me.

Next, I saw a lady outside watering her grass. I rolled up to her and asked her if she would help me.

I told her, "Please help me, ma'am, I'm being kept a prisoner by my husband on Merrick. He already shot me and that's why I'm in the wheelchair. This is my little boy. We need to get out of that house."

She looked at me like I was crazy and went into her house. I didn't blame her; if I had some stranger come up to me and tell me a story like that I might have thought that she was crazy, too. But that didn't discourage me.

I wheeled further and saw another woman getting into her car.

I caught up to her and said, "Please help me. Will you drive me to the Dearborn Police Station? My husband shot me and I need to get away from him and his mother."

She also looked at me like I was crazy and drove off, so I continued.

I saw a man a few more houses down the street and wheeled up to him. I was now getting a little tired, but I persevered on my quest to escape.

I said to him, "Will you help me? My husband shot me and I am being held a prisoner at his mother's house around the block at 3841 Merrick."

He also gave me a funny look, but he pushed me up his driveway and said he would call the Dearborn Police.

I could hear him talking to the police and he said, "I have a young lady with a baby on her lap in a wheelchair saying she is a prisoner somewhere at 3841 Merrick. I don't know her personally, but she sounds sincere and very frightened. Can you send an officer to my address at 3792 Hipp Street? Thank you. Good bye."

He was very nice to me. He offered me a glass of iced tea while we waited for the police. They took about ten to fifteen minutes to get there. When the police car arrived, there were two officers in it. The driver got out of the cop car, while his partner remained inside, and approached the front door. The officer walked over to the man and talked to him first. Then he came over to me. I tried to explain to him how Vic shot me and I was forced to live back at his mother's house again. Just because we were married should not make me his responsibility. After all, I left him.

I told him, "Vic still abuses me and assaults me and even rapes me whenever he wants. I do not feel safe there, and I want to be taken to some kind of shelter away from my husband, Vic, and his psycho mother."

He looked at me sympathetically and said, "As much as I would like to help you, it is not the job of the police department to look for safe housing for anyone. It is totally out of my hands. I see you are in a wheelchair, but you have to find some way to get to a safe place, but we can't transport you. I wish we could, but we can't. I can drive you back to your house, but that's all we can do here."

"I guess," was all I could say.

The only reason I took the offer of the ride was because I was tired and maybe some of Annie's neighbors would see the cop car and start wondering what was going on in that house. The one officer carried me into the house as the other officer was behind carrying my wheelchair. When the officers turned and left, I told Maria not to mention a word about this incident and she didn't. At least a report was on file with the Dearborn Police and it wasn't from me, but a neighbor who was concerned for my safety.

Annie had arrived home from work and started to cook dinner for Vic. I heard Vic and his mother talking, so I knew Vic was now home. I called Vic to come and get Little Vic, so he could also eat. I made sure I ate, too, while Vic was there. Vic had taken Little Vic, so I returned to my room for the rest of the night.

The next morning, I woke up to dead silence. I didn't hear anyone or anything. I thought that I must have been home alone. I got myself up and in my wheelchair and wheeled myself into the kitchen to look for something to eat. Just great, I couldn't reach up into any of the cupboards. I couldn't open or reach anything out of the refrigerator. There was nothing on the counters I could reach. I couldn't even reach the kitchen faucet to get me a glass of water. One time, out of desperation, I actually drank out of the toilet. *I was going to starve to death staying here*, I thought to myself. It would be pointless to ask Maria to help me with anything because she had been instructed to only take care of Little Vic and not my needs.

I was snapped out of my thoughts to the sound of Vic's voice asking me, "What are you doing in the kitchen? Like this was off limits to me."

"I was just looking for something to eat," I replied.

Vic came into the kitchen. He grabbed a bowl, spoon, a box of cereal, and the carton of milk out of the refrigerator. He then placed it all on the dinette table and sat down to eat.

When he finished eating his cereal, he shocked me by asking, "Do you want any cereal before I put it all away?"

"Yeah, I am starving."

"Here, you can have this."

He grabbed a bowl down from the cupboard and a spoon out of the drawer for me, placed it on the table in front of me and walked out of the kitchen. I poured myself some cereal in the bowl, poured milk over it and ate it. When I was finished I put the bowl on my lap, wheeled myself over to the sink and put the bowl and spoon in the sink. I was thankful the bowl was Melamine because it hit a little hard and china would have broken, I'm sure.

I then wheeled myself into my room. I wanted so desperately to go see Little Vic, but I couldn't because Vic had gone back in his room and shut the door. I knocked on his door and asked Vic to put the milk back in the refrigerator, so it wouldn't spoil. Vic stayed in his room with our baby until dinner time. I stayed in my room the whole day watching my television.

I heard Annie yell to Vic, "Dinner will be just a few more minutes."

He yelled back, "OK."

A few minutes later I heard his door open and watched him walk by my door carrying Little Vic. He never asked me if I was hungry, or if I wanted to join them. He didn't even look into my room at me as he walked by. I waited a few more minutes before I got myself up, out of bed, and into my wheelchair. Then I wheeled myself into the kitchen. I was so hungry. Annie fixed fried chicken, mashed potatoes and corn. As I was making my way down the hallway to the kitchen, I could hear Vic and his mother talking. I couldn't hear exactly what they were saying, but when I entered the kitchen, all conversation ceased between the two of them. Vic and his mother were already sitting at the table. Little Vic was beside the table in his Stroll-O-Chair. I rolled up to the table to where the empty seat was. There was a plate already fixed for me. Neither one of them said a word to me. It was as if I was invisible. The only one who acknowledged me was my son. I don't know how I made it through dinner in the dead silence. It felt like we were sitting there for hours, although it was only a matter of fifteen to twenty minutes maybe. After I finished eating, I pulled the tray off of Little Vic's highchair, unsnapped him and pulled him onto my lap. I wiped his face and little hands and then went back to my room with him. I hadn't seen him all day because Vic stayed in the bedroom where Little Vic slept. We were having so much fun laughing and playing together.

It was only a matter of minutes that I was playing with Little Vic when Annie came to my door and said, "Let me take the baby. He needs to get some rest."

"We have only been playing a few minutes and I haven't seen him all day long," I said to her.

"Well, you can see him tomorrow."

Annie acted like the Gestapo and she was the head Nazi. She grabbed him from me and took him across the hall to his crib. I think the real reason she came and took him from me was because she heard us laughing, playing and having a good time, and she didn't like that. I watched her from my room go into his room and she must have laid him down in his crib. I heard my son start to cry. He obviously didn't want to go to sleep yet.

He kept calling my name, "Mommy, Mommy."

She came out of the room and immediately went upstairs to bed because she had to get up at 3:00 a.m. so she could leave by 4:00 a.m. to go to work.

Now that I was all alone and it was starting to get late, I decided I would just get ready for bed. Vic was probably going to be going out soon to party with his friends, anyhow. Shortly after I was in the bed, I heard the side door slam. I knew he had left the house. I didn't care where he was going, what he was going to do, or who he was going to do it with. Of course, I had a good idea where he was going and who he was going to see. I was just relieved to know that I was going to be safe for a little while at least.

Ever since the Detroit Rehabilitation Institute sent me home, I always had a fear that Vic was going to "finish the job" he started. I really believed he was going to kill me. It's almost like I would have to sleep with one eye open. I imagined that he would kill me and Annie would help him cover it up and make it look like a suicide. The police would believe his story and once again he would get away with it—except this time it would be murder. I rolled over, pulled the covers up and tried to go to sleep. All I could do was toss and turn.

I had an uneasy feeling that something terrible was going to happen tonight. My gut feeling was usually right. I had, in the past, been hit, pushed, punched, and slapped by Vic so much that it seemed like an everyday occurrence.

Well, the law saw this behavior as domestic violence, unless you were a married couple, a husband and wife. If you were married, you were unable to press charges against your spouse. There was no protection. A woman could press charges against her boyfriend, father or even a complete stranger for assault, but not against her husband. None of this made any sense to me. I guess, unless I ended up dead, the law could not and would not do anything to protect me.

I started thinking again about how I got back to this house and with the man who tried to kill me. I thought I had a choice; go to a state run institution and be a prisoner there without my son or go to Vic's house, but at least there I was with my son. The choice was a no-brainer. I chose to be with my little boy. I would never leave him. I would rather die than be away from my little angel. The ride from the Rehab Institute was unbearable, dead silence. Then, having to face Vic, my attacker, who almost ended my life, was absolutely unfathomable. How could anyone, with a brain the size of a pea, place me back here? It was beyond comprehension to me. It was impossible for me to fathom or understand the logic behind the idea that I would be safe there. My son and I should have been placed in some kind of a safe house.

I must have dozed off at this point; I was dead tired by now. It had to be close to the time Annie woke up to get ready for work. The TV only had snow on it now; no picture was being broadcast at this time in the morning. I was abruptly awakened by a horrific smell of alcohol followed by the putrid smell of dead fish. It was Vic. He had come into my room and then shut the door behind him tightly. He was drunk and probably high on something. He reeked of alcohol and the smell of dead fish, and he was walking unbalanced, actually, he was staggering like a drunk, but that didn't stop him. He slowly came toward me.

"Hey, Baby. I know you been waitin' for me. I missed you. Why didn't you come to the party with me? You could have danced on the table for all the guys. You are so good at that. I need some love, Baby. Give me some lovin'. I know you want it. Come on, spread those beautiful legs of yours," Vic said.

"Please, Vic, leave me alone. You're drunk. Go sleep it off. You don't want me. Please go," I pleaded.

"What do you mean, I don't want you? Sure, I do, you're my wife and as my wife I can have you anytime I want. So, give it up, Baby. I know you were waiting for me."

"Don't do this, Vic, please. I just got out of the hospital and I don't feel well. I need to sleep and you do too," I begged.

He staggered closer to me and tripped on my leg brace.

"What the hell is this?".

"It's my leg brace. I use it to keep my leg straight, so I can walk. I'm sorry; just shove it out of the way."

"I need you, Chris. Get rid of that thing you got on."

He proceeded to pull up my nightgown. I pulled it back down.

"Oh, I see some panties. They need to go. Take 'em off, Chris. You don't need no panties on."

I was trying to hold down my nightgown while Vic was pulling it up. Then he grabbed my panties and ripped them on one side. Vic fell on top of me. He was fumbling with his pants, but couldn't get them down, so he stood up and took them off. He climbed on top of me again. Now I was trying to lift him off of me, but to no avail. He was so drunk; he didn't realize I still had my panties on as he was trying to have sex with me through my underwear. My panties were the only thing between me and a successful rape by Vic. *He was such a jerk,* I thought.

I started to scream, "Get off of me, get off of me, you son-of-a-bitch!"

Surely his mother would come to my rescue. He put his hand over my mouth. I bit him on the hand. He backhanded me in the face. I was fighting with all my might, slapping and punching, whatever part of his body I managed to hit.

He screamed, "Yeah, Bitch, you like it rough, don't you? I'll show you rough," as he tried to enter me. With each thrust, my head was slamming into the wall at the head of the bed. He realized I still had my panties on and ripped them totally off. With every violent thrust, I screamed with pain for him to stop.

"Yell as loud as you like; no one is gonna hear and if they do, they ain't gonna give a shit. You're my wife and that means you do what I say when I say, got it? Now just lie there and enjoy it and shut the hell up if you know what's good for you!"

, "What are you going to do, shut me up? How are you going to do that? Your two bullets didn't shut me up. Go to hell, you bastard, and make sure you take your mother with you."

As I was trying to fight him off, he grabbed both my wrists and held them down and then tried to kiss me. I moved my head frantically side to side to avoid being kissed by this monster. This continued for what seemed like hours. He finally got off of me, staggered to the door, opened it and was out of sight. I felt so dirty. I knew his mother heard me scream, but she never came to help me. This was her son who was hurting me and yet she did nothing. It took me hours to get back to sleep because I was so fearful of Vic coming back. When I woke up, there, on the floor, were Vic's clothes. It was a horrific reminder of the rape that had occurred earlier.

The next day was an uneventful day until Annie got home from work.

"I went into Little Vic's room to get him and he is not there. Where is my son?" I asked Annie.

She totally ignored me. She said nothing about my early morning hours' screams, either. I stayed in my room watching television all day, except when I dozed off for a couple of short naps. I could hear Annie making something to eat. She never offered me anything. I could hear her washing her own dishes and then go upstairs.

I got in my wheelchair and went into the kitchen. I was going to try again to get something to eat, but the refrigerator door wouldn't open because the dinette table was in the way and being in a wheelchair, I couldn't get close enough. After several attempts to get into the refrigerator, I gave up and went back to my room.

Vic emerged from the bedroom across the hall from me. He didn't say a word to me. I purposely stayed out of his way. He stayed in the living room for several hours and then about 9:00 p.m. or so I heard him leave.

I was forced to go hungry for the whole day and evening. I decided to leave my shorts and shirt on instead of changing into a nightgown for fear of a repeat of the previous early morning hours.

The next day was like the day before. I did not know where my son was. No one talked to me; no one offered to help me. No one asked if I would like something to eat. In fact, I didn't even see Vic all day. I heard him come in around 3 or 4 in the morning and I am so grateful he made a detour around my room. He slept most of the day and left around 7:00 p.m.

Again, when the coast was clear, I tried to find some food. I tried to see if I could figure out a way to get in the cupboards, but they are too high. I tried again to get into the refrigerator, but I just couldn't get the door opened to get any food out because the table was in front of it. I gave up. I didn't know why I kept trying; the outcome was always the same. Everything was just too high for me to reach. Living here was a true test of survival for me.

This was the second day I had not eaten. I went back to my room and turned on my television. I went to bed without anything to eat.

The third day I got an idea. I would use the phone and call my friend, Kathy. I wheeled into the kitchen where the phone was hung on the wall. I didn't realize how high up it was. It didn't seem so high before I got shot. I used this phone hundreds of times, but now it was so high I couldn't reach it. If I could stand long enough I may be able to reach it. I tried several times, but just couldn't keep my balance long enough to reach the phone. I wouldn't give up. I kept trying until finally I was able to quickly knock the phone off the hook. Finally! It sure took long enough. I dialed the number and put the receiver to my ear. It rang four times and then someone answered.

"Hello," they said.

"Hello. Is Kathy there?" I asked. I was praying that Kathy was home.

"Hello, Hello. Is someone there?" they asked again.

"Is Kathy there? Hello. If there is someone there, then answer. Is Kathy there? Can you hear me?"

The person hung up on me. I called back.

"Hello," they said again.

"Hello, Is Kathy there?".

They hung up again. I couldn't believe it. The phone was messed up. I'd try again tomorrow. I went back into my room, so I didn't run into Vic.

I heard Annie come into the house, just getting home from work. I waited until the six o'clock news came on. I went out and could smell Annie had made something for dinner. I stayed in the living room and confronted her about feeding me. Vic once again emerged from the rear bedroom.

"I hope you're hungry. I made meatloaf, mashed potatoes and gravy, and green beans for dinner tonight," Annie said to Vic.

"Yeah, I'll eat in the living room with Chris, so I can watch television," Vic answered.

"OK, it'll be ready in a minute, son," she said.

Annie brought in two plates with the dinner she just described. She gave Vic his plate and carefully put my plate on my lap. I couldn't believe it. She acted like this goes on every evening at dinner time, like I'd been eating each evening.

"I can't believe you. Don't act like you're all nice and have been feeding me each day. I haven't eaten for three days. Do you hear me, Vic? I haven't eaten for three days, that's three whole days. She is trying to starve me to death. This is bullshit!"

As carefully as she put the plate on my lap, I removed it. I took the dinner plate in one hand, food and all. I held it in the palm of my right hand, aimed and threw it at the wall in front of me, above the television set. There was mashed potatoes and gravy running down the wall and meatloaf and green beans on the television and on the floor behind the television set. Lucky for her, the plate didn't break because it was one of those Melamine plates. Well, the good thing was, I just proved Melamine didn't break.

"You bitch, don't put on this big act in front of your son. Tell him you haven't given me any food for three days. Let him know what you are really like. I'm tired of your shit!"

"What the hell?" Vic jumped up and said.

"That's OK, Son, I'll clean it up. You don't think I'd starve her, do you?"

""I don't know. You're both nuts. I'm getting the hell out of here," Vic said and out the front door he went.

I wasn't going without eating one more day, so I took Vic's plate, rolled into the kitchen and grabbed handfuls of food and took it to my room. At least I wouldn't go to bed hungry tonight. For the next week, I had to watch my back. I had to make sure I was in the kitchen when Annie was in there cooking, so I could eat. Three out of the last seven days Vic still came to my room when he was drunk or high or both and I could only imagine what he had been drinking or taking. He forced himself on me. I was so sick of being sexually abused.

Today I was going to call everyone I knew and surely someone would let me stay there. Some of my friends I hadn't seen or talked to in years and others had moved away or changed their phone number. That didn't deter me because I had to get out of there. When I first got to Annie's house, I did not keep up with my exercises, but after the constant abuse, I did start to work out on strengthening my arms and legs. I had gotten a little stronger and it didn't take me as long to get the phone off the hook. I called my parents' house.

"Hello, hello, is there someone there?" my mother said, answering the phone.

She couldn't hear me. I called Kathy's house.

"Hello, hello, hello," someone said.

They didn't hear me, either. I called everyone whose phone number I could remember; each and every one of them could not hear me. Now I couldn't believe the phone could be messed up again. I started to look at the phone. *Why can't anyone hear me?* I wondered. I unscrewed the mouth piece and thought, *maybe there is a loose wire.* When I removed the mouth piece, I was shocked. Part of the inside mouth piece was missing. No wonder no one could hear me.

Was it Vic or was it Annie that removed the mouth piece? *That bitch! I knew it was her,* I thought to myself. She was keeping me literally a prisoner there. I couldn't call out and no one could call in when I was there by myself. Wow! What a diabolical idea! I had to give her credit; she was slick and she knew how to make my life difficult and miserable. I had to beat her at her own game. I got the idea of calling just random numbers and maybe, just maybe, someone would hear me. I called hundreds of numbers. Bingo, finally I hit on a number that could barely hear me.

"Hello, suicide prevention, may I help you?" they answered.

"Can you hear me?" I asked.

"Yes, but just barely. May I help you?" a woman's voice asked me.

"Yes, I'm being held against my will by my husband, who shot me, and his psycho mother. She took the mouth piece out of the phone, so that is why you can't hear me very well. I can barely hear you; talk as loud as you can," I screamed into the phone.

I continued, saying, "Can you call the Dearborn Police for me? I live at 3841 Merrick in Dearborn, Michigan. I'm not sure of the phone number, but I think it is Logan 2-3787. Please tell them I need help," I told her.

"All right. Are you OK? Is there anything else I can do? You're not contemplating suicide, are you?" she asked.

"No. I thought about it in the hospital, but not now. I just need to talk to the police."

"OK. I'll place the call for you as soon as we hang up. My name is Betty Jo if you need to call back again for any reason. Take care of yourself. Good-bye."

"Thank you. Good-bye."

CHAPTER 8

More and More Reports of Abuse

I was expecting the cops to show up right away, but no one came. I got very discouraged. But the next day, while Annie was at work and luckily Vic was also gone; there was a knock on the front door. I wheeled to the front door to answer it. I tried to open the door, but I couldn't believe it. There was a chain lock on the very top of the door, so no one could open the door, but a crack. I cracked the door open. It was a cop.

"We got a call that someone at this address needed help," he said.

"Yes, it's me. I'm being kept a prisoner, as you can see by the door not being able to be opened any more than this. There is a chain lock on the very top of the door. I'm in a wheelchair and I can't reach the chain lock to open the door. My husband, Victor Golden, shot me last December. I was brought here against my will and he constantly physically and sexually abuses me. I hardly get to eat. They even took the mouth piece out of the phone, so I couldn't call for help," I told him.

"Are you married, you said?" the policeman asked me.

"Yes," I answered.

"If you are married, my hands are tied. I can't do anything about problems between a husband and wife. We are not allowed to get involved in domestic disputes or domestic violence issues. I can't help you. I'm sorry."

"You're telling me you can't help me or protect me from my attacker?"

"I'm sorry. I don't make the laws. I only enforce them."

"You have got to be kidding me."

"I'm sorry, ma'am," he said, in a voice that sounded somewhat sympathetic and sincere.

"So, you're telling me if he kills me this time, you can't do anything about it because of your stupid laws?"

"No. Not if he kills you. Then that would be a homicide and he would be arrested, charged with murder, tried in a court of law and sentenced by a court judge."

"In other words, he has to kill me before the law and you will do anything about it. Now that's comforting to know."

"Like I said, ma'am, I don't make the laws, I only enforce them. Is there anything else I can be of assistance for?"

"No, I guess I'll just have to wait until he actually kills me. Then you remember me and our conversation and you will already know who the killer is and where he lives. Thanks, thanks for nothing," I said, now almost in tears.

On that note, the officer turned and walked back to his cop car. *That went well*, I thought to myself. *It's good to know Vic can abuse and assault me whenever he wants and not a damn thing will happen to him. Nice, real nice*, I thought.

I had been here in this hell hole for over two months now. May 6, 1970 was a repeat of so many days before. Vic had woken up from a binger the night before and was demanding my keys to my car. I told him empathetically "No!"

"Where are your car keys?" Vic asked.

"None of your business. Why do you want them anyway?"

"Just give me the damn keys," he demanded.

"No!".

"Never mind, I know where they are. They are in your purse. Where is your purse?"

He started to walk to my bedroom and look for my purse. When he found it sitting next to the TV, I started to go towards the bedroom and try to stop him. When I grabbed my purse, he hit me violently in the head and knocked me down. Instead of leaving, he picked me up with one hand, threw me on the bed and backhanded me again in my face. Now I was in pain. I couldn't do much, but I saw one of Little Vic's balls, so I threw it at him. I don't know what I thought I would accomplish, but I threw it as hard as I could and hit him in the back.

"Give me my purse, you son-of-a-bitch. You got our Malibu and your motorcycle; you don't need my car, too!"

"I'm making sure you ain't going anywhere today!"

With that comment, he got my keys, threw my purse on the couch, started a physical confrontation, I ended up battered and then he left out the front door.

If he thinks he is getting away with that, he's got another think coming, and with that thought I proceeded to call the Dearborn police again.

"I need an officer at 3841 Merrick for help," I told dispatch.

"What is your emergency?" she asked.

"I have been assaulted and am injured."

"Do you need an ambulance?"

"No, but I want an officer out here as fast as he can get here," I said, starting to cry.

"OK, an officer is on his way. Is there anything I can do to help?"

"No, thank you. I'm waiting for them in front," I said and hung the phone up.

When a police car showed up in less than ten minutes, I explained to them what the trouble was.

"I have been beaten up again and my head is hurting really bad. His name is Vic Golden. I want to get the hell out of that house. All I do is keep being assaulted, but I have nowhere else to go. Can you help me? Please take me with you," I begged.

I showed them where Vic hit me one of the times, on my right temple and I felt the blood dripping down my face; I had a knot on my head too.

"We can't transport citizens, but I am getting a taxi for you, so you can come to the station to sign a complaint," one of the officers said.

The officers wrote out a report about the incident and what they saw and ordered a taxi for me and my son, Little Vic. I went to the station, went inside and signed the complaint. At least I had witnesses now. I didn't tell Vic I had called the police. I was afraid of what he might do, but I had to do something or one of these days I would still end up dead.

May 6, 1970. I had to call the Dearborn Police out to the house again for assault on me by Vic. At first, I wanted to talk to the women's division about my problems. I was at a neighbor's house at 3850 Merrick seeking refuge. I made the report about an incident in which Vic and I were arguing and he hit me in the head, causing bleeding and swelling at my right temple. I said I was not going back to that house. The officers said they could not transport me in their police vehicle, but they did get me a taxi to take me to the Dearborn Courthouse to make a formal complaint for assault and battery.

On May 8, 1970, Vic was arrested by the Dearborn police and taken to the station where he was fingerprinted and processed. He appeared in front of Judge Ralph B. Guy. His case was adjourned to May 14, 1970. He was given a $100 bond to appear, which he paid. On May 14, 1970 Vic appeared in court, was found guilty of assault and battery upon me, and was sentenced to 90 days in the Detroit House of Correction plus one-year probation. His sentence was suspended pending his probation.

I thought to myself, *how lucky can one man get? Attempted murder numerous times and yet he is still walking free. There is something very wrong with the current system.* There is no protection for women who are married and are abused by their spouse. I have been an example over and over again and nothing is changing. I am afraid that I will end up dead before laws are passed to protect who they are supposed to be protecting,

COMPLAINT REPORT
(TYPE ONLY)
Complaint File

8A

COMPLAINT NO 70-XXXXXX

3817 Merrick
LOCATION

A & B
NATURE OF COMPLAINT

Gabriele Golden Age   above
COMPLAINANT'S NAME   NO.   STREET   TOWN   STATE   PHONE

above
REPORTED BY   NO.   STREET   TOWN   STATE   PHONE

Dispatcher   X   6 May 70
RECEIVED BY   LETTER   IN PERSON   TELEPHONE   TIME   DATE

R. Maloney, Car 13   D. Stevenson, Car #12
OFFICERS ASSIGNED

DETAILS OF COMPLAINT:—

The complainant stated that she and her husband, Victor Golden,   yrs,
had an argument and he hit her with his fist along the side of her head, she is an invalid
and would like to talk to someone from the womens division about her problem.

POLICE DEPARTMENT

5-6-70 A&B (assault and battery) report made

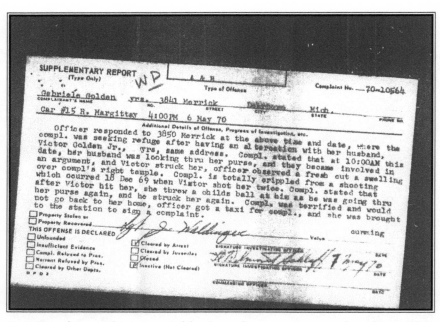

SUPPLEMENTARY REPORT
(Type Only)

WP   A & B

Type of Offense   Complaint No. —70-10564

Gabriela Golden   yrs.   3841 Merrick   Dearborn   Mich.
COMPLAINANT'S NAME   NO.   STREET   CITY   STATE   PHONE NO.

Car #15 R. Margitta   4:00PM 6 May 70

Additional Details of Offense, Progress of Investigation, etc.

Officer responded to 3850 Merrick at the above time and date, where the compl. was seeking refuge after having an altercation with her husband, Victor Golden Jr., yrs, same address. Compl. stated that at 10:00AM this date, her husband was looking thru her purse, and they became involved in an argument, and Victor struck her, officer observed a fresh cut a swelling over compl's right temple. Compl. is totally crippled from a shooting which occurred 18 Dec 69 when Victor shot her twice. Compl. stated that after Victor hit her, she threw a childs ball at him as he was going thru her purse again, and he struck her again. Compl. was terrified and would not go back to her home, officer got a taxi for compl., and she was brought to the station to sign a complaint.

☐ Property Stolen or
☐ Property Recovered_____Value_____
THIS OFFENSE IS DECLARED   cumming
☐ Unfounded
☐ Insufficient Evidence   ☑ Cleared by Arrest
☐ Compl. Refused to Pros.   ☐ Cleared by Juveniles   SIGNATURE INVESTIGATING OFFICER
☐ Warrant Refused by Pros.   ☐ Closed
☐ Cleared by Other Depts.   ☑ Inactive (Not Cleared)   SIGNATURE INVESTIGATING OFFICER   DATE
D P D 3   COMMANDING OFFICER   DATE

5-6-70 taking refuge at neighbor's, police come out and make written report of seeing blood and swelling at my right temple from getting hit in head by Vic.

144

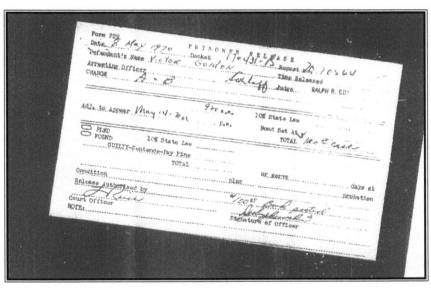

5-8-70 Vic arrested, posted $100 bond, adjourned to 5-14-70.

SUPPLEMENTARY REPORT
– (Type Only)

W.D.

A & B
Type of Offense

Complaint No. 70-10564

Gabriele Golden	3841 Merrick		Dbn		
COMPLAINANT'S NAME	NO.	STREET	CITY	STATE	PHONE NO.

R. Maloney, Car #13   D. Stevenson, Car #12   8 May 70   1:30PM   Wend, Car #5

Additional Details of Offense, Progress of Investigation, etc.

The officers responded to the above location with a warrant for a Victor
Golden,   yrs, and brought Mr. Golden to the stn. Mr Golden appeared before Judge Ralph
B. Guy this date on charges of A & B, per Dkt# 170431-B. The case was Adj. to appear on
May 14, 70, and a $100.00 bond, bond was paid.

Sgt. Vance

☐ Property Stolen or
☐ Property Recovered

THIS OFFENSE IS DECLARED
☐ Unfounded
☐ Insufficient Evidence
☐ Compl. Refused to Pros.
☐ Warrant Refused by Pros.
☐ Cleared by Other Depts.
D P D 3

☐ Cleared by Arrest
☐ Cleared by Juveniles
☐ Closed
☒ Inactive (Not Cleared)

SIGNATURE INVESTIGATING OFFICER   Voids   162   8 May 70   DATE

SIGNATURE INVESTIGATING OFFICER   DATE

COMMANDING OFFICER   DATE

5-8-70 supplementary report to warrant. Adjourned to 5-14-70

146

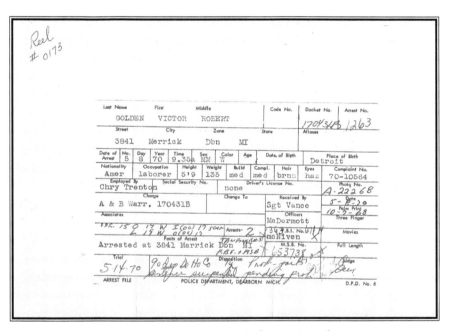

Last Name	First	Middle		Code No.	Docket No.	Arrest No.
GOLDEN	VICTOR	ROBERT			170431B	1263
Street	City	Zone	State		Aliases	
3841	Merrick	Dbn	MI			

Date of Arrest	Mo.	Day	Year	Time	Sex	Color	Age	Date of Birth	Place of Birth
	5	8	70	9.35a	MM	W			Detroit

Nationality	Occupation	Height	Weight	Build	Compl.	Hair	Eyes	Complaint No.
Amer	laborer	5'9	135	med	med	brnn	haz	70-10564

Employed By	Social Security No.	Driver's License No.	Photo No.
Chry Trenton		none	A-22268

Charge	Change To	Received By	Date
A & B Warr. 170431B		Sgt Vance	5-8-70

Associates		Officers	Palm Print
		McDermott	10-2-68

F.P.C. 15 O 19 W I (00) 17 Scam Arrests- 2 36 F.B.I. No. 611
        19 W 0(09) 17   McNiven   Three Finger

Arrested at 3841 Merrick Dbn MI   TFWPUB(s) M.S.B. No. 653738

Trial	Disposition	Judge
5-14-70	90 Sep to HoCo	Sen

ARREST FILE   POLICE DEPARTMENT, DEARBORN MICH.   D.P.D. No. 6

5-14-70 *arrest warrant, information sheet.*

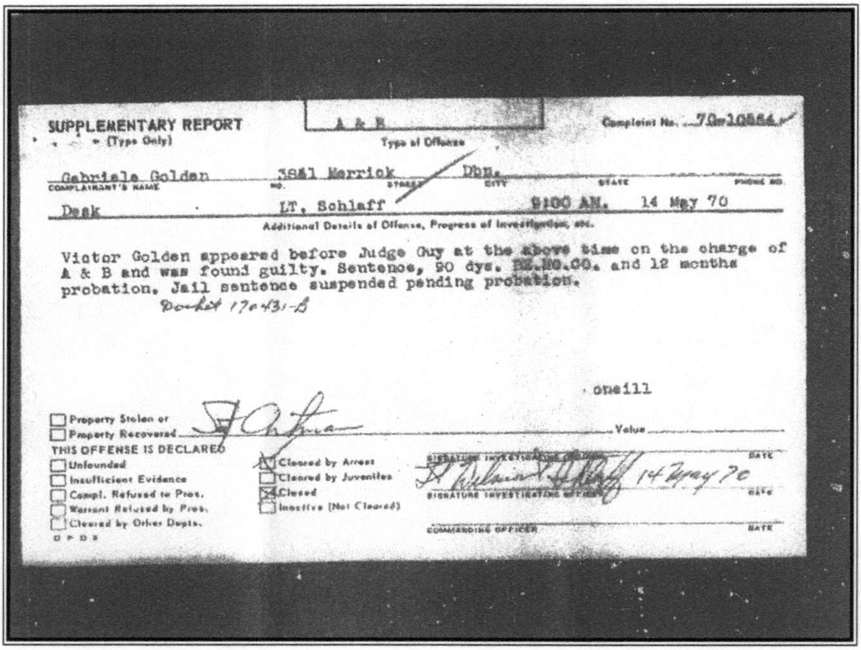

SUPPLEMENTARY REPORT (Type Only)

A & B
Type of Offense

Complaint No. 70-10864

Gabriele Golden	3841	Merrick	Dbn.		
COMPLAINANT'S NAME	NO.	STREET	CITY	STATE	PHONE NO.

Desk LT. Schlaff 9:00 AM. 14 May 70

Additional Details of Offense, Progress of Investigation, etc.

Victor Golden appeared before Judge Guy at the above time on the charge of A & B and was found guilty. Sentence, 90 dys. DE.HO.CO. and 12 months probation. Jail sentence suspended pending probation.

Docket 170431-B

oneill

☐ Property Stolen or
☐ Property Recovered ____ Value ____

THIS OFFENSE IS DECLARED

☐ Unfounded
☐ Insufficient Evidence
☐ Compl. Refused to Pros.
☐ Warrant Refused by Pros.
☐ Cleared by Other Depts.

☒ Cleared by Arrest
☐ Cleared by Juveniles
☒ Closed
☐ Inactive (Not Cleared)

SIGNATURE INVESTIGATING OFFICER ____ DATE
SIGNATURE INVESTIGATING OFFICER ____ 14 May 70 DATE
COMMANDING OFFICER ____ DATE

D P D 3

5-14-70 appeared in Dearborn court, found guilty of A&B, sentenced 90 days De Ho Co plus 1 yr. probation, suspended.

Fingerprints of Victor Robert Golden, Jr.

Today was June 2, 1970. I had been eating irregularly, but at least I'd been eating. I had been exercising my arms, doing better transfers to and from my wheelchair, and practicing using my Loftstrand crutches for the majority of my walking. I needed to get my independence back. I had called the police numerous times in hopes of reaching someone's sympathetic ear, so they would act and do something to Vic for all the abuse, neglect, sexual assaults and any other physical and mental harm Vic and his mother had done to me. At least I saw my son. I wanted to take my little boy out of this house and move where we could be safe and happy.

I was hoping today would be a boring and uneventful day, but as history had proven, I was sure it was going to be a repeat of days, even months past.

The day started like the days prior since I was released from Rehab. I woke up, as I did every morning, not knowing what the day would bring. It was a nice June morning, with July just around the corner, and I knew it would get hotter as the day progressed. I got dressed on my bed in a pair of shorts and a shell top. I walked into the bathroom on my crutches and sat on the toilet to wash my face, clean my teeth and comb my hair.

Now that I was on my crutches, I could reach the phone, get in the refrigerator and even get in the cupboards. How cool was that? It was real cool. I had beat Annie at her own game. Never again could she try to starve me to death. I was a fighter and a survivor and I was not about to give up to anyone. I first made myself some toast and a glass of milk to drink for breakfast.

I had not had a period since I was shot December 18, 1969. I made an appointment, and then went to the doctor for a complete checkup. Maria watched Little Vic while I was gone.

I drove myself in my 1965 T-Bird. When I got to my doctor's office, I walked on my crutches, told the desk nurse I was there and proceeded to sit down and wait for my name to be called.

"Mrs. Golden, the doctor is ready for you now," the nurse said to me.

I was rather nervous. I didn't know why, but I felt very anxious today. I followed the nurse into one of the exam rooms.

"Please wait in here and the doctor will see you in a few minutes." she said.

Like clockwork, the doctor knocked on the door and then announced it was her.

"So, what brings you here today?" the doctor asked.

"Well, I was just wondering why I haven't had a period yet. It has been at least six months now. Is my blood still building up, since I was shot twice and lost a lot of blood?" I asked.

"It is a good idea to get a complete checkup, so I'll check you out and do some tests. We'll take some blood and a urine sample, OK? I'll get one of the nurses to come in and get some blood from you and then you can go down the hall to the bathroom and give a urine sample," the doctor informed me.

"I warn you, I hate needles."

"I'm sure you will survive the needle poke. It only stings for a moment, like a bee sting."

Why do they always lie and say it doesn't hurt? It does hurt from the time they stick you until they take the needle out.

Just as the doctor said, the nurse came in, took my blood and had to put a piece of gauze and tape over the injection site because I tended to bleed longer than most, but I was not a hemophiliac. And by the way, it did hurt. I proceeded to go to the bathroom to give a urine sample and then came back to my exam room. The doctor came back in to check all my vital signs: blood pressure, temperature, heart rate and pulse. She checked my lungs, my reflexes and even pressed on my abdomen. It was a thorough checkup.

"Everything seems to be good. It shouldn't be long for the test results I asked for. Wait here and I will return with the results," the doctor told me.

I waited about twenty minutes before my doctor returned. She had a slight smile on her face when she entered my exam room.

"Well, congratulations are in order. You're pregnant," she announced.

"Congratulations? Pregnant? You're kidding, right? Are you sure?" I asked and then continued, "Vic told me I couldn't get pregnant because I was paralyzed from the waist down and when all that stuff is paralyzed you can't get pregnant. Don't get me wrong, but this is not the ideal time for me to be pregnant."

"Your husband is wrong. He is not a doctor, is he? I promise; you are pregnant."

Finding out I was pregnant was the last thing I would have guessed. In fact, I was shocked. What was I going to do? I couldn't care for my first child like I would have wanted, so what was I going to do with two little ones to care for? This news weighed heavily on my mind as I drove myself back to Vic's house. What would I say and when? Who would I tell this news to? This is ordinarily such great news, and yet I felt it was some kind of act of treason. Vic kept telling me I couldn't get pregnant every time he forced me to have sex with him and I would object for fear of getting pregnant. When I arrived back to the house, no one was home yet. I went straight to my bedroom, turned the TV on and tried to watch it. I ended up falling asleep. I slept until I heard the side door slam, which woke me up.

It was Vic getting home. I stayed in my room until dinner was ready. I joined Vic and Little Vic for dinner, but all I could do was push my food around the plate and pick at it. I fed Little Vic and when he finished eating, I wiped his hands and face and played with him in my room until it was his bedtime—8:00 p.m.

I tried to watch television again, but my secret kept running around in my head. I eventually fell asleep until the following morning. Now I needed to have more calcium for the baby. I first made myself some toast and a glass of milk to drink for breakfast. I still didn't know when or if I would tell Vic. Now, telling his mother I was pregnant was a definite no. I wouldn't tell her the time of day, let alone tell her Vic and I were going to have another baby. She was not fit to be anyone's grandmother. Look how she screwed up her own kids. She was not going to screw up my kids.

Being there all alone seemed a little creepy and yet it felt good, all at the same time. I went out on the front porch and breathed in nice, fresh air. I saw some little squirrels running around, but sadly, it reminded me of my little pet squirrel, Rocky. Vic and his stupid friends shot and killed it. I also missed Little Vic's black Cocker Spaniel, Pepper. Annie never owned up to what she had done with Pepper. I knew she had gotten rid of her because she thought she was my dog, but in actuality, she belonged to Little Vic. Pepper always protected me against Vic's attacks. She jumped up and caught Vic's arm and pulled it down. She was a great protector. I missed her.

One thing I didn't miss was the pair of parakeets we had at the dumpy apartment we lived in behind the Ford Rouge Plant

They crapped everywhere. I was so glad to have gotten rid of them. No more birds for me, ever. I'd never forget my 1969 Plymouth Road Runner. I wondered what ever happened to that. I'm sure Vic knew something about that, but I'd be stupid to even suggest he had anything to do with its disappearance. It would be so easy for him to sell it since he was legally my husband. I beat Corvettes with that car. I knew how to drive, but I knew my racing days were over. I couldn't drive anything with a clutch anymore. Now, an automatic was a piece of cake. I thanked God for me being able to still drive a car. Just like Joe Cocker's song, "I'm Feeling Alright", I was feeling alright, now that I could drive my automatic '65 T-Bird. I wondered what life for me would be like had I never gotten shot. One thing was for sure, I would have been able to carry my own babies and I never would have gotten a job in a bar as a dancer, but I would have gotten a job with a law firm or insurance company, a white-collar job.

Yes, Vic really ruined my life and what's really crappy; he's not even sorry about shooting me. If he was, he would never have treated me like he did. At one point in my life I could honestly say I loved him with all my heart, but he ruined that. Here in this house, I went to bed fearful and I woke up glad I made it through another night and that I was still alive. That was pretty sad.

He had changed me into a person I didn't even recognize. Would you believe, while lying in the hospital and nothing else to do but think, I came up with some horrible thoughts? I dreamed about hiring a hit man and having him shoot Vic in the spine, so he couldn't walk, either. Then I dreamed I ran Vic over in my car, so he couldn't walk again. I even entertained the idea of making Voodoo dolls in his image and making him suffer. I never once wanted Vic dead. I only wanted him to suffer like I was suffering and I'd bet it would only get worse as I got older.

What a crappy future to look forward to. I regretted ever meeting Vic. If I never would have met him, I would be walking today and not living in this concentration camp called Camp Hell. I didn't have anything good to look forward to. My life as I once knew it was now over. I also have wondered why Vic never came to visit me while I was in Detroit General Hospital or even Detroit Rehabilitation Institute. And I have wondered if he ever gave blood for me. After all, he caused all this, putting me in the hospital and causing me to lose so much blood and now, my never being able to walk again.

Did he even have a conscience or was he just pure evil? I have often wondered why he didn't treat me like a queen. After all, I gave him a second chance in life by not pressing charges on him for attempted murder. The detectives were really mad at me for not going through with the prosecution. The Judge, Joseph E. Maher, thought I was nuts. They all wanted to nail Vic to the cross on my behalf, but I was partly fearful and partly still having feelings for Vic. I now regretted my decision, looking back at how Vic had treated me in the last several months. I didn't deserve to be treated like this. This somehow hadn't seemed like a fair trade; my life for his. He ruined my life forever and I gave him back his life forever. He will never serve time in prison. He got money for being on medical at Chrysler's while not working, and then got a good job at Ford Motor's and was making a good living. He was always worried about getting drafted and now he would never be drafted because of the felony he committed. He still had two good legs and me;

I might as well have been cut in half. He should be kissing my feet for not putting him in prison and not giving him a felony criminal record that would follow him for the rest of his useless life. He would never have been able to get a good job or live a decent life if it wasn't for me. He should have been good to me, making sure I had all the medical supplies and equipment I would ever need. I should have had the best that was possible. Someone please smack Vic in the head to knock some sense into him. He could have been sitting behind prison bars for years. Wouldn't you think he should be kissing my feet for that second chance? Shouldn't he be taking care of me, making the rest of life as comfortable, safe, and happy as possible?

Oh man, I was getting really depressed. Reflecting on what could have been, what should have been and what it was, surely was not good for me or my mental health, so on that note I went back into the house and turned on the television to get my mind off of all those thoughts. I was alone most of the day. Annie got home at her usual time, four o'clock.

I stayed in my room until dinner time. When I thought it was ready, I came out of my room. I wanted to know where Little Vic had been all day.

"Where was my son today?" I asked Vic.

Vic answered, "He was with me. I had to go over to Shortridge's house to help him with his shit."

"What? Are you crazy, taking him to that weirdo's house. Don't ever take him over there again!"

"Shut the hell up! I'll bring him wherever the hell I want. He's my kid too!"

"Then you don't bring him to trash like that."

"Just shut up and feed him!"

"Come on, Little Vic. Let's get up in your highchair."

"What is he gonna eat?"

"He'll eat the noodles and sausage, just like us. I'll just have to cut up the sausage real small. Pour him some milk in his Tommy Tippy Cup and please pour me a glass too."

"Why are you drinking milk all of a sudden? We got pop."

"No, I'll have some milk. Women need milk for their bones."

"Yeah, yeah, if you say so," Vic mumbled.

"Why don't we ever go anywhere as a family?" I asked Vic.

"I don't know. You can't go to places where it's fun."

"Oh, pardon me. And who did this to me? You're a real piece of work."

"Shut up and get out of my face!"

"If you're waiting for me to walk again, I wouldn't hold my breath if I were you. It isn't happening, not now, not ever,"

"You don't know that."

"I do know that. The doctors told me I'd never walk again. I have no sense of balance. If that is what you are waiting for, you might as well leave now or let me leave."

"You're not going anywhere, got it?"

"Come on, Little Vic, finish your noodles and we'll go in my room and play with your See N Say," I said to my son, trying to change the subject.

I sat with Little Vic until he finished his dinner and milk. I wiped his face and hands and then brought him into my room, so we could spend some fun time together before Annie ripped him away from me again.

I did what I didn't want to do and that was getting Vic in a bad mood. On the other hand, I wasn't going to stand by and let him take my son to some scumbag's house. I wouldn't take a dog there. I could rarely talk to Vic without him getting mad or ordering me around. I stayed in my room after Little Vic went to bed. Vic stayed in the living room until around 9:00 p.m. I hated it when he went out because he always came back drunk or high or both and he was so mean and violent and uncontrollable. This was beginning to be a routine for Vic— stay out all night, come home drunk or high or both, have sex with me, go to sleep and sleep it off all during the day, and out again at night. On this particular day Vic woke up earlier than usual. He was in a very argumentative state of mind. He had come home so drunk and high on something, I didn't want to be anywhere near him.

I was sitting in my wheelchair in the living room. Vic had come out of the back bedroom.

All of a sudden, he said to me, "Come on, Chris, and make love to me."

"What? I don't think so, you reek of alcohol and the smell of dead fish again," I said.

"I'm not drunk, but I need a little lovin'," Vic said.

"Well, you can get it from your whore you go to see all the time. She only lives a couple of blocks away from here."

Vic replied, saying, "No, I don't want anyone, but you. You're my wife, remember."

"Yes, I am your wife and yes, I do remember, but you sure don't."

"Come on, let's get it on. Let's make love."

"Leave me alone!"

I wheeled myself into the kitchen to get away from Vic, but he followed me. He tried to pick me up out of the wheelchair, but I cling to the side arms. He tried to pull me free. I held on for dear life. Finally, I lost my grip and then he picked me up out of the wheelchair and took me to his old bedroom, which was now mine, where he dropped me on the bed.

"Come on, Baby, work your magic. You turn me on."

"Well you turn me off. Leave me alone!"

"Let's have some of that afternoon delight."

He pulled off his t-shirt and unbuckled his pants. Off they came. I had a blouse and shorts on. While standing at the side of the bed, he tried to unbutton my blouse as I was trying to keep it buttoned, but he was too drunk and couldn't get the last two buttons undone, so he ripped my blouse open. My legs don't move, so all I had were my arms and hands to fight with. I was lying on my back on the bed, but I was fighting frantically with my arms and hitting him. With some difficulty, he pulled my shorts and panties down and then finally off. He spread my legs like a wishbone. I hated wearing that leg brace, but this was one time I wished I had put it on. He walked to the foot of the bed and stood there for a moment, just looking at me. He slowly started to climb toward me from the end of the bed, kissing my legs as he went upwards. I could feel him touching me between my legs.

Vic said, "Why are you not the least bit turned on, do I not turn you on anymore? I am going to have to do something about that."

I could feel the warmth of his tongue all over between my legs. I started trying to roll from side to side. I wished my legs would move, so I could kick him, but I couldn't. Gradually, he moved a bit further up and now started to fondle my breasts. He put his face in-between my breasts and started to kiss them all over. He massaged, rubbed, and worked my breasts like they were a ball of clay. He got on top of me and held my arms down. He tried to kiss me, but I keep moving my head from side to side. He tried to kiss my breasts again, but I started to rock from side to side, trying to get him off of me.

"Get off of me, get off of me! I'm tired of you always forcing me to have sex with you, when you just came from your whore's house. Isn't she enough for you? Why do you want to screw me all the time when you got her to screw whenever you want?"

"I don't want her. I want only you."

"You don't love me. You only want to possess me. You want to hurt me and get even with me for whatever you think I have done to you. We never make love anymore; we just have sex, or should I say 'rape'. What kind of marriage is that, cheating on me all the time and with someone as nasty as Barb?"

"I do love you and you are my wife. Don't you love me, Chris?"

"How can I love someone who treats me like you do? You don't love me enough not to cheat on me, because you are always at that nasty, dirty, and ugly, piece of shit, fish-smelling whore's house. Barb, that name fits her to a tee."

He once again lost interest in conversation and resumed the act of having sex with me. I made it difficult for him, as he had to use one hand to try to restrain my arms and used the other to guide himself inside of me. It took some time, but he eventually was in me. He aggressively moved up and down on me. He once again became victorious over me. He ended up getting his way with me because I couldn't escape him.

I hated him; I hated how he treated me; I hated how he acted; I hated how he drank; I hated how he got high; I hated how he went to see Barb and then came home and had sex with me. I worried constantly if and when he would give me some kind of sexually transmitted disease. I knew he didn't wear a condom, which left me completely unprotected and vulnerable to anything he might catch and bring home. I, most of all, hated it when he forced me to engage in oral sex. His mother knew what was going on and yet she did nothing. After the sex, he fell back into a drunken, sleeping stupor. I pushed him off of me and managed to slide off the bed. I was able to get dressed on the floor and drag myself to the wheelchair. Usually my Loftstrand crutches were in the bedroom, but for some unknown reason they were in the living room. After much effort, I finally made it into the wheelchair. I had to change into a different top because he ripped the last one. I was furious.

While Vic was sleeping it off in my bed that he had just raped me in, I went into Little Vic's bedroom to get him. I had been wondering why Maria didn't come to my room to see what all the commotion was about while Vic was forcing himself on me. I found out why when I opened Little Vic's bedroom door. Little Vic and Maria were not even in there. Maria probably heard all the beating and banging and yelling, so she probably took Little Vic out for a walk. That's usually where she went when she knew something bad was about to happen. I knew she had to have been there at times when Vic was abusing me. Once I heard Vic telling her to go take Little Vic out for a walk prior to his coming into my room and raping me. I couldn't say that I blamed her. She didn't speak much English, mostly Spanish, and she was only a young pregnant teenager. She was probably scared to death and very uncomfortable with all the goings on. With no one here, I turned on the television and watched some shows I liked. Sometime later, Maria returned with my son and told me she took Little Vic to the backyard because she heard loud voices. She fed him and then put him down for a nap. I wondered, *how much loud voices did Little Vic hear and did he understand any of it?* I sure hope not. Maria retreated to the basement. I didn't know what was so interesting in the basement, but she went there a lot. I assumed she slept downstairs.

I watched Annie go into the kitchen. It had to have been getting close to dinner time. I could see her standing at the counter, but I couldn't tell what she was making. I watched her as she peeled and sliced potatoes. I smelled what seemed like hamburgers being fried. I'll bet she was making hamburgers and fried potatoes. I was just going to stay there in the living room until she finished eating and went upstairs to her room.

Annie said to me, "Go get Vic and tell him dinner is ready."

I quickly replied back to her, "I'm not going to get Vic. If you want him, you go get him. He's in my room. Do you know he raped me? I don't want to be anywhere near him right now. In fact, I've had it with him. All the money in the world couldn't make me go and open that door to wake him up, let alone speak to him."

"Well he needs to eat," she said.

"Well then, you go and get him up. I could care less if he eats or not. For all I care he can starve to death."

She fixed her plate and sat at the dinette table to eat her dinner. I stayed in the living room. I didn't dare go in the kitchen where she was. I waited until she was finished in there before I went in the kitchen to fix me something to eat.

Vic woke up again at about 9:00 p.m. He stumbled out of my room and demanded I get him something to eat.

I said to him, "If you want to eat, you fix it yourself. I'm not your sex slave, nor am I your personal waitress."

He answered, "What the hell is your problem?"

"As if you don't know. I guess you had a little too much afternoon delight and it has clouded your brain."

"Oh, that. Hey, man, a husband is supposed to get it on with his wife, remember."

"Maybe if you stayed off the drugs and booze you might remember a thing or two. Why don't you get off medical leave from Chrysler's and get a job again? I'm sure they are getting tired of paying you medical benefits for you to party all night and to booze it up or get high."

"I have more reason than you to get drunk or high to forget my problems, which by the way, you caused. You think it's easy to live with you and all you do that is still hurting me? You haven't done a thing to try to help me or to make things better for me or easier for me. I'm still just your little trophy wife that is supposed to take it."

"Why don't you grow up and act like a man? Do I need to tell you what the word 'fidelity' means? In case you don't know, it means you are loyal, faithful and you don't cheat on your wife. You get sex from me and then you go to your whore's house and have sex again. How much sex does one guy need?"

"You told me I probably can't ever have any more kids because I am paralyzed. You ruin everything. But you go on, eat your dinner, clean up and get dressed and go be with that slut. Just don't come back home to me. I don't think you even know what love is anymore. Sex used to be beautiful with you, but now it is just a dirty word. Go on, get out of here. Get out of here now!"

CHAPTER 9

Felonious Assault by Strangulation

It was June 7, 1970. I didn't know why that night set me off, but it did. I really needed to jump into Vic's shit. All my pent-up anger rose to the surface. He had just raped me earlier that day, and yet, he acted like it was no big deal, an everyday occurrence. Oh, I forgot—it was. That was the norm for him. I swear, Vic is Satan incarnate, the devil, the great fallen angel, Lucifer himself. And Barb, well, Barb is Barb; cheap, fake, homely, and just nasty with no morals, scruples, values, or integrity.

Well, not this night. I was going to do something about it. I waited until he drove off. I grabbed my purse, opened it to get my keys out, but they were gone again. I was so tired of him playing these stupid games of hide and seek with my keys. He had no right to have my keys and he knew this. That was my T-Bird that I bought by myself. He still had his motorcycle and our 1968 Chevelle Malibu. He thought that if he hid my keys, I couldn't follow him and find out where he was going, what he was doing and who he was doing it with. Well, I knew exactly where he was going, what he was doing and who he was doing it with. He was such a jerk. *What did he think I was, stupid?* It didn't take me long to find them. He must have been high or drunk or maybe even both when he hid my keys, because I always seemed to find them hidden in the kitchen.

I didn't have to follow him; I knew where he would be, at the adulteress's house. I walked on my crutches to the kitchen and down two steps to the landing. I then opened the side door and went down one step to the driveway, walked to the street and got into my T-Bird. I already knew where that son-of-a-bitch was. He was at Barb's. This was the one who he told me to stay away from because she was bad news. Well, that part was true; she was bad news. And she was a whore, sleeping with a married man, shame on her. And she had a kid, Rita, whom I felt sorry for. That little girl deserved much better. She deserved a mother that truly loved her, not who used her. I was going to take care of that lying, cheating, good for nothing husband of mine and let her know I knew what was going on over at her house. I put my keys in the ignition and started the engine, put it in gear and drove off. I pulled into the neighbor's driveway to turn around. I went to the stop sign at Merrick and Carlysle and turned right. I went down Carlysle several streets until I came to Dudley and turned right again. I drove towards her house, 3846 Dudley, on the left to make sure our car was there. It was, parked in the driveway and her aqua blue or turquois Cougar was parked on the street in the front of the house.

Someone was peeking out of the curtains. I'm sure it was her. The next thing I knew, the front door suddenly opened and there she stood, big as life.

Barb yelled out, "What do you want, bitch, your man? Well he's with me," like Vic was some wonderful prize or something.

I backed up and pulled closer to the curb parked on the wrong side of the street in front of the Cougar.

I yelled back, "Who are you calling a bitch, you whore!"

"I may be a whore, but I have what you want. Wait a minute, that came out wrong."

"No, you got that right. You are nothing, but a cheap, dirty, nasty, home-wrecking, whore. You can have him, I don't want him!"

"Then why are you here?"

"I just wanted to see with my own eyes that he comes here. He denies it all the time at home. He swears he never sees you, but that's a lie. I want to know one thing from you. Are there any insidious diseases you have that I should know about? He forces himself on me all the time. Can't you keep him satisfied, so I don't have to deal with him? Why does he have to rape me?" I yelled back, feeling like I was in control of this situation and I was getting in all the zingers I could think of to put her down.

"Get the hell out of here you bitch. Vic said for you to leave!"

"I'll leave when I'm good and ready!"

"Go to hell!" Barb yelled out the door.

"I've been there every time with Vic. He can't keep his hands off of me or all his other parts either," I yelled back at her.

"You're a liar!"

"Ask him. Can you not get a guy of your own? Do you have to mess with a married man? He even has a baby. Have you no shame or guilt? He uses you because he tells me you have the best vise grips. Is that true?"

"Shut up you bitch!"

"Here's another question for you. Why do you have such an insatiable appetite for sex? Are you a nymphomaniac?"

"I don't know, but you're what you just said."

"He told me he has to put a paper bag over your head just to have sex with you, because he can't stand to look at you. He says you are repulsive to him. He has always forbidden me to go around you. Bow Wow. Do you want a bone or should I say a boner?"

"Well, at least I'm not crippled, you bitch!" Barb screamed at me.

I knew I had hit a raw nerve with Barb, but she touched on one subject I didn't like, either. You can call me most anything you like, but I hated being called crippled. I didn't know why, but it really bothered me. I had a vast variety of bad things to say to her and about her because Vic at one time or another had said them to me about her. I could throw zingers at her all-night long. She was so easy to put down. I knew I was lowering myself to her level, but I just couldn't resist. I was not ready to let it go.

"I'd come up there to beat your ass, but I might get my hands dirty and I'm allergic to the smell of dead fish."

"Oh, yeah. Come here and try it!"

Truth be known, she couldn't fight her way out of a paper bag if it was soaking wet.

"You are beyond pathetic and I wouldn't waste my time!"

"You're just a crippled bitch and Vic says so, too!"

"Let me tell you a few things you are. You are a whore, slut, adulteress, hussy, trollop, loose woman, strumpet, fornicator, promiscuous, immoral, and of course, let's not forget a home-wrecking bitch! Oh, I almost forgot, you're also a dirty, nasty skank. He should know, after all, he caused all this. He made me crippled. How does that make you feel? You have a guy who is an attempted murderer. Wow, you should be proud of him.

He's such a great catch, more like a booby prize. He's a real man, that's for sure."

There was a brief pause. I guess she couldn't come up with a good come back. I still couldn't let it go, so I continued.

"Then tell him to say it to my face. I don't hear him saying one word."

"It's because he don't want to talk to you, Bitch!"

"You just don't get it, do you?"

"Get the hell out of here!"

"Tell that no-good, two-timing, cheating, son- of-a-bitch, husband of mine to get out here!"

"No," she answered, short and sweet.

I saw Vic standing behind Barb, and he slammed the front door closed. That just showed what a spineless jellyfish-of-a-man Vic was. If he cared for Barb, like she thought he did, he would have come to her defense, but he didn't. I could see her once again, peeking from behind the curtains, watching me. *Well, now what?* I asked myself. What I really wanted to do was drive right across her front lawn and through her front door, so I could tell her face-to-face what I thought of her, Vic, and their little trysts they were having. I was just getting started. I wanted her to know how pissed off I was at the both of them.

I sat in my T-Bird contemplating my options. Then, all of a sudden, looking through my windshield, I saw her aqua blue Cougar parked in front of me. *Well, you asked for it,* I thought. My inner rage was beyond description or repression and I acted with overwhelming anger and hurt. I felt like my blood vessels were ready to pop out of my temples; smoke was ready to blow out of my ears; my heart was ready to jump out of my chest; and my legs were spasming out of control. I pulled into the neighbor's driveway across the street, put it into reverse and then I did the unthinkable. I backed right into the driver's side door of her Cougar. It wasn't much of a dent, but it would be something for her to remember me by. Even if I had to pay for damages, it would be worth it. You don't know how much I hated the both of them. I knew it was wrong and I knew I shouldn't have been, but I was pleased with myself. I took it out of reverse, put it in drive, and drove back to his mother's house. I went back in and went to my room. I was ready for the next confrontation with Vic over tonight. Let him deny now that he didn't go to see that whore, Barb. I was ready for him. Boy, was I ever ready!

Did she think he was going to leave me for her? He would not let go of the strangulation hold he had on me until every glimmer of hope was gone.

I so wished I had somewhere else to go. I would have been gone in a heartbeat. I turned my television on and decided not to think about all the crap that happened today. I had lived through the bad, enough bad to last a lifetime. I needed some good in my life, and I was determined to find it. I changed into my nightgown and got comfortable and lay in my bed. I stayed up to watch the eleven o'clock news. I guess I was more tired than I realized because I had fallen asleep with the television on.

Like clockwork, Vic came home about 3:00 a.m. He came into my room. I heard him, but pretended to be asleep. I did not want any confrontation with the drunk now. I didn't know why he didn't just leave me alone. The sex couldn't be good because I didn't ever respond to him in a loving, passionate way. I just lay there like a bump on a log without moving, or I tried to fight like hell to get him off me. But there he was again, trying to get into my bed and into my panties.

Like settlers of a virgin territory ravaged the land, so too, Vic ravaged my body. He left me sore and in pain from the brutal and abusive sexual assaults, knowing I could never fight back.

"Chris, are you awake?" Vic asked me.

If I answered him, then he would know I was awake, so I tried to pretend I was asleep.

"Chris, wake up. I need you."

Vic stuck his head under my nightgown. I tried to move onto my side, but couldn't and he was getting twisted up in my nightgown.

I asked him, "What are you doing?"

"I'm trying to suck on those beautiful titties,"

"Please leave me alone. I was asleep."

"You need your beauty sleep?"

"No, I just need my sleep."

"You let Little Vic suck on your titties."

"Yes, when I was breastfeeding him. He now drinks out of a cup."

"I don't need a cup."

"Vic, go to bed."

"That's what I'm trying to do."

"In your own bed, not mine," I said, only louder.

"This is my bed."

"This was your room, but right now it's my bed. Please go to your bed."

I felt like I was talking to a little child who didn't understand.

"I'll go after you give me a blow job."

"I don't think so. Go to Shortridge's for that. Why do you want a blow job? Didn't Barb give you one tonight with her vise grips?"

"I think so."

"Get off me!"

"You don't tell me what to do, Bitch!"

"I know you've been with Barb because I smell dead fish on you from her. You stink. You're disgusting, nasty and dirty. Get off me!"

He kicked off his shoes and then took his pants and skivvies off, but left his T-shirt on. He climbed on top of me, very precisely, sat on me, and pinned my arms down with his knees. He was trying to force me to have oral sex. I didn't know which style of sex I hated more with Vic—oral or just straight sex. He had forced me in the past to have oral sex with him. I started screaming, and then I stopped and just turned and watched television since it was still on. I was as lifeless as I could possibly be. I was hoping he would lose interest in me. Instead, he got off of me, stood up, picked up the television, pulled the cord out of the wall and threw it at me. I ducked and it just missed me by an inch and it hit the wall. It was smashed into a million pieces.

"Now your boyfriend can buy you another TV. Is there anything else you would like me to get rid of for you from your boyfriend?"

"That was not necessary! You didn't have to break it. It was a get-well gift, not a gift from a boyfriend. I never went out with him. He was just a nice guy who cared about me."

"Well, now he can be a nice guy again and buy you a new one, you stupid bitch. I'm getting my blow job now or else!"

"Or else what? Just get out, you stupid son-of-a-bitch! I'm not taking your shit! I'm sick of you. Get out! You could have killed us if you would have hit me with the TV!" I screamed as loud as I could scream.

"What do you mean, us?"

"I mean I'm pregnant," I blurted out.

"You're whoring around on me? I know it's not my kid, you whore. Whose is it?"

"Well, it's either yours or your mother's. Take your pick," I screamed back, trying to be just as demeaning as he was.

I was not talking to Vic, but was screaming at him. I heard Little Vic crying across the hall. I wanted to comfort my baby, but I couldn't get free from Vic. I had never heard Little Vic cry as hard as he was crying right now. Vic backhanded me and I started hitting him back as hard as I could. He must have split my upper lip when he hit me because I was bleeding from the mouth. The more he hit me, the more I screamed. All of a sudden, he put both hands around my neck and started choking me while I was lying on the bed. I was screaming bloody murder. I could feel the extreme pressure on my throat and the air being cut off. I screamed and screamed until I gave out one last blood-curdling scream before he cut off my air entirely. I couldn't catch my breath. I tried to breathe. I was gasping for air. I could feel myself start to lose consciousness. He was literally squeezing the life out of me. I knew I was going to die this time. I had had a bad feeling about today and now I knew why. I was near blacking out. I lost any fight I had in me. I felt lifeless and my arms finally went limp. Vic did not let up and was still choking me with all his strength.

Surprisingly enough, just in the nick of time, Annie threw the door open and said to Vic, "What are you doing? Let her go. Get your hands off her throat! Let loose, Vic. The baby is crying. Go get your son. Stop it! Let go! You'll kill her if you don't let go now!"

Vic let loose of my neck and left my room. I was gasping for air. I was coughing. I was having a hard time catching my breath. I was dizzy. I couldn't believe Annie intervened. I guess she didn't want a murder taking place in her house. I was sure she was concerned what the neighbors would think if there was a murder committed next door or across the street from them. I was so thankful I was still alive. I asked Annie to sleep in Little Vic's room because I was so fearful of Vic. Annie told Vic to go upstairs to sleep. I could not go to sleep. I stayed awake until the morning light appeared.

When Vic left, I called the Dearborn Police. An officer came to the house and I showed him my neck where Vic had choked me and my lip he split open from hitting me. I made a report and he seemed genuinely concerned for me. Surprisingly enough, he took the report and said I would be notified of a court date very soon. I got notified by the Wayne County Recorder's Court of Vic's impending court date and went there to testify against him. Judge Joseph E. Maher sentenced him on June 24th to six months in the prison, the Detroit House of Correction. He was admitted to De Ho Co on June 26th. I was told he would not spend the entire six months in the Detroit House of Corrections, or De Ho Co as it was called for short, because he would get time off for good behavior. Vic was charged and convicted of Felonious Assault. I was also told the reason this case got to court was because of my persistence and the numerous complaints that were made for the same thing, domestic violence.

That was fine because it would give me time to get the hell out of his mother's house and find a new, safe place for my son, me and my new baby due in January of 1971. I never thought I would see the day when I would have my day in court. I should have done this when Vic first shot me. He was charged with **"Felonious Assault to commit great bodily harm with intent to commit Murder" or "Attempted Murder,"** for short. I was just too afraid of him and worried that he would serve very little time in prison, get out and then finish the job. Then I would be dead and my kids would have no mother. I also had mixed emotions about Vic. I still loved him, or so I thought, but then I hated him, too, with such a red-hot intensity.

Regrets? Maybe. With Vic going to De Ho Co, I had some time to find us three a new place to live. I would have to get a paper to see the "For Rent" section of the Detroit News and the Detroit Free Press. Then I had to find someone to help me move out of this hell hole. Where was I going to get the money to move with? I was sure Auntie Anne would give me the money to move with. So many things to deal with, but I was determined to get the hell out of there, no matter what, and it would be before Vic got out of De Ho Co. He was sentenced to stay in De Ho Co until December 23rd, but he got out December 5, 1970 for good behavior.

Sometime before Vic went to De Ho Co, surprise, surprise, Vickie came to visit. She didn't look happy. She was talking to her mother about her husband, Jack.

"Mother, you are not going to believe what I caught Jack doing. I caught him wearing my bra and panties. Oh, Mother, my marriage is over. I don't know what to do. What is the matter with Jack? How can he do this to me? I am devastated," Vickie tearfully said to her mother.

"I don't know what to tell you. That certainly is not normal for a man to do," Annie answered.

"I can't live with that man for one more day," Vickie said.

"What are you going to do?" Annie asked.

"I don't know, but I am not living with him one more day. He is getting out or I am moving home," Vickie said, hinting that she wanted to move home.

"Where would you and Jack stay? There is no room here. I have Chris to contend with, Vic and Little Vic. I have a full house," Annie explained to Vickie.

"You never help me. You are always there for Vic, but you are never there for me," Vickie yelled at her mother.

"That's not true," Annie answered.

"It is true. You have done everything for Vic and nothing for me. I'll deal with this by myself like I have done all my life with everything else," Vickie screamed.

"Vickie, honey, don't be mad," Annie said.

Vickie had a flair for being very dramatic. Vickie stormed out the front door and drove off in her big Ford Crown Victoria. *Well, that went well,* I thought to myself sarcastically. Now I wanted to get the hell out of there even more, the sooner the better. I hadn't seen Vickie in forever and now, all of a sudden, she appeared. *All my problems seemed so unimportant and so small,* I thought to myself again sarcastically. I am trying to nap, but I can't because my door is wide open and I can hear all the drama going on in the living room. Vic came in as Vickie was leaving.

"What is she doing here?" Vic asked.

"Don't ask. You know your sister. She can't handle anything by herself," Annie answered.

"So, what did that fat-ass do now?" Vic asked.

"Vickie caught him wearing her bra and panties," Annie said.

"You're kidding. What a queer. Maybe I'll set him up with Shortridge," Vic said, and then started to laugh.

"Now, Vic, you shouldn't make fun of your sister or her husband," Annie said, trying to sound nonjudgmental.

"I always thought he was a faggot. That just proves it. Man, Vickie can sure pick 'em," Vic said.

CHAPTER 10

Too Young to Die

One day in September of 1970, I had decided that it was going to be now or never for me to find a place of my own for Little Vic, my new baby that would arrive at the beginning of next year, and myself to live. I had been there in the same house with the man who shot me, my husband, and his mother since April. If I didn't find somewhere to move and get out soon, one-day Vic might actually succeed in killing me. My son and my new baby would then be raised by a murderer and/or his mother. Maybe he wouldn't even want the children and they would end up being raised by complete strangers. Oh, I knew that I needed to stop thinking like that again and just find a place for me and my babies. I was at the point at which I would rather be living under a bridge than there. Now that everyone was gone, I could start making plans to get the hell out of there. Vickie got married to Jack and they moved into their own apartment on Snow Street in Dearborn, Vic was still in the Detroit House of Correction for attempting to kill me once again, and Annie was at work, so I could safely leave to go house hunting.

I had gotten a *Detroit News* and a *Detroit Free Press* and now looked in the classifieds for a place for rent. I would need someplace that was furnished since I didn't have any furniture I could take with me. All I had was Little Vic's crib, his Stroll-O-Chair, my clothes and Little Vic's clothes. I opened the first newspaper and it was overwhelming. There were a ton of places for rent. I began at the beginning of every heading that started with 'furnished'. I looked under rooms for rent, apartments and houses. I knew I wouldn't be able to afford a nice place, but any place was better than where I was moving from. It would be my own place, just me and my children. I would be independent once again. I would not have to worry about anything or anyone, just me and my babies. That sounded so wonderful to my ears; finally, something positive may be beginning to happen in my life. I wanted to be excited, but I also knew I should be cautious. I did not want to get my hopes up only to be shot down.

I really wanted to stay in Dearborn or the surrounding areas. I would first try looking in Dearborn, Dearborn Heights, Taylor, Melvindale, Inkster, Lincoln Park, and Garden City.

I started calling each and every listing under 'furnished' in those areas. I was totally shocked when the first person I spoke with who had a place for rent in Dearborn, was asking $200/month for a two-bedroom, one bath furnished house, and no kids or pets were allowed. That did not include utilities, either; I had to pay all my own utilities on top of the rent. I could not believe what I had just heard. After hearing the price, I had no reason to ask any more questions about that place. I wondered if I was going to even be able to find a place that I could afford; only I didn't know what I could afford because I had no income. I would figure all that out when I found a place. I continued to call other ads. I called one that was a two-bedroom, furnished, all utilities included and for under $100/month. I just knew this was going to be the one. I wrote down the directions and gathered up Little Vic, his diaper bag, and headed out to go look at it.

The disappointment I felt when I arrived! There in front of me was a two-story house. I parked in front of the house and just stared at it. It was so cute. The front yard even had pretty flowers planted up the walkway to the front door, where I counted seven steps to walk up. It was at that moment I remembered that I was not able to walk; I was in a wheelchair or using my ugly crutches now since Vic had shot me. This would not even be possible. I could feel tears rolling from my eyes and down my cheeks. Just then, a very nice-looking gentleman approached my car on the driver's side. My window was down.

He said, "Hi, I'm Dennis. Are you the young lady who is interested in the house for rent?"

I replied, "I was very interested. This is a cute little house. I know me and my children would create some wonderful memories here."

"Well, what are you waiting for? Let's go in and see if you like it. If you do, it's yours. Is that your son? He sure is a cute little fellow. I'll go and unlock the doors," the man said.

"There won't be any need in doing that. You see, I have to use crutches or my wheelchair to get around. There is no possible way for me to get into the house. I don't want to waste anymore of your time mister, but thank you for coming to show it to me," I politely told him.

"I'm so sorry. I would have loved to have you and your children as my tenants. You seem like a very pleasant young woman. Well, good luck and I hope you find a place that will work for you," he said as he got in his car and drove off.

I was now discouraged. Vic had really screwed up my life. This was going to narrow down my search for places dramatically. I drove home and began my search once again. I was determined to find a place as quickly as I could and get out of that hell hole. Little Vic and I had driven to several addresses at which I was told they couldn't rent to me because I was disabled and would be a liability for them if I fell. After looking at several houses, I was getting very disappointed with the same comments geared toward my being handicapped. I couldn't believe these landlords, using my handicap as a reason not to rent to me.

I wished that my house was available, but the real estate agent had gotten it rented for me for the next three years. I was so glad the real estate company was taking care of my Detroit house, so I didn't have to worry about that, too. I needed to raise the rent after the current lease had expired. They really got a super good deal because of my situation. I was just thankful it was rented and taken care of.

I felt so bad that I sat in my car and turned on the radio. "Band of Gold," by Freda Payne played. Just what I needed, a song that reminded me of Vic. Next, they played "I'll Be There" by the Jackson 5. "We've Only Just Begun" by the Carpenters, "The Love You Save," by the Jackson 5, and "Turn Back the Hands of Time" by Tyrone Davis. With that song, I had to turn off the radio because it made me think too much of Vic. It was over. I wondered if he hurt as much as I did.

I almost didn't go to see the last house for fear of the same hurtful disappointment. But I did go and it turned out to be a good decision. The owners were an elderly couple and were very nice. They could see I was pregnant and had a young child, also. They told me the rent was $60 per month plus utilities. I said I would take it. It would be available October 1, 1970.

I then went to the local DSS and applied for emergency help. They gave me a check for $100 and a food stamp coupon book. It was for $40 and I would get this monthly for the next six months. I also got medical insurance for Little Vic and myself since I was pregnant.

With that completed, all I had to do was wait. I never spoke a word about this move for fear of something going wrong. I wanted to get out of Annie's house more than anything at any cost.

October 1, 1970 had come and with it came a move that was so very important to me; it was my new independence. Vic was still residing at the Detroit House of Correction for his assault on me by choking me and Annie was at work, so I had some time to move out lock, stock and barrel. Vickie should also be happy, since now she can have the whole house to herself. I packed up all that I could gather that belonged to just me or my son. I did take my two-slice toaster and the sheet sets I had gotten as a wedding or shower gift. I didn't dare take the furniture Vic and I had bought when we were still together. I left that behind for fear that Vic would hunt me down just to get the furniture back.

I had put my clothes in the back seat of my '65 T-Bird and some boxes in my trunk. My friend had a truck, so we put the large things in his truck. I put Little Vic in his car seat, and buckled him securely in the front seat. I took one more look at the house I had been imprisoned in. This was one place I would never miss. This is one house I would never come back to, ever. I put my keys in the ignition, started the engine, put it in drive and finally I was on my way. I drove down the street and never looked back. I turned the radio on and "Only the Strong Survive" by Jerry Butler was playing. I turned it up so maybe, just maybe, I could forget all the hell I had been put through in that house. I would never return.

I was facing a new future, a new adventure in another episode of my life. I had found a house in Hamtramck, just outside of Detroit. It was an older house in a poor neighborhood, but it was all I could afford since I had no funds or income. The best thing about it was that it was all mine. No one was telling me what to do, or how to do it. I pulled up to our new house, Little Vic's and mine. I just sat in front staring at our new residence. It wasn't much to look at, but it would be our first new home and our family would grow from two to three in just a few short months.

Some kids came up to my car door and asked if I was the new tenant. I told them 'yes' and introduced myself and my son to them. They introduced themselves also as Ronnie Hodges, Shelley, Marie, Libby, Danny and the smallest was Teddy. The name fit him to a tee since he was as cute as a little teddy bear. Ronnie told me he was twelve years old; Shelley was eleven years old; Marie was nine years old; Libby was eight years old; Danny was seven years old and Teddy was five years old. He told me his older sister, Cheryl, was seventeen years old. The kids offered to help carry the things from my car to the house. It took us awhile, but finally all my belongings were inside the house. I politely thanked the kids for their help. I finally did it. We were moved into our very own place, away from harm.

I had a little trouble walking up the two steps on my crutches, but I did make it into the house. Thank goodness it was only two steps and then one more from the enclosed porch into the house. Little Vic picked out his room and I took the other one. We unpacked our boxes and put them in the drawers. I was thankful this house was furnished since I didn't have any furniture yet. That would have to come later when I figured out what I was going to do about an income.

Auntie Anne had told me to apply for Social Security Disability, which I did. Can you believe I was denied? How could they deny me? I was as disabled as any person could get. Thanks to Vic, he would make the rest of my life miserable. I was paralyzed from above the waist on down. My left leg I had to use as a peg leg because it would not bend or move at all and I could not feel hot or cold. My right leg is what I depended on for my mobility. Luckily it did bend and move, but it had a constant numbness and tingling sensation. I really didn't have any normal feeling in either one of my legs. There were also the spasms. I was prescribed Valium to help with the spasms. It helped some with my leg spasms. I had stopped taking it because I was pregnant. But the worst thing was, I had no sense of balance. I did appeal the decision of the Social Security Administration and now I would play the waiting game.

I did get my friend to take apart Little Vic's crib, so he had a place to sleep. When we arrived at our new house, he put Little Vic's crib back together again. I took the Stroll-O-Chair with me which made into seven different things like a high chair, play and feed table, chair, stroller, pram, and bassinette. I would use the bassinette for the new baby.

After putting most of our things away, I realized we needed some food in the house. Little Vic and I went to the grocery store and got some food with our $40. We went to the Farmer Jack

183

grocery store, which was not too far from our new house. We went in together. I politely asked a stranger if they would please pick up and put my son in the shopping buggy, which they did. We got milk, stocked up on TV dinners in every variety, animal cookies for Little Vic, bread, butter, eggs, pepperoni and an Appian Way pizza mix to make. I pushed the buggy with my crutches hanging from my arms. I hated all the looks and stares I got. I actually had people come up to me and ask me if I had Polio.

I had one lady say to me, "How long have you had Polio, honey?"

I told her, "I don't have Polio."

Kids were the worst, always pointing and staring at me. I felt like saying, "Take a picture, it will last longer," but that would be too childish. No wonder I felt like a freak of nature.

When we were done shopping, we went to the checkout. The cashier rang up all our groceries and it came to $29.16. I gave her $30 in food stamp coupons and I got back $.84 in cash. My groceries were put neatly in the paper bags and a young man helped put them in my car.

I once again put Little Vic in his car seat, buckled him in securely and then I put my crutches on the front passenger seat of my car while holding on to my driver's side car door for balance. I got in, started the car and off we went back to our new house.

All the kids were waiting for us when we pulled up.

Ronnie said, "Need some help carrying in your groceries?"

I said, "Sure, just put them on the kitchen table."

I slowly went into the house and turned on the radio. The Carpenter's song "Close to You" was playing. One by one the bags of groceries went inside.

I said, "Hold on, let me give you some cookies I just bought."

"Ok, but you don't have to," Ronnie replied.

I unpacked the bags, but there were no cookies. I was sure I bought some of Little Vic's favorite cookies. I guess not. I told Ronnie next time I got some cookies I would give all of them some. They left out the back door into the backyard. They lived next door to me.

A few days later Ronnie came over with three small kittens in his arms, a tabby, a black and white one and an orange one.

He said to me, "Do you need any kittens? We got lots of them and my maw said we gotta get rid of some of them."

"I don't think so, but thanks, anyway," I said.

"Just these three?" Ronnie asked.

"I can't. I don't have a litter box or food for them," I told Ronnie.

"We got a litter box and some food too."

"Well, I'll try it, but I can't promise anything."

"Ok. Here are your kittens and I'll go get the litter box and food for them. Just stay here 'til I get back," Ronnie told me.

"Ok, I'll wait on you Ronnie."

Ronnie came back with a big plastic container which was used as a litter box and the cat food. The kittens wore out their welcome in exactly three days. They were litter trained, but they climbed and scratched on everything; the couch, chair, curtains—I mean everything.

The neighbor on the other side of me had given me their newspaper since they were done with it. I couldn't take care of these kittens, nor did I want to while I was pregnant and getting such little money to live off of.

I looked in the paper under "pets" for sale and free. I couldn't believe how many kittens were for sale, $5 each. That gave me an idea. I could sell these kittens and get some money to live off of and get them a good home at the same time, and it would keep them out of the shelters. I knew anyone who was willing to pay for an animal usually would take better care of them than ones who got them for free, so I put an ad in the paper under the "Wanted: kitten" ads. I sold those three kittens all in the same week for $2 each. That was the start of my new little business.

I looked up ads for free kittens and went out to get them. At first, I would only get one kitten from each place, but as I quickly learned, the owners wanted to get rid of them as soon as possible, so I asked for more than one, sometimes as many as four at a time. I had a cardboard box I put the little kittens in to bring them back to my house. I turned around and sold them for $2. Now that the kittens were paying for themselves, I also got good kitten food for them instead of cat food. My attitude changed toward the kittens from their being just an annoyance to being sweet pets that would help me pay the bills.

Little Vic loved all the kittens we had, and at times, we had many. I remember one time we had a total of 18 kittens, in every color and type you could imagine. I had long haired, short haired, and tabby, black with white markings, white with orange patches, young kittens, and older kittens. No matter what the callers asked for, we seemed to have it. I saved every dollar from the sale of the kittens and kept the money hidden in the freezer in a sandwich bag under all the TV dinners. This was not the safest neighborhood, not like Dearborn, and I didn't think a robber would think to look in the freezer. It proved to be true. It also allowed me to get off of welfare really quick, so I had no one to answer to. I did not like depending on welfare.

I had lived there for a couple of months when I figured out why the next-door-neighbor kids were so anxious to help, especially with groceries. They had a system. For every two bags of groceries that came in the front door, one bag went out the back door to their house. I guess my being on crutches and slow moving, I was an easy target. When I figured this out, I confronted the kids. They did admit to their criminal act of stealing my groceries. I told them if they continued I did not want them over to visit anymore.

I did give them some things that I could afford to give them like some apples from the bag of apples or cookies out of the bag of cookies. But I could not tolerate stealing, no matter what the reason. I knew their mother had her hands full with seven kids, but she also drank and their fathers were absent from their lives. I did feel sorry for them. I wished I had a lot of money, so I could help more, but I had Little Vic and a new baby on the way to worry about. My family came first. With gas only $.40 per gallon I did give them rides to where they needed to go. I also took them to the movies sometimes and paid for the show. The matinees were only $.50 per child. That was only $3 or selling one kitten if all six of the kids went. Their older sister on occasion would baby-sit for me. She had a nineteen-year-old boyfriend named Justin.

One day while I was gone, my house was broken into. Not much was missing. My jewelry box was gone. Most of the jewelry contained in it was just costume jewelry. The only three things that mattered to me were the blue heart earrings I wore as a little girl from Germany that my real mother had given me, his wedding ring, and my wedding rings from Vic. The earrings were little blue hearts and my rings were only one-quarter karat diamonds. His ring was also white gold with diamond chips all around and an inscription inside of it. It wasn't the money, but if I had a little girl, I wanted to give it to her because they were very precious to me. They only had sentimental value to me. I made a police report, but the jewelry box was never recovered. That made me very sad.

One day I turned on the television and I couldn't believe what I was hearing.

The reporter was saying, "A twelve-year-old boy was shot and killed early this morning by the bar owner while trying to rob a local bar. In custody is his older sister's boyfriend, nineteen-year-old Justin Dunkin. A shoot-out ensued, causing the death of the twelve-year-old. No charges have been brought against the bar owner, stating it was self-defense. The boy's name is being withheld until full investigation."

I got a sick feeling in the pit of my stomach. I knew it was Ronnie Hodges next door. I didn't need to know his name. I knew it was Ronnie and it made my own shooting come flooding back into my memory. I started sweating and crying. Ronnie didn't seem to have a chance for a good life with all the negatives in his life. He had no role models who could have a positive effect on his young life. I didn't understand why God allowed him to die and yet he saved me. Don't get me wrong, I was so thankful I was saved, but I wished Ronnie could have been saved, too. He was too young to die. He was so young and impressionable. This was the last straw.

I decided I would look for a better place for us to live. With the money I had saved, I would be able to find a better, safer place to live. The only good thing about this place was that no one knew where I was, so I was safe from Vic and his mother.

On the other hand, I couldn't risk the safety of my precious children. They came first in my life and I only had a few more days before the baby was due. Once again, I looked in the newspaper for houses for rent.

CHAPTER 11

New Baby, New Beginnings

December, 1970, once again I found myself looking through the newspapers to find a place to rent for me and my two children. I had called and had spoken to a gentleman about the first ad I saw which sounded promising. We set a time for one o'clock to meet at the first rental. I pulled up and parked in front of the house. The owner of the house was walking toward my car to meet me. I unbuckled my seat belt, opened my car door, and reached around back to get my crutches out from behind my seat.

As I grabbed my crutches, the landlord looked at me for a moment and then he said, "I don't think this is going to work. I can't rent to someone like you."

I replied, "What do you mean, someone like me?"

He replied back, "You got polio, you can't walk. I don't wanna take a chance of you falling and suing me."

Very angrily I then informed him, "First of all, I don't have polio, and second of all, I am very capable of getting around as I drove here by myself."

"Well, I don't care. I don't have to rent to you. I think you need to leave."

"Well thanks for nothing," then I turned to my son and said, "Let's go on to the next place."

Luckily the second house I was going to look at was only a couple of blocks away, also in Dearborn Heights. Again, I pulled up in front of the house and parked. I waited a minute and seeing no one come out, I unbuckled myself and Little Vic, opened my car door and once again grabbed my crutches from the back. We started up the front walk and went up just two steps when I saw a woman standing at the top of the steps.

She looked at me and said rather rudely, "Lady, you can just turn right around because there is no way I am going to rent to somebody like you. I'm sorry you have polio, but I just can't take a chance of you getting hurt on my property. Besides, we don't want no kids and you got one and one on the way."

"Just to be clear, I don't have polio, but I don't guess it matters, anyway. Have a nice day," I replied very sarcastically and then said to my son, "Come on Little Vic, we didn't want to live here anyway."

The next house on the list was in Taylor, but the rent was a little more and it was further out. I had also found a quadplex apartment on the corner of Beech Daly Road and Dartmouth Street. I called about the ad and made an appointment to go see it. There were four separate little apartments with the one I was inquiring about on the main floor.

"Maybe we'll go look at the one in Inkster," I said to Little Vic.

We pulled up to the side of the building. This was not a single house, but an apartment building with four separate apartments. I saw kids playing outside. That meant they allowed kids, which was good. I went through all the motions to get out of my car, but instead of talking to the landlord first, I talked to the kids and the one guy in front. I asked if they allowed kids and I asked the guy if he thought the landlord would rent to me.

"I have looked at a couple of other houses, but all I got was shot down because I had kids or I am on crutches. Do you think he will rent to me without hassling me about being on crutches?" I asked the guy.

"Yeah, we got kids and besides the owners are husband and wife. They just care about the money, so long as you don't make no trouble. They are round the back," he answered.

"OK, thanks for the information. Wish me luck," I said very hopefully.

"Mommy, can I play with the kids? They said I could." Little Vic asked me.

"OK, but don't go nowhere else," I instructed him.

I walked around to the back of the apartment building and saw the owners. I met the owners and we talked about how much the rent was, what the tenants paid and the rules of the building.

"Hi, I'm Christi Golden. I talked to someone about the apartment available. Could I see it? I have a son and a baby, which is due anytime now."

"I believe you spoke with my wife. It is a main floor apartment with storage in the basement. It's unfurnished, but the utilities are included. Pay up front the first month rent and a one-month security deposit. It will be ready in a couple of weeks. The tenant gave their thirty-day notice to vacate the premises. The rent is

$200 per month. If that suits you, I have the papers for you to sign and a receipt book for your deposit," the landlord replied.

We went around to the side of the building and up the couple of steps to get to the apartment. It wasn't the Ritz, but it would have to do, especially after the previous turndowns. I can't believe how prejudiced people are against people with disabilities. By shooting me, Vic threw me into a whole new world, a world where people stare, point, whisper, and make you feel uncomfortable. No wonder I felt like a freak of nature.

It didn't take me long to accept the lease since I felt I had to move from the Detroit house as soon as possible. Since I had been shot and now the 12-year-old boy next door had been shot and killed while trying to rob a bar with his older sister's 19-year-old boyfriend, I no longer felt safe. I had a little boy and a baby on the way to worry about. I handed the owner my deposit and signed the lease. I had to wait until the previous tenant moved out before I could move in.

January, 1971. Finally, the day came. I was able to get a few friends together to help me move into our new apartment. It took the better part of the day to move and rearrange my furniture and put things away, but we did it. I was so excited about our new apartment. Even Little Vic was happy and he had already met two new friends—a 10-year-old boy, Gary Kudos, and his older sister, Roxanne, from the upstairs apartment. There was a full basement and each tenant had a section in which to store their belongings. All in all, it was the right decision for us. I was a little concerned and nervous that we were living so much closer to Vic, but I would deal with that situation if it ever arose.

*7-4-71 Little Vic with Gary Kudos
and his sister, Roxanne*

After we got settled, we started to do some decorating. We first put the large picture of the line of trees that at least a million-other people had. We put up some posters on the walls, my trophies on the TV and started a collage of pictures on the wall over the couch. The apartment consisted of a living room, kitchen, two bedrooms and a bathroom. The bedroom off the living room was for Little Vic and our new baby. I would take the bedroom off the kitchen. It wasn't the Ritz, but it was nicer than the rat-traps of Detroit that we had just moved out of and a lot nicer than the apartment Vic and I had behind the Ford Motor Rouge Plant. I also called Auntie Anne to let her know we moved.

Since we didn't have a tree for Christmas, Auntie Anne said, "I know you are in the middle of moving, but Uncle Glenn has something for Little Vic. I think he will like it since he has been asking for one. I would tell you what it is, but I promised to keep it a surprise. How are things going? Moving right along? I know moving can be such a big chore and you have your hands full. That baby is due anytime now. Didn't you tell me the baby should be here January 23rd?"

Feb. 1971, I am 10 mos. Pregnant with Annemarie

"Yes, the doctor told me the 23rd, but you know babies, they come when they feel like it, not when the doctor says," I said.

"You keep me posted. Make sure you call me when the time comes to have this baby. I will take care of Little Vic for you, so no worries there."

"If you remember, Little Vic was supposed to come in April, but he decided to come in March. He fooled all of us. I sure hope this baby will not take as long as Little Vic did. 32 hours is a long time and very exhausting."

"I'm sure it won't."

"I think it will be a girl this time. I carried Little Vic low the whole time and I gained 50 pounds with him. With this baby, I only gained 15 pounds and I am carrying it high. I know there is nothing scientific about it, but I did think Little Vic was a boy and I turned out to be right. Besides, I'd like to have a little girl, so I have one of each."

"Where are you going to have the baby?"

"Same place I had Little Vic, at Metropolitan Hospital."

"Have you thought of any names?"

"Yes, but just girls' names. This baby caught me off guard. I didn't even know I was pregnant for several months because I didn't have any periods, nor was I showing until after six months. I have had a burning desire to find my real mother ever since I was sixteen and her name is Annemarie. Then your name is Anne, but Vic's mom's name is Annie, so I don't know. I'm still leaning towards Annemarie, but I can just see all the problems.; People will spell it wrong, say it wrong, shorten it like it's two names."

For a split second the name *'Penny Lee'* crossed my mind. It was the name Vic had picked out for a girl when we were in love and wanted to have a baby, but now, no, no way.

"You could name her after your adopted mother."

"I don't think so. I really don't like her first or middle name, too old-fashioned."

"Well, Glenn just walked in the door, so I am going to have to cut it short, but keep in close touch and let us know when that baby comes. Take care of yourself and that baby and Little Vic, too. Bye."

"OK, I will. Bye, bye."

The next few weeks seemed to drag on. I was getting so uncomfortable. I couldn't sleep well. It was a bit more uncomfortable and difficult to balance on these crutches when I walked; even sitting bothered me. I was ready to have this baby. January came and went and no baby. I went to my doctor weekly, but nothing new. The baby was not in the birth canal. All I could do was wait it out.

It was the morning of February 23rd. I was fixing Little Vic breakfast.

"What do you want for breakfast?" I asked Little Vic.

"I want pancakes, my favorite. The ones with the eyes and the beard."

"Let me see if I have any pancake mix or raisins. I know I have Reddi Whip."

"Do you? I want pancakes because you buy yucky cereal."

"You're in luck. I have what we need. And I don't buy yucky cereal. Just because they don't have a ton of sugar on them; you like Kix, Cheerios and Rice Krispies, don't you?"

"Yeah, but I like pancakes better."

"OK, then pancakes it is."

I made Little Vic's favorite pancakes. The eyes are raisins, the nose is a grape or maybe an M&M chocolate and the beard is Reddi Whip.

"Bring your plate and your cup over and put it in the dishwater so I can wash it when you are done," I told Little Vic.

He insisted on eating off of his own plate and using his own cup for milk. It was a cute set of unbreakable Melamine with a plate, cereal bowl, cup and silverware with Peter Rabbit on it. Little Vic finished two pancakes, carried his dishes to the kitchen sink and put them into the dishwater. I cleaned up the kitchen and then made my way to the bathroom.

I was now using a wheelchair for the last couple of weeks because I felt unsteady and with all the weight in front I didn't want to fall. I wheeled myself to the bathroom and I no sooner got in the bathroom, I had an overwhelming urge to pee. There was no stopping it. I soaked the wheelchair and I flooded the bathroom floor. I knew I had to change out of these wet clothes, so I transferred onto the toilet. When I wiped, I got scared at first, but then I remembered about that pink or red mucus plug. I wasn't bleeding, my water broke and I was going into labor. I turned the TV on so Little Vic could watch *"Sesame Street"* and so he would not feel panicky. I then proceeded to call Auntie Anne.

"Hello, Auntie Anne. I think I am finally in labor. One month late, but better late than never. I thought I was bleeding, but it was that mucus plug I saw," I said to the voice at the other end.

"Are you sure? I hope so. It certainly is time. I'll meet you and Little Vic at the hospital," Auntie Anne replied.

"Little Vic has eaten. I have to change clothes and then I'll hop in my car and we will be on our way to Metropolitan Hospital."

I got changed, grabbed my purse, the homecoming outfit for my new baby, the baby book I bought and my keys. The outfit and the baby book were both pink and white. That is how sure I was that I was having a little girl. Little Vic carried my overnight bag for the hospital. I locked the apartment door and got into my 1965 gold T-Bird and off we went, all three of us.

When we arrived, Auntie Anne and Uncle Glenn were waiting at the emergency entrance.

Boy, do I remember being here before, I thought. It was when I was in labor with Little Vic for so long. I sure hope this baby is not so long getting here.

Auntie Anne came over with the hospital attendant to help me get out of my car and into a wheelchair. Uncle Glenn took my keys, got in my car and drove it to the parking lot. The attendant wheeled me over to the registration desk to get me registered and then put a hospital bracelet on my left wrist. Auntie Anne had grabbed a hold of Little Vic's hand and was still holding tight to him. I was taken to the labor and delivery room immediately because my water had broken. I had no contractions, but the doctor told me he would wait for twelve hours for the baby to start contractions. The doctors did not want to risk infection for me or the baby. I had been put on high risk because of my being shot in the spine. At ten months pregnant, I weighed in at 119 pounds. I had gained twenty-seven pounds. I remember them putting a mask on me and the awful smell of rubber tires. I remember nothing after that.

When I woke up, I had a little girl. I came in at around noon and I had delivered a beautiful little girl at 3:32 pm. She weighed six pounds, fourteen ounces and was nineteen inches long. Just moments later I was taken to a semi-private room. There was no one else in there. So, in the blink of an eye I went from a semi-private room to a private room. It was nice and peaceful for me and my new daughter. Our first interaction was breastfeeding. She let me know in no uncertain terms she was hungry. When she was full, she fell asleep in my arms. What a precious moment. As she slept, I kept looking at her. She was small with big blue eyes and blonde peach fuzz on her head. I was thinking of all sorts of names, but I kept coming back to the name, 'Annemarie'. This baby was not planned, but neither was I. I thought to myself, *what a great way to honor the woman who gave me life. I didn't have to fool with names from Vic's side of the family because he did not deserve to name this precious baby. He denied that she was his. What good father denies his child? Your name will be Annemarie Christiane Golden. You will be named after my mother, me and Christ. You will be loved.*

I watched her sleeping, I knew this little baby would be someone special and do great things. How could she not? She was planned by God himself. I was glad I brought the baby book. During our stay, Annemarie had her hand and foot prints taken and the person was nice enough to also put them in her baby book. I put both wrist bands, hers and mine, in the baby book. I wrote in it, adding pertinent information. I had gotten her delivery doctor to sign her book and added newborn pictures. Later I added her belly button when it fell off, each little tooth she lost with the date, and coins of the year she was born, 1971.

Auntie Anne came to visit me while Uncle Glenn watched Little Vic. I was ordered to stay for six days because of my high-risk status. When I was finally released, Little Vic rode home with me while Auntie Anne and Uncle Glenn drove with my baby, Annemarie, to our apartment in Inkster. We arrived safely and Auntie Anne carried Annemarie into our apartment. She placed her into the Stroll-O-Chair bassinet, which was all done up in white eyelet and lace. This is the same bassinet that Little Vic used as a new baby. Little Vic was now sleeping in a crib. He was now officially a big brother at the tender age of two years, eleven months. You could definitely tell they were brother and sister.

It was so much easier with me breastfeeding and my bassinet was one with wheels, but now I had new obstacles to overcome. *How was I going to carry this precious bundle? In the apartment I could roll the bassinet around, but how was I going to get her out to my car if I had to go somewhere?* All these thoughts went in and out of my head.

So many hurdles to jump, so many mountains to climb. But I was not going to give up or give in. Where there is a will, there is a way, and I was determined that I would find that way. You could bet your bottom dollar on that. I didn't need Vic, nor did I want Vic. I never understood why Barb thought Vic was such a prize. Enough dwelling on the past and fantasizing. I needed to deal with reality and the reality was--Vic was not coming back. He deserted me and his children. He was not looking back. He was going on with his life, the life I gave back to him by not pressing charges. I wondered, *had he ever thought about what he did to me and how he changed my life, not for just a little while, but forever? Did he ever think of just how much pain, both physical and mental, he inflicted on me? A better question—Did he even think before he acted? How would he feel if the tables were turned and he was at the receiving end of two bullets?*

Stop it Christi, stop it Christi, or you will drive yourself crazy. Get all those bad thoughts out of your mind. Think positive, not negative. Think happy, not sad. Think good, not bad, think forgiveness, not revenge. Think new beginnings, not the past. Maybe you should just stop thinking to yourself.

I did not take Annemarie out until after she was a full month old. Being inside made it easy to care for her and Little Vic loved his baby sister and helped wherever he could. He would bring me a clean cloth diaper and shook baby powder on her. He rubbed baby lotion on her after her bath. He wanted to give her a bath, but I thought he might fall standing on a chair at the kitchen sink. Bathing Annemarie in the kitchen sink made it easier than bending over in the bathtub. Standing at the kitchen table with no sense of balance made it harder, but somehow, I managed. He brought her baby toys. He would shake the baby rattles to make Annemarie laugh.

7-23-71 Annemarie in the baby bath tub on the kitchen table.

March 6, 1971, today was Little Vic's birthday. He was three years old and was such a good helper. We had a birthday party for him with cake, ice cream, and the number three candle for the top of his cake. We invited the kids that lived in the apartment and across the street.

I remember one incident that made me very nervous. It was the day of Annemarie's six-week checkup. I had made the appointment while I was still in the hospital, so I did not know who would be around. By this time, Little Vic had been carrying Annemarie around quite often in our apartment. He knew how to hold her, making sure she would not flip out of his arms. I had forgotten to call someone to come with me. It was a long-distance call to the Detroit area and who knew when I could get another appointment. I took a deep breath and told Little Vic he would have to carry his baby sister.

7-15-71 Little Vic holding his baby sister, Annemarie, in front of his crib. Such a big helper.

"Little Vic, I need you to help mommy by carrying Annemarie out to the car. Do you think you can do that? You will have to walk slow and hold on to her real tight." I asked Little Vic.

"Yes Mommy, I do that," Little Vic answered excitedly.

"You are such a big boy, Little Vic."

"Me a big boy. I can carry sissy."

Very reluctantly I walked out the door with Little Vic carrying Annemarie. I locked the apartment door and went to my car. Little Vic was right behind me, so if, God forbid, Little Vic fell with Annemarie, I could block his fall. I kept thinking during that short walk, *what a piece of crap you are, Vic. You should be here helping. After all, you caused all this. If it wasn't for you, I could be caring for my baby like normal, capable people. Instead, I am putting both of my kids in danger. I hate you and I hate that piece of white trash, Barb. I wished I never would have met you. God forgive me for all the hatred I feel. Why me? It's not fair. He has a great life and I have this. How I wish Ronnie Turner and I would have stayed together forever.* Then a little voice snapped me out of my negative thoughts,

"Mommy, can you get Annemarie now?" asked Little Vic

"Sure, just let me put my crutches on the rear floorboard and get in."

I had a little plastic carrier and put Annemarie in it. Then I buckled the carrier with the car seat belts in the front seat. I had to put Little Vic in the back seat and make sure he was buckled in, too. We drove to the pediatrician and I learned really quickly to depend on other people, sometimes complete strangers.

I parked and saw a woman coming from the next aisle over and made sure she heard me, "Excuse me, but could you help me carry my baby into the doctor's office?" I asked.

"Sure, I would be glad to. It's been a while since I held such a tiny little baby. How long have you had polio? How old is she?" the woman asked.

"I don't have polio. She is six weeks old," I answered.

"She's my baby sister. I'm her big brudder," Little Vic proudly chimed in.

I couldn't help thinking, *why does everyone think I have polio? I hate it. I wish I didn't have these crutches.* But then I wouldn't be able to walk independently. *Thanks Vic, thanks a lot.*

With the help of this stranger, I got Little Vic and my baby safely into the doctor's office. I checked in and waited for our name to be called. When our name was called, the nurse politely took Annemarie into the room with me and Little Vic right behind. The pediatrician gave Annemarie a clean bill of health. I knew Annemarie would pass her first check-up with flying colors.

I did not know it then, but I would be using the kindness of total strangers to help me for many things. I would also make decisions I would never have made had it not been for my disability. I have so much to thank Vic for, and none of it was good.

4-14-71 Annemarie in the same christening gown her brother wore.

May, 1971. Today was a day of celebration. Annemarie was being baptized at St. Paul American Lutheran Church in Dearborn, the same church I attended all the years I lived at home and the same one Victor III was baptized in. Auntie Anne and Uncle Glenn Lake were the official godparents. Annemarie wore the same christening gown that her brother, Little Vic had worn for the baptism. I chose St. Paul's because I had some roots and familiarity here. I remember Vic and I standing at the front of the church at the baptismal bowl with Little Vic. Vic held our son and I stood beside him so proudly and with such hope for the future. That was all gone now. Vic ruined that like he ruined everything else. I watched from the front pew the private ceremony going on. Annemarie was being so good, quiet and not crying. Pastor Sund was officiating and asked for the godparents to come forward.

"Whoever gives this child to God, please come forward," Pastor Sund said.

"We do, Anne and Glenn Lake," Uncle Glenn said.

"Do you promise to raise up and keep this child in God's word?"

"Yes, we do," both Uncle Glenn and Auntie Anne replied.

"I baptize you, Annemarie Christian Golden, in the name of the Father, Son and Holy Ghost," Pastor Sund said with a soft smile.

Just then, Annemarie let out a short cry as the pastor was sprinkling the holy water on her head. I had brought my camera and naturally took several pictures of our small party to commemorate this special occasion.

June 9, 1971 was a day for visiting. First Auntie Anne and her friend, Annie Gabauer, brought Little Vic a pedal car he had been wanting for a long time. Since Auntie Anne and Uncle Glenn were Annemarie's godparents, she naturally wanted to hold her goddaughter.

"Chris, I can't believe how much Annemarie has grown and such a beautiful baby, too. It seems like only yesterday that I was at the hospital waiting for her to make her grand entrance." Auntie Anne said.

"Yes, she has grown, and yes, she is beautiful. You can tell Little Vic and her are brother and sister. They both, I think, look like their dad. They definitely take after my German side, blonde-haired and blue-eyed," I answered.

"You remember my friend, Mrs. Gabauer? She has been to my house when you were there."

"Yes, I remember her," I said.

"And I remember you, even as a little girl, when you came from Germany. Ah, such a sweet and beautiful child. I'm sorry to hear about your mother dying," Mrs. Gabauer said.

"Yes, she died of breast cancer after losing both breasts. She died July of 1970. I was not able to attend her funeral because of matters I had to deal with concerning my husband and my own health. My daddy disowned me because of Vic, my husband," I told her.

Little Vic was also excited to show her his pictures he had scotch taped to the wall over the couch in the living room.

Little Vic chimed in by saying. "I cut out all those pictures and put them on the wall. I made it for my baby sister. It's pretty, huh?"

Mrs. Gabauer replied, "Yes, those are a lot of pictures and you did a good job. I'm sure your mommy likes them, too."

"Yes, I love them. That is the best decorated wall in the apartment. Thank you, Little Vic," I said.

I told them all the updates on Annemarie's accomplishments and health. She couldn't believe Annemarie was already four months old. It was such a nice day that we all decided to take Annemarie for a short stroll outside, down Dartmouth Street. I was glad and thankful that I kept in touch with Auntie Anne over the years because she had helped me in several situations.

6-4-71 Annemarie in stroller.

6-9-71 Auntie Anne, Mrs. Gabauer,
Little Vic in his new pedal car from Uncle Glenn

6-9-71 Vic III and his aunt Vickie Valian
with her son Jack Curtis Valian, born May 1971

June 9, 1971. We were going to visit Vickie, my sister-in-law, and her baby, Jack Curtis Valian, who was born three months after Annemarie, in May of 1971. I was determined to be cordial for the kids' sake, and after all, she and her baby were family, too. I had gotten both Little Vic and Annemarie dressed nicely, because Auntie Anne had come to visit, so I didn't need to change their outfits. Since she married Jack, she was all about everything being prim and proper. I was expecting just her and the baby, but her mother-in-law was there, also. Now I had to put on airs and act all snobby and couth. I certainly could talk with refinement when I needed to. I could also act cultured and well-mannered. She was still living at 21726 Snow Street in Dearborn, in an apartment. I'm sure the Valian's were not as well off as my adopted father, who owned two Tool and Die companies, Republic Tool and Engineering, not to mention all the vending machines all over town. They did own an insurance company and partnership in The Chicago Road House Restaurant. I could pull that off. I parked the car and went to the door and knocked.

When the door opened, I said, "Hi Vickie, we decided to visit to see the baby."

"Come in, here, let me get Annemarie from Little Vic. You are such a big helper carrying your baby sister."

Walking on my crutches, I stepped in and noticed the lady on the couch and said, "Hi Mrs. Valian, I'm Chris, Vic's wife. We came to see baby Jack."

I walked over to the couch and sat down. I brought my camera, so I could get a couple of pictures of the kids together. Vickie was all dressed up and her hair was all done up; she looked nice. She allowed me to take some pictures of her, baby Jack, Little Vic and Annemarie. I took maybe, a half dozen.

"So, how have you been?" I asked Vickie.

"Just fine," she replied.

It was hard to make small talk with someone you were not close to, but I suffered through it.

"Do you want something to drink?" Vickie asked me.

"No, thank you," I said.

"So, what do you think of your first grandson?" I asked Mrs. Valian.

"We are all happy. You know he is the third Jack," she said.

"Yes, I know. We heard. He certainly looks like your side of the family," I said.

"I'm hungry," Little Vic said to Vickie.

She gave him a banana.

"Thank you, Aunt Vickie," Little Vic told her.

"You're welcome," she said.

Little Vic had sat beside baby Jack, so I decided to take some pictures. I grabbed my crutches off the floor, stood up, balanced and walked in front of my son and baby Jack.

"Can you smile for me, Little Vic, so I can take a picture of you and baby Jack?" I said and which he did. baby Jack was not as cooperative.

We talked about nothing just to pass the time. We stayed about an hour and then I announced that we would have to leave. I politely said our good-byes. Vickie was kind enough to carry Annemarie to my car and put her in her plastic carrier in the front seat. Little Vic climbed in the back seat and buckled himself in. I got in, turned on the car, rolled down the passenger window and told Vickie thanks and good bye. She walked back to her apartment and we were off, heading back to our apartment.

June 11, 1971, I decided to visit Shirley Anthony. We had remained friends after all that had happened between Vic and me. Shirley and Larry now had three boys; Rodney, Roger and Michael. Rodney was Vic's age and Michael was Annemarie's age. They lived in Taylor, so it was a little drive for me, but I always enjoyed visiting them. I just recently had to have a heel cord lengthening because of the severe drop foot on my left foot. It made it even more difficult to walk on the crutches with my foot in a cast. Shirley came out to meet me and got Annemarie for me. As usual, I had my trusty camera with me and asked Shirley to take a picture of me with Annemarie and with Little Vic, which she did.

6-11-71 Me leaning on my car, holding Annemarie

6-11-71 Me leaning on my car, holding Vic III

July 16, 1971. Today we went to visit Helen Shortridge and her baby, Tina Shortridge. I couldn't believe Larry and Olivia did not stay together, but then, I figured she got smart and left him. I have never liked Larry Shortridge. I hated to admit it, but I was rather curious as to who Helen was and what she was like. I could not see anyone wanting to marry Shortridge, but Helen obviously did. She was actually a nice person. She welcomed me, my kids and Sharon Rockey in. Rose Chaffer was there too.

"Hi, Christi. C'mon in," Helen said very welcoming.

I walked in with Little Vic and Sharon was carrying Annemarie.

"I heard Larry had a little girl. I didn't believe it at first. I just couldn't see Larry married and with a baby, no less," I said.

I sat in a chair across from her couch. I had my camera with me. Helen and Sharon sat on the floor with the kids.

"Yeah, I know. He shocked a lot of people. He's different now. He's settled down," Helen said.

"How old is Tina now? She's not much older than Annemarie, is she?" I asked.

"She's almost eight months old. Look at the size difference between Annemarie and Tina," Helen replied.

"To be honest, I never liked Larry much. He was so much older than all of us. He called me a broad a lot, which I hated. New Years Eve of 1965, he almost got us tossed in jail because he got into a fight at a bar in Toledo. He tried to kill my pet squirrel with a bb gun. And, talking about a bb gun, he shot out my parents' big picture window. That was not cool and I got in trouble for it," I informed her.

"I heard about the window, but I don't remember the squirrel, Helen said.

"Yeah, but he did have a nice Vet. He let me drive it a few times. He didn't know I loved a three or four speed on the floor. Does he still have that burgundy, 1963 Corvette?" I asked.

"No, he sold it before we got married. Do you want something to drink? I got iced tea or pop. Which do you want?" Helen asked me and Sharon.

"Nothing for me. I can't stay real long, but thanks for the offer. Sharon, do you want a drink?" Then I continued to say, "I brought my camera. Do you care if I take some pictures of the kids together?

"No, that's fine. We can just sit here on the floor"

I took five pictures of Helen and Tina, Sharon with Annemarie and Little Vic. I didn't have much film left, so I could only take a few pictures and then I could get this roll developed. We ended up staying for about two hours. We talked about the kids and each updated the other on current affairs. All in all, it was a nice visit and the kids got along and behaved very well. I could tell we would never be best friends, but we would be friends.

7-16-71 Helen Shortridge holding Tina. Vic III & Sharon Rockey
holding Annemarie,

7-16-71 Helen & Tina, Sharon & Annemarie

CHAPTER 12

The Party Crasher

I was now in a new, safe place with my children. I had placed an ad for a roommate in the newspaper when Annemarie was a couple of months old and a young girl, Sharon Rocky, had answered the ad. She was eighteen years old, a little younger than me, but we became good friends. She helped me with the baby for which I gave her free rent. We got along and it worked out for the both of us. I wanted to celebrate the next chapter in our lives, so I decided to throw a party and invite some close friends. I called several friends, including Kathy Budai, and Larry Anthony. I had invited at least a dozen people. I was so excited and wanted this party to be absolutely perfect and go off without a hitch.

August 5, 1971, I got the kids dressed and ready to go. Sharon was at her mother's in Wayne, so luckily, I ran into one of the other tenants who carried Annemarie to the car for me because otherwise I would very reluctantly have had to have Little Vic carry her for me.

Sharon Rockey - graduation picture 1971

We arrived at the store and bought some snacks; chips and dip, pretzels, nuts, and pop, which included my favorites, Dr. Pepper and Vernors ginger ale. While shopping with my kids, I held onto the buggy, for balance and pushed as my crutches dangled from each arm. It was extremely difficult. I was wearing out and out of breath very quickly. I looked around, but did not see anyone around that could reach the bag of chips off of the top shelf for me.

I asked Little Vic, "Can you climb in the buggy and reach that big bag of chips way up there on the top shelf for mommy?"

Little Vic answered, "I can reach them. Can I have some animal crackers, too?"

"Of course, you can. You are such a big helper."

Little Vic climbed into the buggy, grabbed the bag of chips for me and off we went to the next aisle to find some pop. As we turned the corner into the pop aisle, I noticed a lady walking toward us with her two children. As they got closer, I noticed her kids pointing at me as they stared down at my legs. I had forgotten that I was wearing my left, full-leg brace. I wanted to ask them what they were staring at, but I just kept my mouth shut as hard as it was. I hated wearing that thing. People were so rude. Every single time I wore it, people would stare at me like I was a freak of nature. I just wanted to run home and hide from the world. This was my motivation for hurrying, although hurrying was impossible as I had to hike my left hip up while dragging my left peg leg behind. This leg brace may have brought me some independence in walking; however, it created and brought me a whole lot of negative, embarrassing, unwanted attention. I couldn't believe no one had asked me how long I have had polio today as that question was usually asked every time I went out in public.

We had the chips and dip, pretzels, nuts, pop, and Little Vic's animal crackers, so we headed toward the checkout. The girl rang my order up and placed my things in the paper bags. I asked her if she could double bag my order and find someone to help me carry the bags to my car. A young boy carried my groceries to the car for me. I opened the driver side door and sat down on the seat. My left leg was in the straight, locked position. I had to unlock my leg brace, so I could bend my knee. I got my right leg in the car and then I grabbed my left leg by the brace and lifted it into the car. My leg felt like it weighed a ton. The doctors referred to it as dead weight. I asked the boy if he could hand Annemarie to me, so I could put her in her car seat that I had next to me, which he did. Little Vic climbed into the back seat and buckled himself up. The boy then went around to the passenger side of my car and placed one bag on the front floorboard and the other two in the back, one on the backseat and the other on the back floorboard.

As the boy was placing the last bag in the backseat he said to me, "My uncle has polio, too. How long have you had polio?"

I knew it was too good to be true as I answered, "I don't have polio, thank you. I was in an accident and severely injured my leg."

"I'm sorry ma'am, I thought you did because my uncle has the exact same kind of crutches that you have. Have a nice day."

"It's ok, I get that a lot. I didn't mean to snap at you like I did. I know you didn't mean any harm," I replied, although I was furious on the inside.

I knew he was just a kid and probably didn't know any better.

I put my key in the ignition, started the car and off we went back to the apartment. I parked on the side street and saw Paul playing ball with his son.

I asked Little Vic, "Will you go and ask Paul if he would carry Annemarie into the apartment?"

"OK, Mommy. I will ask him," and off he ran to ask Paul.

Paul walked over and said, "Sure thing, what do you need, Christi? I see you have some groceries and the baby and you need help getting them both in, right?"

"Yes, if you don't mind," I said and then continued, "Will you get the baby in first and put her in her playpen which is in the living room? Here are the keys to unlock the door," and I handed him the apartment keys.

Little Vic looked in the bags for his animal cookies and when he found them, he asked me if he could stay outside with Paul and his son, Gary Kudos. I told him that would be fine, but not to cross any streets and if they went in, he would have to come in, too.

I sat in my car while Paul carried Annemarie and then the groceries into our apartment. I got on my crutches, locked the car doors and went in. There was Annemarie, playing happily with her toys in the playpen. I put the groceries away and started to do some cleaning, organizing and rearranging. I put a couple of posters on the wall by the kids' bedroom.

I heard Little Vic come in and yell, "Gary and his dad went in, so I came in, too. Is dinner ready?"

To answer him, I said, "No, I haven't even started it. What do you want? I can make noodles and sausage or how about hamburger ring surprise? Or I can make TV dinners. So, what will it be?"

"I want noodles," Little Vic replied, "with chocolate milk."

"What vegetable, green beans, carrots or corn?" I asked.

"Corn," he yelled out loudly.

I took two sauce pans out and put them on the stove. I emptied the bag of noodles into the water to start boiling, opened the sausage and cut them into quarters, added them to the noodles and opened the can of corn. I got Annemarie out of the playpen and sat her in the highchair and fed her first. She ate chicken and rice and for dessert, apricots. Just then Sharon came through the door. She saw I was fixing dinner, so she helped by carrying the noodles to the sink to drain when they were done. In about a half hour everything was cooked or heated up. Little Vic said his prayers and then we all ate. I fed Annemarie tiny pieces of noodles and sausage off of my plate. Sharon and Little Vic put the dirty dishes in the kitchen sink so I could wash them.

I put the kids to bed at the usual time, eight o'clock, and then Sharon and I watched some TV.

We watched "The Brady Bunch" on ABC at 7:30 p.m. with Little Vic and after he went to bed we watched "Nanny and the Professor" on ABC at 8:00 p.m., "The Partridge Family" with David Cassidy on ABC at 8:30 p.m. "That Girl" with Marlo Thomas on ABC at 9:00 p.m., and then the CBS Friday Night Movies. I watched the news and then I went to bed. I tried to go to sleep, but I kept tossing and turning, going over every detail of my party for tomorrow night in my head.

August 6, 1971. The morning eventually came. The day passed as any other ordinary day until about seven o'clock. I asked Little Vic to pick up his toys from the living room floor. Sharon and I put the snacks and pop on the kitchen table. Earlier today, I made sure I had ice cubes made in the ice cube trays in the freezer. I was getting a little nervous now as nine o'clock was fast approaching. I changed into a little peach and white mini dress and wore my hair down on my back. It was long, almost to my waist. Everything was ready and now we just had to wait for my friends to show up.

The kids stayed up until their bedtime and at eight o'clock they were both in bed. About fifteen minutes later I checked in on both of them and they were both sound asleep.

The first ones to show at nine o'clock were Kathy Budai and three girlfriends. Then Larry Anthony and two more guys, Tony Rhodes and two girls, and by 9:30 p.m. I had a house full. Some sat and talked, others munched down on the snacks, and a few even danced to my records. I was taking pictures of my friends, because I wanted to remember what fun I had at my first party since I got shot by Vic.

Tony walked over to the record player, turned around and asked, "Does anyone have any requests?"

Sharon yelled out, "Yeah, I got one. How about 'Starting All Over Again' by Mel & Tim or 'Everybody Plays the Fool' by Main Ingredient."

Tony answered, "I can't find 'Starting All Over Again', but I found 'Everybody Plays the Fool'. Will that make you happy, Sharon?"

"Yeah, that's great Tony, and if you're lucky, I'll even let you dance with me."

I was in the kitchen when Tony yelled to me, "Christi, someone is knocking on the door."

Sharon heard Tony and said to me, "I'll get it, Christi. I wonder who else it could be?"

I said, "Go see who it is, Sharon."

Sharon yelled at me, "Christi, you might want to come here now."

I grabbed my crutches to see who it was and as I was making my way to the door, in walked Larry Shortridge carrying a little black and white dog under his left arm. Behind him were Glen Hensley and some guy I had never seen before. The song, "Mr. Big Stuff" by Jean Knight, just started to play.

I asked Larry Shortridge, "What are you doing here? I don't remember inviting you and why did you bring that dog in?" I grabbed my camera and took a picture of Larry and Glen with that strange guy. He obviously didn't want his picture taken since he covered his face. I guess he knew something was not right and he did not want to be implicated.

Before Larry could answer, in walked Vic, big as life and acting like he owned the place.

I got in front of Vic and yelled, "Vic, get the hell out of here! You weren't invited!"

"I came to see my kids and I told Shortridge you would take the dog, it's for Little Vic, cuz he can't keep it," Vic replied.

I answered, "Both of the kids are sound asleep. You need to make a time when you want to see the kids, not just drop by whenever you feel like it. Besides, why all of a sudden do you want to see the kids now? You denied my daughter was yours and haven't come to see Little Vic in forever and now you just show up. I don't think so. Get out now!"

Vic gave me a shove and I landed on the couch. I still had a hold of my camera and I started taking pictures of Vic. He went into the kids' bedroom and woke both of them up. Larry showed Little Vic the dog and told him it was his. Vic had the nerve to put on a record on the record player. The one he chose was "Oh How Happy" by the Shades of Blue. *Why did he do that? And why that song? That used to be our song.* Then he closed the kids' bedroom door with Annemarie crying and went into my kitchen. He went into my refrigerator and poured himself a drink.

Tony came over and asked me, "Do you want me to escort these guys out?"

"Yes, well… no, because then there will be a fight and things may get broken and the cops will be called. I just want him to leave with his friends. I thought, *first Vic has to ruin my life and now he has to ruin my party. I wish it was him that was disabled, not me and then he would see what an ass he acts like. I hate him. I wish I never met him.*

Vic came over to me and said, "Those are my kids, too, and you can't keep me from seeing them. I'll see them whenever the hell I please."

"It would be nice if you paid some child support, but that is not the issue. You are causing a scene, so just get out, leave, make like a ghost and disappear. No one wants you here, especially me," I informed him.

I looked over at Larry Anthony and he just sat and talked to some of my friends. I could tell he did not want to get caught up in this mess. When Vic went over to him, he acted cordial toward Vic, but did not offer to get involved. Their conversation lasted only a minute, then Vic turned and walked back towards my kitchen. I told Vic again to leave; however, he kept walking, ignoring me. Instead of him going into my kitchen as I thought, he suddenly turned left into my bedroom. Now I was beyond angry with him, so I yelled, "Get out of my bedroom! There is nothing for you in there! Get out of my bedroom you son-of-a-bitch! Get out of my house now! If you and your friends don't leave, I'm going to call the cops!"

As Vic rounded the corner, coming out of my bedroom, he was carrying one of my trophies that I won at the Detroit Dragway with my '69 Plymouth Road Runner. I became livid. My legs started to spasm bad causing me not to be able to get up off the couch and onto my crutches. If I had made it off the couch, I would have tackled Vic and beat the shit out of him. That was the last straw. I grabbed my camera again to take pictures of him crashing my party, going through my entire apartment, waking up my kids, and stealing my trophy, so I would have proof of who was harassing whom, if I had to call the cops. Now, the song "Never Can Say Goodbye" by the Jackson 5 was playing. How appropriate.

Vic continued walking towards the door, walking right past me. It was then I yelled again, "Bring back that trophy you son-of-a-bitch!"

Kathy chimed in, "Hey Vic, why do you gotta steal her trophy? Can't you win one of your own?"

Then Larry Anthony said to Vic, "Hey man, you don't want no trouble. Just give her back her damn trophy."

Larry Shortridge said to Vic, "Let's get the hell out of here. You know she'll call the cops, and I don't need no trouble from them. C'mon man, let's go."

"Yeah, Shortridge is right, let's just get the hell out of here," Glen Hensley said to Vic.

Vic, Larry Shortridge, Glen Hensley and the guy who did not want to be identified left out my front door and was gone. The little dog was sitting on the floor, scared to death, so I asked Sharon to put her in my bedroom for now until the party ended. I would deal with the dog later. Vic left with my trophy. I thought to myself, *what did he want with my trophy? I wonder if Barb, that piece of white trash, knows that Vic was at my apartment?*

8-6-71 Kathy Budai giving little Vic a sip of pop,
Tony Rhodes in fridge.

8-6-71 Kathy Budai, Janet Huffine, Sue Arquette, Jackie Wells

8-6-71 Larry Anthony, Sharon Rockey

8-6-71 Larry Anthony

8-6-71 Larry Shortridge with dog

8-6-71 Glen Hensley, Vic going into kid's bedroom

8-6-71 Vic in my refrigerator.

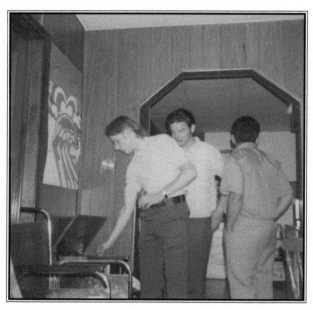

8-6-71 Vic changing record, Glen Hensley, some guy

8-6-71 Vic with drinking glass.

8-6-71 Victor Robert Golden, Jr not welcome.

8-6-71 Vic stealing my trophy, Shirley Idiot

8-6-71 Glen Hensley, guy covering his face.

8-6-71 Larry Anthony, friends

Yes, Vic showed up where he was not invited and he took advantage of me by embarrassing me in front of my friends and stealing my trophy, which meant a lot to me and he knew that, but he did not totally ruin my party. After his rude appearance and then disappearance, the party continued as planned and we all had fun. Now I was determined to plan another party, one that Vic would not find out about and if he showed up, I would be prepared for him and his entourage. We did keep the little dog, part Border Collie, and we named her Trixie. She turned out to be a good little dog. Denis Waitley once said, *"Don't dwell on what went wrong. Instead, focus on what to do next. Spend your energies on moving forward toward finding the answer."* I ended up taking that good advice and just moving on with my life.

http://www.brainyquote.com/quotes/authors/d/denis_waitley.htmlSkip and Linda Janik were friends of mine for several years. Linda was Vickie's friend first, but being Vic's girlfriend, we too became good friends. Kathy Budai had thrown a baby shower for the two of us. It was a combined baby shower since we were due so close together. Little Vic was born on March 6, 1968 and their daughter, Ronnie Ann was born March 11, 1968, just five days after Little Vic. I was sure the kids were what kept our friendship going. I was happy that after Vic shot me, Linda and Skip Janik and their daughter, Ronnie Ann, remained friends with Little Vic and me. Vic's friends remained his friends and not mine.

August 16, 1971. We decided to go see Ronnie Ann and her mom, Linda Janik. Linda and her husband, Skip, were living in Garden City with her parents. It was a beautiful warm day. The sun was shining and Ronnie Ann and Little Vic went into the backyard to play. Linda carried Annemarie and the three of us sat in the backyard. I sat on a chair and lay my crutches next to me on the grass. Ronnie Ann and Little Vic immediately started to play. The backyard was huge and there were many things for the kids to play with including a huge cardboard box, some big balls to sit on, a spring horse, and a variety of other toys.

"Hi, Chris. How have you been? It's been a while since we last saw you. I'm so sorry for what happened to you, but it looks like you are moving on. Where are you living now? Last we knew it was at Vic's mom's house," Linda told me.

"I was forced to live there, but when Vic went to De Ho Co, I made my escape and moved to the rat traps of Detroit and then to Inkster, where we live now," I replied.

"Little Vic sure has gotten big and Annemarie is so cute. She looks just like her brother."

"Yes, she does resemble him and they both look like their dad. Can you believe Vic had the audacity to say once that Annemarie was not his? I can't believe the nerve of him; she looks just like him. I wish she looked like me, but she doesn't. Oh, did I not tell you, my name is Christi now, not Chris. It's a long story about work changing my name, but I like it. It fits me and with a new name comes new changes and a new life."

"OK, Christi."

"Look at our kids; they play so good together. It's like nothing ever happened."

"I don't know how you do it, but you are doing great."

"I have a roommate, Sharon Rocky and she helps me with the kids a lot."

"Do you ever see Vic anymore?"

"Very little, only when it suits him. He is shacking up with that bitch, Barb, you know, his mistress. I personally stay far away from him. I've had all the abuse I need to last a lifetime. He's ruined my life. I still can't believe how he turned out. I thought I was so in love with him and he turned out to be such a bastard, always hurting me one way or another. If it wasn't for him literally raping me, I wouldn't have Annemarie. He just couldn't keep his hands off of me. Let's change the subject. He is such a depressing subject that I would rather talk about something else. Have you seen Kathy Budai lately?"

"No, have you?"

"Yes, she came to my party I had on August 6th. Naturally, Vic showed up with his bunch of loser friends and crashed my party. She still looks the same; pretty and with that gorgeous hair of hers. She's not dating anyone in particular. She came with some of her girlfriends. Vic was the life of the party when he stole one of my trophies. Oops, sorry, but he ticks me off so much I can't help fuming. Change of subject."

"Can I hold Annemarie?"

"Sure, she likes to be held instead of being in this carrier."

We stayed for several hours and visited and we got to catch up on so much that went on.

Since the shooting, most everyone avoided Vic's mom's house like the plague. While living with them, I never saw anyone come over anymore. Then, when I moved out and lived in the rat traps of Detroit, it was too far to go to see anyone. This was the first time I had seen Linda in a long time. As we sat and talked, it seemed like we just picked up where we left off.

8-16-71 Linda Janik, Vic III, Ronnie Ann.

8-16-71 little Vic on horse, Ronnie Ann Janik.

8-16-71 Ronnie Ann and little Vic sitting on big balls.

8-16-71 kids in big box.

October 31, 1971. It was Halloween and Linda Janik and I had made plans to spend Trick or Treat time together with the kids. I drove out to Garden City to meet at her parents' house. The kids were dressed up in cute costumes. Skip and Sharon Rockey took Ronnie Ann and Little Vic out to Trick or Treat. Linda, Annemarie and I stayed behind and waited for the kids to get back.

9-30-71 Ronnie Ann, Vic III in same outfit at our apt.
on Beech Daly

10-31-71 Skip Janik, Sharon Rockey, Ronnie Ann, Vic III

10-31-71 Ronnie Ann Janik, Vic III

10-31-71 Vic III, Ronnie Ann in costumes, Annemarie

*10-31-71 Linda Janik holding Annemarie, Vic III and Ronnie Ann
going through all the candy they got from Trick or Treating.*

CHAPTER 13

The Lavender Raincoat

It was the beginning of December, 1971 on a Friday night. Sharon Rockey, Little Vic, Annemarie, and me, had just recently moved from Beech Daly Rd. in Inkster to Westminster Townhouses, 23631 Kensington Street, in Taylor. Sharon would normally watch the kids for me or she would accompany me, but on this particular night, she also had plans. I took my two kids to a neighbor's home.

I was driving down Telegraph Road in my 1965 Thunderbird, not speeding, not swerving, driving perfectly fine when a car pulled up next to me and started motioning for me to pull over. Now I had just been to a party with some friends, and I use the term loosely, where most, if not all, were smoking pot. You need to understand, at this point in my life I felt like a freak of nature, an ugly imitation of a human being. I had not been able to shake my negative self-image or self-worthlessness because I couldn't walk without those ugly polio-type crutches and I had to wear a brace on my left leg. That was truly the biggest turn off I could think of. Yes, Vic had really done a number on not just my body, but also on my mind. He destroyed me totally.

My thinking was a little screwed up and because I thought I was worth nothing; I was lucky to have any friends. I was not choosey when it came to making friends. Any friend was better than no friend at all. I had to admit, many of these so-called friends were simply low life, pot smoking, good for nothing people. But that was my perception of who should be my friend. The only good thing about this self-perception was since I never smoked cigarettes, I had no desire to smoke pot, either. Well, let me stand corrected. In eleventh grade, Eddie Glomb tried to get me to smoke a cigarette, but I didn't like the taste, so I never took up the bad habit of smoking. But on this particular night I think I may have been a little high from the second-hand smoke from the pot. It was around eleven o'clock Friday night.

1965 Ford Thunderbird interior

I was coming from a party in Redford, Michigan and going home to my townhouse in Taylor. I noticed the car beside me when I went under Michigan Avenue. I was in the far-right lane and this car continued for about a mile driving to the left of me in the middle lane, and I was starting to wonder, *why doesn't this car pass me? Did I sideswipe or hit this car?* Not thinking clearly, I turned right onto McDonald Street after going through the light at Annapolis. I was in no mood to get into a confrontation with anyone; however, I was not the type of girl who puts up with anyone's crap, either. I was not afraid to face anyone or stick up for myself. I was pretty sure I didn't do anything to this person in that car. I had been driving slowly and carefully since I left the party. There weren't a lot of cars on the road. I'm sure if I would have hit another car or run someone off the road, I would have remembered it. I just wanted to get home, so I could be with my babies. I drove down a couple of houses and pulled over next to the curb. I wasn't sure what was going on. A woman came to the passenger side of my car. Like a dumb ass, I let the window down to ask her what her problem was. The next thing I knew; her arm was reaching into my car trying to open the door lock. My T-Bird was all power and I tried to put up the electric window, but it was too late. She had pulled up the lock and opened the door and sat in the passenger bucket seat. Now I freaked out. I asked her what she wanted. No answer. Then all I could think about was getting killed. I thought about Ted Bundy, but this was a woman, not a man. I imagined someone finding my body cut up into little pieces, stuffed in a large green trash bag along the side of some street. Then I flipped out.

I started to cry and between the gasps of air I said to her, "What do you want? Why are you doing this to me? My husband shot me, so I can't walk or get away. I have two little children waiting on me at the neighbor's. They are expecting me to be there any minute now. My sweet, first born child is now three-and-a-half years old. His name is Little Vic. He is named after his father. I also have an adorable, precious little girl. Her name is Annemarie. She is only ten months old. I named her after my real mother. They both need me. They just can't grow up without a mommy and be raised by the man who shot and almost killed me less than two years ago. I just can't have that happen. They are with a neighbor and are expecting me to get them soon. Please don't hurt me for my kids' sake."

I kept crying.

She grabbed my arm as if trying to pull me out of my seat. I pulled my arm back, trying to get her to loosen her grip on my right arm. I was not believing this. It couldn't really be happening. J.D. Salinger once said, "Among other things, you'll find that you're not the first one who was ever confused and frightened and even sickened by human behavior." I got what he was saying by this woman's actions. I was confused and frightened. Would I die? I was sickened by her tactics and aggressive pawing of me. *Why me?* I thought.

"What do you want with me? Why me? What did I do to you? Please don't hurt me. If you are trying to scare me, you have succeeded. Did someone tell you to do this, to pick me up and hurt me? I get it, Vic or Barb told you to find me and hurt me. Are you going to kill me?" I asked her.

Somehow, I accidently turned the interior light on and saw her. She had bleached blonde hair, her lips were painted blood red with lipstick, and her face was a pale white, which looked like she had an inch of make-up on it. She had very dark and thick eyeliner outlining her brown eyes, and had a hideous, shiny, lavender raincoat on.

She finally spoke and said to me, "Turn that light off, now!"

"I didn't mean to turn them on, I'm sorry."

"Why haven't you tried to run? Oh yeah, you said you got shot. Where exactly did you get shot?"

"I got shot through the lung, just missing my heart. When I made a run for it, he just aimed and fired and the second bullet hit me in the spine, paralyzing me instantly."

"Was there a lot of blood?"

"I guess, because I felt the warm, wet blood going around me. It was like I was in a pool of blood."

"Who was it that shot you again?"

"My husband, Victor Robert Golden, Jr."

"What happened to him?"

"Nothing."

"Why not?"

"Because I was afraid of him and afraid that he would finish the job for revenge. I made the mistake of not pressing charges against him. The detectives wanted me to press charges, so Vic would go to prison. I guess I still loved him a little; after all he is the father of my two kids."

"I would have killed him."

"Right; me weighing 92 lbs. and five foot two and him five foot ten. Look in the back, on the floor of my car. Can you not see my crutches I have to use to get around?"

She took her stare from me and focused on my crutches for a few seconds.

"Wait a minute. You don't know Vic or Barb?"

"No."

Then what do you want with me?" I said, with a very puzzled look on my face and in my voice.

She did not reply.

Ted Bundy kept entering my mind. *What did she want with me?* I thought. Did she somehow see the car seats and was planning on kidnapping my babies? It just didn't make sense to me why a woman would pick another woman to pull over and what could her motive possibly have been?

She spoke again and said, "If you don't scream, do what I say and stay still, I won't hurt you."

What did she mean by that—I won't hurt you? I thought to myself.

How could I stay still? My legs had already started to spasm. They were shaking uncontrollably. My whole body was shaking, but I did try not to cry. My left foot kept hitting the brake pedal and because my legs both were spasming very violently and my left leg kept hitting the brake pedal, I couldn't help but notice through my rear-view mirror that my brake lights were flashing off and on continuously. I was hoping and praying that someone would drive by and see my brake lights flashing off and on and stop to see if anything was wrong or if I needed any help. Not one car passed the whole time we were parked there. Now I was starting to have flashbacks of the day when I was shot by my husband, Vic.

I said to her, trying to get some sympathy, "I was shot, not once, but twice. The first bullet went through my left lung, broke my left floating ribs and still remained in my abdomen surrounded by scar tissue. The second bullet hit me in my spine at T11 and fragmented. I lay in my own pool of blood, and was in the hospital for over four months."

How could I have survived all of that just to lose my life at the hands of a complete stranger? I thought. We sat there in dead silence, which seemed like forever, but in reality, it was only about fifteen minutes. I was so afraid for my life. My heart was pounding so fast and hard that I thought it was going to explode right out of my chest. The anticipation of not knowing what her intensions were with me made me that much more fearful. It was the unknown that was really freaking me out. All I could think about were my babies. Was I going to live to see and hold them again? Was I going to end up in the hospital again with another bullet in me? Was anyone going to find me? Would anyone even care that I was missing? Was I going to live or die? I wished she would do or say something else, at least let me know what she wanted and why she pulled me over. The dead silence was really creeping me out. I couldn't take it anymore. I might have ended up dead, not by her hands, but from having a heart attack—I was that scared.

Suddenly, as quickly as she got in, she pulled up the door locks, opened my car door, got out and slammed the door shut. I immediately locked the doors with the power door locks. My body was still shaking, but my mind was relieved she was gone. She pulled out from behind me and with split second thinking I looked at her license plate as she drove past me. I saw her rear license plate and started to repeat it. I somehow was able to make it around the block and pulled into a gas station on Telegraph Road. I noticed all the lights were on, so I knew they were still open. Since it was lit up so well, I felt safe stopping there. I pulled right up to the door and put my car in park. All I could do was babble her license plate numbers. The gas attendant came out and walked around to my driver's side and tapped on my window. I was too busy repeating her license plate numbers to even hear or notice someone was trying to get my attention. I guess after the guy had been tapping for a while, I eventually looked and saw the attendant. I pushed the power window button down and when the window was down, the attendant asked me if I was ok. All I could do was repeat the license plate numbers. He must have thought I was crazy because, since I wouldn't answer him, he must have suspected something was wrong. He walked back inside the gas station and, I would guess, called the cops because the cops showed up in just a few minutes. Two officers approached my window and asked me if they could see my driver's license and registration. I was not able to respond to them because all I kept thinking was I needed to remember those numbers. They must have seen my purse sitting on the passenger side floor and they proceeded to walk around my car, open the door and grab my purse.

The officer asked, "Are you all right, Miss?"

I did not reply, I just kept repeating those numbers.

The officer opened my purse and removed my driver's license from my wallet and asked me, "Are you Christine Golden?"

I couldn't even tell them who I was, for fear of forgetting the license tag number, but they got the information from my driver's license in my purse.

"Are you all right? Do you need an ambulance?"

All I could do was repeat the license plate numbers.

"What exactly are those numbers you keep repeating?"

"License Plate, License Plate, License Plate."

"Whose license plate?" the officer asked.

Again, I just repeated the numbers. The officer called dispatch and asked them to run the license plate numbers I kept repeating. A few minutes later, dispatch came back on the radio and said the plates came back registered to a person in California. They had outstanding warrants, so they issued an APB (all-points bulletin) on the vehicle license plate numbers.

The officer walked back to my car and said, "Are you going to be ok? Do you think you need an ambulance or need medical attention? We are definitely following this up with an investigation. You seemed to have stumbled upon a fugitive from California. I don't know all the information yet, but I believe you are a lucky little lady. Things may not have turned out so well and we probably never would have known about this fugitive if it wasn't for you. I'm glad you are all right."

"I'm feeling a little better now that you have the tag number. My mind went into overdrive. I just couldn't forget them. I don't know why she picked me." I told the officer.

Now that the cops had the plate numbers, I proceeded to tell him the whole story about what had happened just the other side of the block.

"If you would feel safer, I can follow you home to make sure you are not accosted again."

"Yes, I would like that. I just live a little further down Telegraph at the Westminster Townhouses in Taylor."

"I have to fill out this incident report. Can you sit tight for a few minutes?"

"Yeah, it'll give me a chance to get it together."

I stayed at the gas station for several minutes until I got a little more pulled together. I then drove home with the cop car following me. I arrived at my neighbor's home to get my babies.

"What's with the cops?" she asked me.

"You wouldn't believe me if I told you. I'll tell you tomorrow. Thanks for watching my kids. I appreciate it," I told her.

She carried Annemarie and the cop offered to carry Little Vic to my apartment. They were both sound asleep. He made sure all three of us were safe inside my apartment. He told me he would call the Taylor police to drive by the apartments and also tell them to be on the lookout for the license plate I informed them of.

About two weeks later I got a summons to appear in court at the Dearborn City Hall Courthouse. I had been asked to stay in another room just off the courtroom. When I finally was called to testify, I was shocked. Sitting at the defendant's table was a blonde wig and a lavender slicker or a raincoat, and a guy, not a girl, who had terrorized me for such a long time that fateful night. I walked, on my crutches, to the witness chair, put my right hand on the Bible and swore to tell the whole truth and nothing but the truth. I felt uncomfortable recalling that horrible night, but I shared with the court all the details and the fear I experienced. I found it hard to look at him, but I occasionally looked at that lavender raincoat and blonde wig. They gave me goose bumps.

After testifying, I went back to a bench in the courtroom and listened to the judge's verdict. He was found guilty of assault and attempted kidnapping. I watched as the bailiff and another police officer took him out of the courtroom in handcuffs wearing his jailhouse uniform. I was so relieved that they caught him and he was now in jail. I found out this guy was from California and had done this to women in several states many times, except he beat them up and raped them. At that moment, I had to count my blessings. God had protected me once again. He got jail time and after serving time in the Michigan prison system, he would be extradited to the other states for prosecution. The judge and prosecutor thanked me and told me they were sorry for what I had gone through. I'm just glad they apprehended him. No thanks needed, God took care of me, again.

It was now nearing Christmas of '71. I purposely stayed away from Vic and Barb. I heard rumors she was pregnant, but I didn't want to believe any of them. I didn't know if I could stomach the thought of a baby being the result of a union between Vic and Barb. I knew he was screwing her for a long time, so nothing would surprise or shock me. I also knew she would try to get pregnant to trap Vic. I couldn't understand why she just couldn't wait for Vic and I to get divorced. It was inevitable that we would get divorced, but she just couldn't wait to ruin our marriage, if there was anything to save. That would have been the decent thing to do, but decent was not her thing nor did she know the meaning of the word. To me, it seemed to be only an act of desperation. I know a lot of girls get pregnant deliberately to trap their boyfriends, and Barb was no exception. I also heard that the rumors of Barb's pregnancy proved to be true, so I deliberately took a picture of her pregnant stomach. This not only verified that the rumors were true, but it also proved she was the whore and home wrecker that she was. Now let her say something about me or how good she was. She could never redeem herself in my eyes. She would forever remain the whore, harlot, tramp, slut and every other word that describes her kind in my mind. Forgiveness would become almost impossible for me in years to come.

It was only for my children that I would be congenial, or at least reserved, while the kids were exchanging presents. I bought, out of a feeling of pity for Rita, a Christmas present for her.

"Hi, Victor," Rita said to us excitedly as we entered the house.

"Hi Rita," I said and then said to Little Vic, "Give Rita her present."

Rita was very giggly and happy and started to tear off the wrapping paper, but then stopped and got two presents and handed them to Little Vic. She then finished tearing off the wrapping paper.

"Are you gonna stay here and play with me?" Rita asked.

"No, we can't because we have more places to go," I told Rita.

"Will you bring Victor and Annemarie to visit me again?" Rita sadly asked.

"I will, or you can come to visit us sometime," I said.

I don't know why I told Rita that, since I dreaded the thought of Barb in my apartment.

12-23-71 Barb Noe and her pregnant stomach,
proof of adultery on Vic and Barb.

12-23-71 Rita Lynn Smith giving Vic III present.

CHAPTER 14

D S S Steals Kids

I t was June, 1973. We had lived in Taylor from December of 1971 to June of 1973. As if things had not been bad enough, I could not believe they were only going to get worse, much worse. This would be the worst nine months of my life. My precious children would be taken from me for nine long months. And why? Because someone thought they could hurt me by taking what was most precious to me, my two kids. It all started from a lie, a report anonymously called in to DSS (Department of Social Services), stating my kids were neglected, malnourished and so hungry that they were eating cat shit, I mean, cat feces. Just keep in mind, no matter how hungry a kid was, they would never eat cat shit. I had a very good idea who called DSS, Barb and/or Victor Robert Golden, Jr. With that said, "…and now for the rest of the story," as Paul Harvey Aurandt, an American radio broadcaster, would say.

I was living in Wyandotte, Michigan, but I was not happy there. It was too far from my friends and my hang outs, so I decided to find a new place to live. June 1973 was a great month to move in. It was warm, very little rain, so moving was not bad.

I hated moving in the rain or when it's cold. I once again got the want ads for houses to rent. I checked several out and a couple would not rent to me because I was handicapped, but I didn't let that get me down anymore. I found one I liked and I could afford. It was a nice three-bedroom brick, ranch style house, all on one floor, no upstairs and no basement in Dearborn Heights.

Another reason I was moving was once again because of Barb and her gossipy meddling. Every place I have moved to she managed to find out about and then she would talk to the neighbors and told them I was shot, so they freaked out and usually then wouldn't let their kids play with my kids. She, of course, did not tell them it was my husband and her so-called live in boyfriend who shot me. So, the end product was my kids didn't have friends. She was really getting on my last nerve. Why was she so obsessed with me and my life? My life was nothing to brag about and yet she constantly interfered, just like Vic's mother.

I got a couple of guys to help me and my roommate, Sharon Rockey, to move. We got the big things like furniture in the truck we borrowed and the rest of the boxes we put in the trunk and backseat of my car. I now owned a 1966 Chevy Caprice, burgundy in color and plenty of room. It definitely was a full-sized car; power everything including a reverb and 8-track stereo system. We got all the furniture in the house, the bunk beds put together and some of the dishes put in the cupboards. What we didn't have were groceries, so I asked Sharon to baby-sit while I went to get some food for us to eat. I was gone for about two hours and when I came back with the groceries, I didn't see my kids.

I asked Sharon, "Where are my kids? I didn't see them as I drove up. Are they next door meeting the neighbors?"

"No. The Dearborn Heights police and some DSS worker came and took the kids. I couldn't get in touch with you, so I had no way of telling you they were taking the kids," Sharon told me, very upset.

"I know who did this. It was Vic and that bitch, Barb. When I was leaving I thought I saw

Barb's Cougar, but there was no one in it, or at least not that I could see. So, I thought it was just coincidence and didn't think about it again. I'm sure I'll hear from them and this will get straightened out. There is no reason for them to take Little Vic and Annemarie. Sure, there are still unpacked boxes in each room, but what do you expect when you are moving? We haven't even moved in to make a mess. Maybe because there was no food in the house, but I was getting the food and here it is."

Sharon went out to my car and brought in the groceries.

"We need to get the phone hooked up immediately," she told me in a desperate tone of voice.

"I'm going up to the gas station to use the pay phone to call the Dearborn Heights police to find out exactly what is going on here."

"Ok and I'll keep unpacking and putting things away."

I drove up to the gas station to use the pay phone, but I had to wait because there was someone using the pay phone. I asked them politely if I could use it because it was an emergency, but they didn't listen to me, so I waited until they got off the phone. I called the police and asked to speak to the officer who came out to my house and took my kids. The officer on the other end of the phone told me that officer was off duty because of shift change and I would have to call back tomorrow. I took the phone book hanging in the phone booth and looked up the number for DSS and called them. They told me that that worker had not come in from the field yet and since I didn't have a phone yet, they couldn't call me back. I told them my name, address, my kids' names and that I would definitely be calling tomorrow. I drove back to the house and helped Sharon unpack the rest of the boxes. All I could do was cry.

I thought to myself, *why was Vic so damn vengeful and Barb so damn spiteful? She has Vic. Isn't that enough? I know she doesn't want my kids; she has kids of her own who she doesn't seem to care about. Well, maybe the baby, because she says it's Vic's. Can't they leave me alone? Everywhere I move to, it's the same thing. I can't live in peace nowhere.*

Sharon and I did as much as we could to straighten the house out, but there were still boxes to unpack, clothes to hang up or to put in the drawers. It was six o'clock and we were both hungry, so we made an Appian Way pizza from the box. Since we didn't have any pepperoni, we used cut-up ham. It wasn't the greatest, but it cured us of our growling stomachs. I washed the pizza pan and Sharon threw away the paper plates. We brought our drinks into the living room, so we could watch some television. We watched "The Mod Squad," "Ironsides," and "The Streets of San Francisco," and then the news came on. It was the same old stuff; people in Detroit getting shot, criminals on the loose and the mayor getting caught on corruption charges. No wonder Detroit was called the murder capital of the world. It seemed like every day a person was getting shot. Since I was a victim of a shooting, it really bothered me to hear it and especially when the camera got an angle where someone was aiming the gun right at me. That freaked me out. I knew it was on TV, but it still bothered me intensely. We both went to bed right after the news.

As soon as I got up, I went back to the gas station, so I could use the pay phone. I called the DSS department first to try to find out where my kids were. I got the run around. No one seemed to know what happened at first. After talking to several people, I got a person who could give me a little information. First, they told me an anonymous call came in and said the kids were in immediate danger. Secondly, they were informed that I was disabled and could not care for my kids and that there was no food in the house and the kids were being starved to death. Thirdly, they told me the complaint was that there was cat crap that the kids were eating because they were so hungry.

Now let me explain; first, I didn't even have a cat there, second, I was out buying groceries, and, finally, that my disability did not stop me from parenting. That is one reason that Sharon Rockey lived with me. I believe that was a lot of nerve for Vic and Barb to use my disability against me since he was the one who caused it in the first place. No one who is moving gets all the furniture placed and all the boxes unpacked in one day. It took us a couple of days to get settled, but we did get moved in and settled. I wanted my kids back immediately, but they said I would have to go to court for that to happen. Think about this, if Vic was innocent in this situation then Vic would have stepped up and should have wanted to take the kids until I got moved in, so the kids would not get into the DSS system. But no, Vic never offered at all. He just wanted the kids to be taken away from me to hurt me. This was all new to me. I had never been involved with the child protection department of the DSS system, but I would soon find out how treacherous and malicious they could be. They keep your kids, no matter what. June was such an unhappy month for me. All I did was sulk around the house.

After a month or so I had an interview date and that did not go well. I demanded my kids be given back immediately. They had other plans for my poor kids. They definitely did not like me standing up to them and speaking my mind. They wouldn't even let me talk to them. I found out they were separated from each other, so now they were with total strangers.

When I went down to the DSS department I was placed in a room. A big, fat, black woman, and not the least bit jolly, came in to speak to me, and she was not patient either. The first incident I went ballistic over was when I found out my little boy was placed in a home with a family who had a little girl who was a couple of years older than Little Vic. Little Vic was already five years old now and their daughter was seven or eight. They had a two-bedroom house and my son and their little girl were sleeping in the same bed. I felt that that was very inappropriate. They were not related as family, but total strangers. My poor baby, Annemarie, was put into another home with a family who had a ton of kids where she was lost in the shuffle.

"I am Mrs. Jackson and I understand you want to talk to me about your kids," she asked.

"Yes, you people have both of my children, but you had no right to take them. They were just fine with me. Granted, I was gone when you came, but I was at the grocery store getting food and my sitter, Sharon Rockey, took care of them. Whoever called told you lied. I believe my husband or his mistress called you. They didn't even have the guts to say who they were. That should tell you something if they wouldn't even leave their name. Nothing like relying on an anonymous tip, right? I was told that my son and his sister were separated. Why is that? I was told DSS is supposed to keep a family together, and yet you split my two kids up. Why is that? You people are useless. I did a better job of caring for my kids then you are doing. I want my kids back immediately due to the fact of your incompetence," I said angrily.

"Sometimes it isn't always possible to keep siblings together. This is what probably happened in your case. There is a shortage of foster homes."

Raising my voice an octave or two, along with my blood pressure, I said again, "If you have such a shortage of foster homes, then why did you take my kids? They were in no danger and the decent thing to have done was to wait until I returned back to the house."

"When we are called to pick up a child, we cannot wait around for the parents to show up. Many times, the parents never show up. They are too busy getting high or drunk or even worse."

"Well, that is not me. If you would have waited just a lousy fifteen minutes, I would have been there. And besides, why do you think Sharon was there? She was there to watch the kids, which she did. She told you I was coming back soon, and yet you took my kids, anyway. What is wrong with you people? Do you enjoy ripping families apart on the say so of a person who doesn't have the guts to tell their name? I said, raising my voice again at her.

"We have a report and that is what we go by. We have to investigate each complaint," she said.

"Well, whoever investigated did a lousy job. They should be fired. Was there a mark on either of my kids? No! Were they skinny and malnourished? No! And I know they were not eating cat crap, because we do not even have a cat. Besides, no kids would eat crap, no matter how hungry they were."

"You need to lower your voice now or this meeting is over."

"Hey lady, if you haven't figured out yet, I am angry, very angry and I want my kids back now!"

I had stood up for a moment, but then sat down again. All I could think of was Vic and Barb laughing about this, but this was no laughing matter. This was serious. I thought to myself, *yes, Vic, you think you have hurt me, but it isn't over yet. I just got started. I'll get my kids back and you will pay and pay dearly. You will pay child support for two kids and that will take some food out of the mouth of that woman, and I use the term loosely, you are living with. I am so sick of the both of you.* Was I angry? You bet I was. Did I let that DSS worker know how I felt? You bet I did? Was I done fighting? No, not by a long shot!

I made such a big stink about my son sleeping with the girl that DSS eventually moved him out of that house and placed him in another home. What I also found curious was to this point I was not given an attorney, neither were my kids given a Guardian Ad Litem, which is just another word for an attorney for the kids. I could not afford an attorney on my own, so I continued to fight solely on my limited knowledge of the law and based on sheer assumptions and hearsay.

Aristotle once said, "Anybody can become angry - that is easy, but to be angry with the right person and to the right degree and at the right time and for the right purpose, and in the right way - that is not within everybody's power and is not easy."

I needed to be careful who I picked my battles with and how I showed my emotions toward them. I needed to be able to control my anger and resentment and just try to stay positive and focused on getting my children back. I learned that day that DSS was not a friend of mine. They were not here to help reunite my family; rather, my children were just a pawn in this game they were playing with our lives and for the money they received from the state of Michigan.

I returned home after spending hours fighting with DSS. Sharon must have heard me pull up, because she greeted me at the door.

"So, how did it go?" Sharon asked me.

"As well as to be expected, I guess," I replied.

"When are you getting little Vic and Annemarie back?".

"As it looks now, never."

"They can't keep them forever, can they?"

"The complaint is all bullshit is all I can say. It is nothing, but lies and half-truths."

"I figured you would be all day, so I started dinner. I made us TV dinners. Is that OK?"

"That's fine. Actually, I'm not even hungry. I am still fuming from talking to that stupid woman.".

"What do you have to do to get the kids back?"

"According to that idiot woman, the things mentioned in the complaint have to be resolved. The problem is that there is nothing to resolve. We now have food in the house; we never had a cat, and the kids were never hungry or malnourished. We even have the house settled now and everything put away. So, you'd think I would get the kids back today, but no. She says someone from DSS has to come out to verify the situation has changed. What the hell do they want from me? Short of drawing my blood, I have done everything they want me to do. She told me a worker in the field would come by unexpectedly to see my housing situation.".

A few weeks later a skinny, white, older woman came by the house and rang the front doorbell. Sharon answered the door.

"Are you Mrs. Golden?" the woman asked Sharon.

"No," was all Sharon replied.

"Is Mrs. Golden home?"

"Hold on, I'll get her. Wait here," Sharon told her and shut the door.

I went to the door and said, "I am Mrs. Golden. Who are you and what do you want?"

"I am Mrs. Atwater from the department of Social Services, Protective Services Division."

"What do you want? Are you here to see my house? Come in," I told her.

"I need to see your whole house, the refrigerator and food pantry and your pets," she stated.

I answered, rather a bit sarcastically, "There is the fridge and the food is in those cupboards, pointing to the refrigerator and food cupboards. There is our dog. Her name is Trixie and she belongs to my son, and you can see the house, just look around."

"Where is the cat?" she asked.

"We never had a cat, well we had a cat, but not at this house, just the dog." I answered

She proceeded to go through the house like she was looking for an escaped fugitive or a hidden treasure. She looked in every room, in every closet, in every drawer of every dresser, in the bathroom; even behind the shower curtain. She must not have been a dog lover, because she kept waving her hands at the dog and saying, "Shoo, go away," so Trixie finally came back into the living room where we were waiting for that drill sergeant to finish her inspection. I knew she found nothing wrong, but what she would write in that stupid report of hers was another story. I found out that DSS workers do lie, add negative facts and leave out the truth.

"That concludes my visit and inspection."

"When will I know that I am getting my kids back?"

"We have a forty-five-day timeframe to inform you of our findings and decision. You will be hearing from us. Thank you," she said and left.

July 4th, 1973 was very lonely. I had planned to get some fireworks like bottle rockets and sparklers for the kids to enjoy watching. But since there were no kids here, I never bothered to celebrate the 4th of July. DSS was not working with me, but against me. They did everything to keep me and my kids separated. They did little to nothing to get us reunited. That was supposed to be the goal. I had been told that it might take a couple of months to get my kids back. It would take much longer than that. I was given a court appointed attorney, but that was a joke. I saw him exactly twice and he did exactly nothing for me. He never got me a court date or visitations—nothing. He was there for the easy money because he didn't do any work to earn however much the state gave him for my defense.

I found out that once kids were in the system, they were there to stay for a long time. There was no such thing as a short snatch. I also was told, but not by DSS, that for every kid DSS takes away from the parents, they got money from the state. Well, that certainly was a great incentive for taking and keeping kids. That's almost like selling kids. Once DSS got the kids in their clutches, it was very difficult to get them back. It was never a short timetable, but they would drag it out for months and months. I had heard horror stories that kids had even been gone for years. I was not going to allow that to happen if I could help it.

Every month I had a type of review, but I never was able to please them. They always found reasons not to give my kids back to me. It didn't take long for me to cop an attitude. I loved my kids and I would do everything in my power to get them back.

"Are you Mrs. Golden? I am Miss Ferguson. I am working on your case. I see your son has had to be moved twice. Was he having trouble at home acting out?" she asked.

"Just wait one minute. You are not going to blame the moves on him. He was a well-behaved child until you people go a hold of him. It is your foster homes who are not worth a crap. One home had him sleeping with a little girl a couple of years older than him and in the next one he got hit all the time, even leaving bruises, which by the way, I saw," telling her and coming to my son's defense.

"If you think something is going on, you need to make a report," she told me.

"I have complained. Why do you think he eventually got moved? You sure didn't move very quickly, though. DSS is hurting my son physically and mentally," I spewed.

"We do our best and have only the best interest of the child in mind," she said defensively.

"Your best is not good enough, because if you did your best, my kids would be home by now."

"What would you like me to do?" she asked, like she was going to listen and act on my request.

"You can release my kids out of the strangle hold DSS has on them. But you won't let them come home, so you can at least put them together. Do you realize how much harm you have done to my two kids, especially my baby, Annemarie? She is only two, is so confused, is very impressionable and you don't care."

"I will see what I can do, but you have to be patient and do what they ask of you."

"I don't even know where my daughter is right now. No one will tell me anything. You want to do a nice thing, find where my baby is, so I can see her,' I told her, now almost in tears, but still angry.

Throughout this whole ordeal, Vic never once offered to take the kids, so they would be with family. I made sure I asked about that. He just didn't want to pay child support and he wanted to pay me back for whatever he thought I did to him, like leaving him. Pay back is a bitch and I believe that is what Vic thought he was doing to me.

It was now August, 1973. I had not seen or knew anything about the whereabouts of my baby, Annemarie. DSS refused to divulge any information about her to me. I had to tell my attorney to petition the court in order for me to be able to see my daughter. Finally, I was granted a visit with her. She was in a home in Westland. I showed up right on time for our visit. I could not wait to hug and kiss my little girl. I had not seen or heard anything about her since they took her from me. I don't know why DSS was keeping all information about her a secret. I brought with me one of Annemarie's baby dolls. I felt she needed a familiar something from home to comfort her. I rang the doorbell and waited for someone to answer. I had butterflies in my stomach. I hoped Annemarie hadn't forgotten me.

A young boy answered the door and said, "Who are you?"

"My name is Christi Golden and I am here to see my daughter, Annemarie. Will you please go and get one of your parents?" I told the boy.

The boy turned around and yelled, "Someone is here!" And then the door slammed shut.

I waited several minutes until a woman finally opened the door and said, "Can I help you?"

"My name is Christi Golden and I am here to see my daughter, Annemarie."

"Oh yes, Annemarie. She's here somewhere. Come on in," she told me.

As I walked in, I thought that it looked and sounded like a circus instead of a nice family home. Kids were all over the place, jumping on the couch, yelling, screaming; some were crying. I couldn't believe my poor baby was in this mess. Just observing the house and all that was going on, I knew I was going to insist she be removed from this zoo. As I looked all around, I couldn't see or hear Annemarie anywhere. Suddenly I spotted her in the corner as two boys had just taken a toy away from her. I was reluctant to try walking towards her for fear that one of these rambunctious little monsters would knock one of my crutches right out from underneath me as they ran all around the room. I called to Annemarie; however, she couldn't hear me over all the yelling, screaming and the television. As I made my way toward her, I called out her name again. This time she heard her name, looked up, saw me and started running toward me.

"Mommy!" she yelled as she ran to me with her arms wide open.

When she got to me, she hugged my leg tight, looked up and said, "I wanna go home, Mommy. Let's go!"

I had to ask one of the kids if I could sit in the chair they were jumping on. I couldn't stand for fear of getting knocked into the chair and falling. I sat down and lifted Annemarie onto my lap.

"I have missed you so much, Annemarie," I said.

I hugged her so tightly that I thought I would squish her. I kissed every inch of that innocent, little face of hers.

"I don't like it here. I want to go home with you now. Let's go now," she said insistently.

I wouldn't be able to make her understand, but I said to her as simply as I could, "I came to see you because I missed you so much. I am working on getting you and your brother out of this situation, but it will take a little time. I don't want you here, either, but a lady said you have to stay for now. She doesn't know us, but when she learns she is wrong then we will all go to our new home. I am getting a three-bedroom townhouse. You and Little Vic will have your own room with all your toys. When it is ready, we will move into it and we will all be together again."

"I wanna go now. I don't like it here. The kids are mean. Let's go," she said, as she grabbed my hand and tried to pull me up off the chair while waving with her other hand.

"What do you do here?" I asked.

"Nothing, just play," she answered.

"Whose clothes do you have on? Where are your clothes?"

"I don't know."

"What is your favorite food you eat here?"

"Candy."

"You must eat more than candy?"

"The lady makes yucky food. I don't like it," she said, while making a face of disgust.

"I have got you spoiled on TV dinners, but I am sure the food she makes is good for you."

"Let's go, Mommy. Get up. Now, Mommy," Annemarie pleaded with me.

"Do they have a book you like here? Find a book and I will read it to you."

"They don't have Cinderella here. Let's get my book at home."

"We can't, but go get another book and I'll read it to you, OK?"

Annemarie found a book, *Snow White,* and I read it to her. As I read the book, she held onto me very tightly and placed her little head on my chest. While reading, another little girl came beside me and listened to me reading. When I was done, the other little girl got me another book to read. During this reading, Annemarie fell asleep. I just sat there with my precious baby girl sleeping in my arms. She slept for about forty-five minutes. While still sleeping, another kid threw a car and just missed Annemarie's head. It landed on the end table next to us and the noise woke Annemarie up.

The lady came over to me and said, "You should get ready to leave now because my husband will be home soon."

"But I have the whole afternoon to visit until six o'clock," I informed her.

"Well, they didn't tell me. I told them you needed to leave before five o'clock," she replied.

"It is only four o'clock now, I have two hours left with my daughter," I told her.

"My husband gets upset if there are people here, so please leave."

I immediately gave her a piece of my mind, which I had wanted to do all afternoon, and said, "I will be reporting this. I have my rights and I don't like my daughter being here, just so you know. And the next time I come, I expect my daughter to be wearing her own clothes, not someone else's. And feed her food she will actually eat besides candy, and learn to take care of all these kids. It is a mad house in here."

I put Annemarie down, grabbed my crutches and stood up. Annemarie grabbed my one leg and held on with all her might. She started to cry as I tried to walk with her attached to my leg. It did cross my mind to just scoop her up in my arms and make a run for it, but Vic took care of that. I can no longer lift either of my precious children in my arms. That got me angry again.

The woman came over and picked up Annemarie and then my daughter started screaming, I mean really screaming like someone was killing her.

"Mommy, Mommy, don't leave me! Take me too. Mommy, Mommy, don't go! Don't leave me here no more! Put me down! Mommy, get me, get me! Put me down!"

That broke my heart to hear my daughter crying, no, screaming, because her mother was made to leave. She should not have been there in the first place. That terrified look on Annemarie's face was etched in my mind. I was now more than ever determined to get Annemarie and Little Vic back home where they belonged. I left without a scene, but I would return for Annemarie to either bring her home for good, or at least to get her moved out of this zoo. She deserved better than that.

October 31st was hard on me. I was going to take my kids out to go trick or treating and dress them up in cute costumes. Since my kids were still not back with me, I had no desire to celebrate that holiday, either. I was getting very angry and frustrated with DSS.

I finally got a new court appointed attorney. He was a young guy, just fresh out of college, most likely not very experienced, but he had a heart like a lion. He believed in me and thought my situation was very unfair and possibly even illegal.

I had an offer to live with my cousin, Jean, so I decided to give up this house where my kids were stolen from me. Sharon and I had a very long talk about some major changes for the both of us.

"We need to talk about this whole situation. It doesn't look like I'm getting my kids back any time soon. You have been a great friend and helper. We certainly have had good times and some not so good. Can you believe we have lived together for over two years? We have partied down with the kids not here and consoled each other over guys we liked, and many other things. I feel like I am keeping you from enjoying life. I don't want to live in this house anymore because all it reminds me of is the tragic situation with my two kids. I was talking with my cousin and she offered to let me live with her until I get my kids back, and I will get my kids back, come hell or high water," I told Sharon.

"I understand. I can move back in with my mom in Wayne," Sharon said.

We both started crying and hugged each other. After making the decision to move, we both started packing up and making arrangements to get some friends to help move us.

The landlord turned out to be a real piece of work. During one of the trips to the storage building where I had taken my things, the landlord came in and stole some of my belongings. One thing she stole was my good set of translucent china I had bought piece by piece over a couple of years because it was so expensive. That was one of the few things I owned that had any value. I couldn't dwell on that though, I needed to get moved so I could focus on getting my kids back.

Sharon moved back in with her mother, sister, Linda, and brother, Mike. I moved to Canton and put my stuff in storage. I had my own room and had someone to talk to. We talked about me swallowing my pride and not being so angry, so I could get my kids back. My cousin was a pillar of the community and DSS could never say anything bad about her.

My young, court-appointed attorney got me a court date, so the kids could be together. So far, DSS had refused to find a home who would take the both of them, so they would be together.

When I got in front of the judge in family court, I said, "Your honor, my kids have been taken from me wrongfully. I was in the middle of moving and an anonymous call was made to DSS and stated the kids were in danger. This is an out and out lie. My two kids were just fine and happy. I just want them to come back home. I have jumped through all the hoops that DSS has asked me to do. My kids have been made to sleep with complete strangers of the opposite sex, hit and abused, neglected and the worst of all is they have been separated from each other. I ask that you order the return of my kids to me, and if that is impossible, then at least put them together in a loving home where they will not be neglected or hit and where they can wear their own clothes." I pleaded with the judge.

The judge replied, "I just can't return kids without a report from DSS stating all the problems have been addressed and corrected, which I do not see one at the moment. When this is done, have your attorney petition the court again. In the meantime, I will order that the two children be put together in the same foster home. Your attorney knows what to do to finalize the process.'

I did not expect much, but I hoped the kids would get moved and put together.

Little Vic once again had to be moved because the home he was in was abusing him by hitting him. I saw the bruises on him. I was supposed to have my kids for Thanksgiving, but something got screwed up and DSS couldn't get the two kids together. I ended up celebrating Thanksgiving with Jean. I sure didn't feel like I had anything to be thankful for. But I kept up my fight. I would never give up on my kids. I had made such a stink about the homes Little Vic had been in that he had now been moved twice. The first time was when I found out he was sleeping in the same bed with a little girl, and now the second time, because I saw the bruises on him. This second home was also very uncooperative with following the instructions from DSS that I had the right to see and visit with Little Vic. Every time we set up a time for me to see Little Vic, they would cancel. My attorney was constantly petitioning the court for visitations that were never fulfilled. I had insisted that he be moved to a safe and happy home until they decide to give my kids back to me. I wanted to choke someone for what my kids were going through.

Once again, I went to the DSS office and demanded to be seen. I saw another uncaring social worker. I threatened to see them in court if my kids were not put together. I reminded them of the last judge's order, which was to put my two kids together in the same home.

I said to the worker, "I am here to make sure my kids get moved from their present homes into the same foster home where they will be together. Make sure you get my kids' clothes, too. The last move my son made, he did not get all his clothes and had to wear some rags that were given to him."

The worker replied, "We have the court order and are looking for a home where the two children will be placed together. As soon as one comes available, we will move the children."

"How long will that take?" I asked.

"I don't have a timetable, but as soon as we find one, we will be moving the two children," she said.

"I would like to be notified when that happens. Need I remind you, this is not a request from me, but an order from the judge?"

"I told you when we find one, we will move the children. I can't make any promises."

"Well, why can't you let me know when and where the kids get moved?"

"Because we don't know when that will be. We have a shortage of foster homes right now, so it will be a little while is all I can tell you now.

December 25th, Christmas, would be a time to celebrate. I was able to see both of my kids, together in the same home. I had caused such a ruckus that both of my kids were moved and put together in the Kennedy home in Livonia. This was the third home Little Vic had been in and the second home Annemarie had been in.

I brought my friend, Bob Rice, to see my kids with me. I brought both of them presents, watched them unwrap them and play with them. I took pictures, lots of pictures. I was so happy. After that, I started to get regular visits. My attorney really fought for me and my kids and he actually accomplished some things I thought would never happen. I spent the whole day there. They had to ask me to leave or I would have stayed longer. I was not impressed with this home, either, but at least Little Vic and Annemarie were together, and that's all that mattered for now.

4-26-74 Bob Rice, drummer, with Annemarie,
little Vic. at his brother, Michaels's wedding.

Another good thing happened to me. I was asked to join a rock and roll band as a singer. Bob was the drummer; Don Autio was on bass guitar; another guy was lead guitar, and I was a singer. We all sang good, but when we practiced "Proud Mary" by CCR (Credence Clearwater Revival), I just could not get it. Bob picked me up each week in his beautiful, huge, yellow Cadillac. I really looked forward to those jam sessions. I had always loved to sing and this helped me cope while my kids were away from me. Bob was simply wonderful. We practiced in Don's basement and sometimes his wife and two girls would come down to listen. I got the impression Bob may have liked me. I valued him too much as a great friend that I did not want to mess it up by dating him. That may have sounded a bit crazy, but that was me. Some guys I liked as friends and other guys I liked to date. Dates are for a while—friends are forever.

It was around this same time that I also sang at the Confetti Lounge in Dearborn, Michigan. It was cool, because I sat on a chair and you couldn't tell I was disabled until I had to get off the stage. I sang mostly oldies, but some current songs, too. The most requested song I had was "Angel Baby" by Rosie and the Originals. Music was such a huge part of me.

I had the good fortune to sing a song with Bob Seger at a lounge he frequented. I loved his music. He was a true R&B singer with that raspy voice, belting out the words with such feeling. When he sang, you could feel it down deep in your soul.

I had put in an application for a three-bedroom townhouse at Canton Commons and was waiting for one to become available. In the meantime, I met a nice guy, Ed Burnette, who went with me to see my kids. We started dating and we did fun stuff together. He even took me to Windsor, Canada to go see

BTO (Bachman Turner Overdrive) in concert. He put me on his shoulders, so I could see better. That lifted my spirits, and my attorney gave me hope and showed me there is a light at the end of the tunnel. February 23, 1974 was a wonderful day. Ed Burnette had driven me to the Kennedy's home and I was able to take the kids out to celebrate Annemarie's third birthday. Naturally, I had my camera and I took lots of pictures of my kids and Ed. We went to McDonalds since it was Annemarie's favorite place to eat.

2-23-74 Ed Burnett with Annemarie at McDonalds.

2-17-74 Ed Burnette with kids in Kennedy foster home

Unbeknown to me, my attorney had worked it out to get Little Vic and Annemarie moved to a family living in Dearborn Heights called the Meaders. They were a loving family that bent over backwards to help get me and my kids reunited. They were aware of how my little boy had suffered in more than one home from getting hit to the point of abuse. It was such a short time and then I finally got my kids back, for good, forever. I can't thank Vic for anything because he did nothing. I was told he went to see the kids once in nine months. Father of the year he's not.

I had gotten my own townhouse at 1481 Stacy Drive in Canton Commons. My kids made new friends and finally we were a family again. It was a total of nine, long, excruciating months that my precious children were ripped from me and kept from me, their mother. One more reason I hated Vic. I knew in my heart Vic and Barb made that call to DSS. I hoped they were proud of themselves. I thought that it would come back to them sevenfold. All that mattered was that I had my two precious children back home with me. The townhouse at 1481 Stacy became available and we moved into it nine months after the kids first got taken by DSS. We made new memories, and the kids made lots of friends here; the best thing was they were happy here. I also made new friends and welcomed old friends over to visit us. One of those special friends was Brian Docherty. I had known him since 1971. I will never forget that beautiful, gray and pink 1956 Chevy he owned.

I met a single mom named Diana Kay Kessler Jennings. She had two kids, like me, and they were the same age as my kids, one boy and one girl, Joey and Caroline. They lived in the next building from us. Diana made a lifelong, lasting impression on me. We became great friends and we were there for each other. With friends like Brian and Diana, I knew my future was heading in the right direction. We became very close and our kids became best friends.

CHAPTER 15

Thrown into The Detroit River

It was a warm, sunny day in July of 1973. I had just recently gotten my two kids, Vic and Annemarie, taken away by DSS. The reason was that my ex-husband and/or Barb had called the police on me because I moved again. He and his mistress, Barb, would harass me and my neighbors wherever I lived. This started early on when I moved to Inkster, Michigan at 3902 Beech Daly Road. in December of 1970. In my opinion, I think Barb had some kind of obsession to know where I lived and what I was up to. She even got a wig to imitate me and dressed like me, but she did not look good in low slung hip-hugger bellbottoms since she was not thin like me. Barb would find where we lived, tell my neighbors I was shot, which freaked them out. Then they did not want my kids playing with their kids. Of course, she did not tell them it was Vic, the guy she was shacking up with, who shot me. Maybe the neighbors thought I was a criminal who was evading the police and got shot by them. I don't really know what the neighbors thought. I lived only six months to a year at each new residence. Every time we moved, my kids made new friends. Annemarie was a bit shy, but she was very smart. Little Vic was very outgoing and very sports oriented.

I seemed to drag around this ball and chain. No matter how hard I tried, nothing ever seemed to turn out right. Look at my track record thus far: my real mother gave me away at the tender age of five years old; my adopted father spanked me a lot, which turned into beatings; the love of my life, Ronnie Turner, and I were broken up; my husband shot me; I couldn't walk without the stupid crutches; I saw double; and now DSS had my kids. *How much bad could one person take? How much suffering did one person deserve?* I thought to myself.

I still carried the feeling of being a freak of nature. The people I hung out with were not true friends of mine, but merely acquaintances I had met along the road of life. I had real friends when I was still in high school and several in my childhood neighborhood. I suppose I would have had real friends if I would have felt better about myself, but that was not the case. Every time I took, or attempted to take a step, or looked in the mirror, I reminded myself what a freak of nature I was. I felt uncomfortable being around me, so why would I have expected others to feel any differently?

As I was sitting on the couch, watching TV, I heard a knock at the door.

I yelled, "Hold on, I'm coming."

As I reached down to grab my crutches, I looked over at the door and through the glass of the front door I could see Gary Goodman standing there.

I made my way to the door, opened it, and said, "Hi, Gary, what are you doing here? Come on in."

I turned around and went back to my couch and sat down.

Gary said, "I got invited by Fred to go out on his old man's yacht next week and I just thought about you."

"Why did that make you think about me?" I asked.

"Well, I know you've been down cuz of your kids, so I thought this might give you a chance to get your mind off of things and have a little fun. You don't have to bring anything except your gorgeous self."

"I'm not really in the mood for having fun. I don't think it's possible to have fun without my kids being with me."

Gary pleaded with me in such a sweet voice, "Aw, come on. Fred always throws a great party. I promise you will have a great time. There will be lots of good food, music and plenty of beer and maybe even a couple of joints."

I said to Gary, "Well the food and music sounds good, but I'll have to pass on the beer. I'm just not a beer drinker, but I guess I can bring my own Dr. Pepper. I don't smoke, either, but OK, I guess I'll come. All I do here is sit alone and cry over my kids. Maybe you're right; I need to do something to help me pass the time until I get them back."

"Great. We are all meeting at the docks, near where Woodward Ave. ends by the river, Saturday at 12 o'clock and parking our cars there. I'll pick you up or meet you there and we can walk down to the river together, sound good?" Gary asked.

"I'll meet you there, so I'll have my car with me if I need it," I answered.

It was nice of Gary to include me. I certainly was not having much fun, not for the lack of things that were going on, like Pink Floyd performing at the Olympia Stadium June 23rd, and Led Zeppelin was going to be at Cobo Hall on July 12th. I was so terribly depressed about my kids. I just didn't want to do anything, but Gary talked me into actually having some fun. I was determined to have fun with Gary and the gang.

I did some things to keep busy like laundry, which was not much, since I didn't have the kids' clothes to wash. I didn't feel like eating. I didn't have many dishes, either because I ate TV dinners, making clean up a breeze. I just had to throw the aluminum trays in the trash. I didn't even make my bed when I got up. I didn't feel like doing much of anything. These were dark days for me, but with Gary's invitation came a little ray of sunshine. I was going to have fun even if it killed me. Never did I dream how close to true those words were.

Saturday came and I was actually a little excited about going down the river on a nice boat. I still had to shake my head in disbelief that my adopted dad painted his nice, big, elegant yacht gray for duck hunting. Oh well, today I would be on an elegant yacht to have fun. I had to keep reminding myself—I was going to have fun. I now had a burgundy 1967, Chevrolet Caprice with a 327 under the hood. It was fully loaded complete with a great stereo, 8-track and reverb system, not to mention leather power seats and power windows. I was riding in style from Wyandotte to Detroit's Cobo Hall. It didn't take me long to arrive and to see Gary waiting for me. I pulled in and parked.

"Hi, Gary," I said.

"You decided to show up? I was worried you might not come, but I am really glad you're here," Gary told me enthusiastically.

"You made me see that I need to get out more and stop moping around. I hate being sad. This is not the person I really am. I was always out-going, fun-loving, even a loud mouth at times. Now I just sit around and cry. Crying leads to feeling sorry for myself and that leads to more crying. God help me, but I hate Vic for what he did to me. Gary, stop me before I cry me a river," I said.

"OK, OK, I get it. So now shut up. Today you are with me and all of us are going to have a blast," Gary told me in no uncertain terms.

Gary opened the driver's door, so I could get out. He reached behind my seat to get my crutches and handed them to me. I stood up, grabbed my stupid crutches, locked and slammed the car door and started walking to where we would meet the rest of the gang.

I was able to walk with Gary to the river's edge where the yacht was, but I couldn't climb into it. Gary, like the gentleman he was, did his white knight routine by offering some assistance.

"Christi, need some help getting into the boat?" he asked.

"Yeah, I can use some help, if you don't mind?" I answered.

"How about if I pick you up and carry you over?"

"Sure, that would be great."

I held onto my crutches and with one fell swoop he picked me up, stepped into the boat and stood me up, so I could get my crutches on my arms and get my balance.

"Thanks a lot Gary," I said.

"You're most welcome," he said.

"Do you know who owns the yacht we're on?"

"I think it's Fred's dad's boat. He is some head honcho at Ford Motor Company."

"My dad also has a big cabin cruiser, but like an idiot, he painted it gray, so he could go duck hunting. Can you believe it?"

"Man, what a waste of a nice boat. If I had a boat like that I'd be cruising with all kinds of chicks and party down."

"So how many are supposed to be here today?"

"I think 12 plus Fred."

"Do you know all the people?"

"I know you and Fred and Nancy, Derek, Mark, Paul, Steve, Sarah, Sue, Marie and Tom. So yeah, I guess I know them all."

"I only know you, Mark, Marie, Sue, Nancy and Fred."

"Fred brought a shit load of food and some good smokin' weed. We are all going to go swimming later, too. Just dive right off the side of the boat. Man, will that be cool."

"I don't think I'll be joining you for that."

"Why not? You don't know how to swim?"

"I did know how to swim. In fact, I knew how to dive, too. My parents belonged to the Dearborn Country Club, and I learned how to swim and even do back flips off the high diving board at a fairly young age. I hated golfing, though."

"Well, it's like riding a bike. Once you learn how, you never forget."

"Here comes Nancy and Marie. Where are Sue and Tom?" I replied, then added, "I thought we were going to Bob-Lo Island or Belle Isle?"

Belle Isle was located just a ferry ride across the Detroit River and on the shores of Amherstburg, Ontario, Canada. It was located down East Jefferson Avenue in the middle of the Detroit River. Bob-Lo was 24 miles down the Detroit River, which the Columbia and the Ste. Claire shuttled the people there and back, starting point being the foot of Woodward Avenue and ending at the island near Grosse Isle.

"Let's go over and find out. Hey man, where is my man, Tom?"

"He'll be here in a few," Nancy said.

"Yeah, you know Tom, always late and holding things up. If you mean six o'clock you might as well tell Tom four o'clock and he might make it on time," Marie said.

"I'm glad you showed up or I would be the only girl," I said to Marie.

"Well, look who decided to grace us with his presence," Gary said.

"How the hell are you, my man?" Tom asked Gary.

"Enough with the intros. Is everyone present and accounted for? If so, then let's get this party started," Fred announced to everyone on board.

"Nice yacht, what is it?" I asked Fred.

"It's my old man's, a forty-five-footer, 1954 Chris Craft Corsair. He named it, 'Fantasia Isle'." Fred replied.

1954 45 ft., Chris Craft Corsair yacht.

"Where's the kegger, Fred?" Tom asked.

"Right where it should be, on board," Fred replied.

"Hoist up the anchor and let's boogie," Fred commanded.

Someone pulled up the anchor and started the engines of the boat, and off we went.

Fred did supply a lot of food. There was fried chicken, ham, burgers, potato salad, chips and chip dip, and chocolate brownies for dessert. There was beer, lots of beer. I chowed down on chicken and potato salad and chips and I even ate a brownie. Luckily, I brought my own Dr. Pepper to drink because I couldn't stand the taste of beer. You would think I would love beer since I was born in Munich, Germany, which is the beer capitol of the world, but I didn't. There was a radio on board and there were some good jams playing.

I heard someone yell, "Kick out the jams!"

"Bang a Gong-Get it on" by T-Rex was playing. I was enjoying myself because I loved listening to the music. "Clean Up Woman" by Betty Wright came on which reminded me of Vic and Barb.

Unconsciously, I yelled out, "It's the cleanup woman."

I was sitting in a nice comfortable chair on deck. I wore a pair of white, short-shorts and a cute, little, white halter top, and I was catching some rays. My hair was down to my waist, so I had to lay my hair over the back of the chair and let it hang down. As I lay there, listening to the music and seeing the others having a good time, I began to think of Annemarie and Little Vic. "Mother and Child Reunion" by Paul Simon started to play. My eyes teared up a little. *Where were they? Were they missing me? Were they being treated well? Were they even together?* I thought to myself.

313

That damn DSS would not let me know anything about my kids. They shouldn't have even been taken away from me to begin with. I was still moving into the Dearborn Heights house when the police and DSS came. Yes, boxes were everywhere, but so what? What do you expect when you move? We were getting things unpacked and put away. I couldn't believe they came when I was at the grocery store getting some food for us and the kids were left with the babysitter. Their beds were already put together and my furniture was there. I just couldn't believe my kids were not with me. I missed them so much. I hoped Vic was proud of himself. He wasn't hurting me as much as he was hurting my kids. I wished he could find something else to do besides keeping tabs on me. I didn't want to live without my kids.

*1960's Looking at the Detroit River and
Detroit from the Canadian side*

"Christi, wake up. Come on and go swimming with us," Gary said.

Before I could answer him, he scooped me up in his arms, lifted me over the side of the Yacht and dropped me into the water, the Detroit River. The last thing I heard was the song "Too Late to Turn Back Now" by Cornelius Brothers and Sister Rose. Splash. I hit the water hard and became disoriented. *What was happening?* I went from being warm from the sun to cold from the engulfing water. I continued sinking deeper and deeper down into the river. As I looked up, I could no longer see or hear anyone or anything. It was pitch black.

I thought, *two bullets didn't kill me, but now I'm going to die by drowning. Everyone was too high to even know I was gone. How long would it take for anyone to know I was missing?*

I kept going downward, deeper into the cold, dark, unforgiving water. I was surrounded by black, cold water. I didn't want to live without my kids, but I didn't want to drown, either. I was holding my breath. Oh God, please help me just once more. I was beyond terrified. My heart was racing in panic mode. I feared I would have a heart attack if the lack of oxygen didn't kill me first. Drowning, I heard, is not a good way to die. It is painful and you look awful when they find you, all bloated up and discolored. That's if the fish don't eat you first.

A voice whispered to me, "Christi, you've survived worse. Start moving your hands and kicking your feet, at least your one leg that still moves. You know how to swim, so do it."

I started doing the breast stroke upward. I kept going downward. I finally stopped my downward decent. I couldn't let fear paralyze me. I had to move if I was going to survive this plunge into the water's depths. All of a sudden, I was going upward. I had stopped my spiral downward and now was inching my way back to the surface. It felt like an eternity in the cold, dark, murky waters, but I could finally see some feet kicking in the water above and the sun casting down on the water. I broke the surface of the water like a fish jumping out of the water.

When I hit the air, I breathed in the air like there was no tomorrow. I coughed and spit out water, but I was alive. I started treading water at first, and then I tried swimming with my head above the water. I was swimming. I could swim. Gary was right. Once you know how to swim you don't forget it. What a rush that was. *Nothing like a near death experience to make it interesting,* I thought to myself. Then it hit me like a ton of bricks. It was God talking to me under water and giving me the directions to save my life.

Gary swam over to me and said, "There you are. I was wondering what happened to you."

I answered him by saying, "You don't want to know."

I looked up at the sky and said, "Thank you, God, again."

And then I continued to paddle around in the water with the rest of the gang.

THE END

To end this book on a happy note,
I wanted to add these updates.

I met Brian Docherty in 1971 and remained friends until I moved from Canton Commons into our first house I was determined to turn into a home for the three of us, which I did. I found him, or should I say, he found me, while I was living in Garden City. Then we lost touch again. I just found Brian again in October, 2016. Sadly, one of his sons told me Brian had passed away about five years ago. He had married four times and had six children. He was such a great guy and we had so much in common. Since we were both unlucky in love maybe we should have married each other and we could have saved each other from so many marriages; his four and my two (wishful thinking). My only regret is that I did not find Brian sooner, while he was still alive. In speaking with one of his sons, it sounds like they are all great kids.

Brian Dockerty, kids, 1971

Brian Dockerty at Canton Commons 1974

Brian Dockerty with Vic, Annemarie, at our new Townhouse.

I met Diana when I moved to Canton Commons in 1974. We fast became friends, and I considered her my best friend. We had so much in common. She was beautiful, smart, caring, kind, giving—all the attributes to be the best person around and was even the same age as me. One of the best times the kids and I had was when we went to visit her family in Wisconsin on the farm. That was a perfect vacation for all of us. We lost touch for a couple of years, but I found her again. I remember her peach-colored Chrysler K-car and that she was involved with a strange religious group. We lost touch again, but I found her with a man who did not deserve her. Once again, we lost touch, but I wasn't about to give up, and in 2012 found her again through relatives and have been keeping close communication with her and her kids. The future is once again bright for all of us. Thank you, Diana, for all you have done for me and my kids. Now it is our time to shine.

12-23-74 Diane Caroline, Joey at Westland Shopping Mall

12-24-74 Christmas presents for my kids from Diane

7-18-75 Diane with all four kids in Wisconsin

7-19-75 Carolyn, Vic, Annemarie,
Joey visiting Diane in Wausau, Wisconsin.

7-20-75 Diane, the Kessler family, my kids at the farm in Wisconsin.

EPILOGUE

On my life's journey, I have had many twists and turns. For those who have wondered or asked about this, here is a roadmap. The one most important thing in my life, and I have never found, is love. All I ever wanted was a kind, gentle, beautiful Christian man to love me unconditionally. I thought I found it in Ronnie Turner and then I thought I found it in Vic, but I was wrong. I am still looking and will never give up, but the years get shorter and my chances at finding true love diminish more and more with each passing day.

In the meantime, I will answer the most commonly asked questions: "What have you been doing since you got shot? How has your life changed? What are you doing today?" Well, to answer all of you curious people out there, I have done a lot. I shall address these questions in chronological order.

First, I fought like hell to get my life back. Like Mel and Tim sang, "Starting All Over Again," is gonna be rough, so rough, but I'm gonna make it. I was not about to give up my life. I fought hard and with the help of God, I made it back to the living. I was in Detroit General Hospital for three long months and then I was transferred to Detroit Rehabilitation Institute where I stayed for one month. I accomplished getting from the bed to the wheelchair, then maneuvering in a wheelchair, walking on a walker and finally walking on Loftstrand crutches. Those were gigantic steps for me. It was the start of my independence and my admittance back into society. I was shot on December 18, 1969, ironically, on Vic's twentieth birthday. I had closed on my first house the end of December of 1969, while still in the hospital, but ended up having to rent it out. In April of 1970 I was sent by the rehab center to Vic's mother's house, the house from hell. The whole time I was living in the house of horrors, being verbally and physically abused, starved to death, raped, and strangled, I finally caught a break from the Dearborn Police. Vic was found guilty of felonious assault when he strangled me for the last time and almost killed me again. While Vic served his time in the Detroit House of Corrections, I made my escape out of Annie's house and vowed never to step inside that house again. I also found out I was pregnant.

I had some friends pack up my belongings and found a place in the Detroit area. I lived there with my son for several months. I also started my first business selling kittens I feared for my son and unborn baby, after finding out that the next door twelve-year-old boy and an older teenager tried to rob a bar with the twelve-year-old being shot to death. I moved to Inkster. We lived there only a month or two before I went to Metropolitan Hospital and gave birth to a beautiful baby girl on February 23, 1971. We lived in Inkster about a year and then moved to Westminster townhouses in Taylor in 1972. We lived there for another year and then moved into a brick ranch house in Dearborn Heights in 1973. That was where my two children were stolen from me by DSS. After nine long months of battling with the courts and DSS, I got them back and we moved to Canton Commons townhouses in 1974. Vic and I did end up divorcing. That was where I met Diana Kessler Jennings who became my best friend. By this time, I had already applied for disability benefits, but was denied, so I filed an appeal. After six years of fighting with the government, I received my first check and in 1975 I bought my first house to live in. I fixed it up and after living in it for only about two years, I rented it out and in 1978 bought my next house to live in. That was where I met Brian Zarbaugh and dated him for three years. He even asked me to marry him, but I said no. I couldn't believe anyone would actually want to marry a freak of nature.

My next house was a Spanish ranch house, which I had fun fixing up. I enrolled myself at Schoolcraft College and got my Business Administration degree. But I wasn't done there. I took a class in real estate and on the first try passed and got my real estate license. I met another guy, Don O, also in real estate, and we became partners. I bought another house as an investment and then in 1981 another one to live in. We lived in this four-bedroom brick ranch house for three years.

In 1983, I made my second biggest mistake. I met a guy over the phone in North Carolina. The long and short of this disaster was I ended up moving to North Carolina and marrying him. He didn't want to move to Michigan because of the snow. He owned a little S-10 truck and a used, single-wide trailer, which he let get repossessed. I cleaned up his credit, balanced his check book, and refiled his taxes, so he would get a refund with deductions. In 1984, I bought a three-bedroom brick ranch house. I owned a full size custom van and a Z-28. When my oldest son, Vic III, was nineteen years old, he kicked him out of the house. After being married to him for many years, I got wise and divorced him after he assaulted me over a fight over his pornography obsession. He thought I stole his porn. Not me, no way. It turns out my middle daughter stole it and sold it.

My first and second husband had one thing in common, they hated paying child support. Another thing in common was that I enrolled myself in college after each divorce. I got my certificate in child development and added a few more electives after the second divorce. One of those electives was creative writing, which I got an "A" in. After having so many people ask me how long I had had Polio, I turned the conversation around to tell them the real reason I was on these crutches and they most always would say, "You should write a book about your life." Since 1971 to present, I would venture to say there have been thousands of people telling me that, so in 2012 I started a journal and in July of 2015 my first book was published. Now I am struggling to finish this second book while battling Shingles since September, 2016.

Some of the most exciting things to happen to me because of the books were being interviewed by Karen Wynne of TV station WLOS, Bill McClement of radio station Mix 96.5, and doing book signings at Barnes & Noble.

In April of 2015 I started a support group for abused and battered women called Overcomers of Domestic Violence. We were given the use of a small church, so we could hold our meetings and we met each Wednesday from 12 noon to 1 p.m. I also started a writing group called Writers Reign of Asheville for writers who wanted to become published, just brush up on their techniques or bounce ideas off of other writers. The setting was informal and held at my home. I hope this answers some of your questions about what I have been doing thus far.

Lastly, my family has grown. I have 5 children, 12 grandchildren and now 3 great-grandchildren (Adalyne & Oliver & MaKenzley) and 1 baby angel, MaKenna, in Heaven.

Thanks again to all my fans and loyal readers.

Christi Golden-Clark

AFTERWORD

Writing these two books, *FAMOUS LAST WORDS: "If I Can't Have You, No One Else Can"* and *FAMOUS LAST WORDS: "I Will Survive"* has been the hardest thing I have ever done. As with my first book, I cried, I laughed, I smiled and I got angry. It brings out so much emotion in me, so many memories, both good and bad. Sharing these books with the reader is a very humbling experience. I hope every reader takes away some good advice, some good instincts, some good insights and some good experience, so they can see and know the dangerous warning signs of domestic violence. I was a classic case of domestic violence. Some of the signs I was not aware of, other signs I did see, but I just didn't want to see them. I knew in my heart they were wrong, they were bad, but still I ignored them. I thought I loved Vic so much that I could forgive him for anything. I know Vic loved me, but sometimes a guy can love you too much and then it gets into the realm of obsession and insane jealousy. That is not healthy for either of you.

Forgiveness is hard to do. I forgave Vic 17 years after he shot me, but in my heart, I never fully forgave him. I still carried some resentment and anger. I carried a bitter hatred for Barb, because she could have handled the whole situation very differently. She should not have slept with my husband. She should have waited to see if we would end up divorced, which was the direction it was headed for, but she chose to be the sleazy mistress. Instead she carried on an illicit affair by having sex with my husband and then getting pregnant, while we were still married, to trap him. Waiting until we were divorced would have been the decent way to have handled it. I, on the other hand, chose to remain the faithful wife until we got back together or we divorced. I guess that is where our upbringing comes into play. I was not raised to do things like that, but then Vic got me to do things I never would have done, like stealing my mother's ring or living together in sin. I never could have ever carried on an affair with a married man. I find it amusing that this is the girl Vic told me to stay away from because she was bad news. I guess he was right on the money with that statement.

Love comes softly. A relationship is not meant to be violent and abusive, but caring and sharing. It is soft strokes on the cheek, holding hands, a warm hug, his arm around your shoulders, and a soft kiss. We, as women, are born with all the tenderness and nurturing attributes. On the other hand, men are born with the leadership, take charge, bossy traits. In a relationship, you need to blend these qualities of both. Then, and only then will it work smoothly. You have to have the hard with the soft, the loud with the quiet, the strong with the weak. Men cannot rule women, nor do women want to be ruled. Women love to be loved, to be treated with kindness, respect, and equality. Men need to take heed of over-bearing actions. Forewarned is being forearmed.

Violence and abuse should never be tolerated. Signs of domestic violence are: cursing or name calling, throwing objects, hitting, slapping, pulling on, kicking, biting, hair pulling, beating, breaking bones, cause bleeding, stabbing, knocking unconscious, shooting, and the ultimate betrayal is death from any of these acts.

My advice is and has been for a long time: The first act of violence, you can choose to forgive, but never forget. The next act of violence, get out and find someone new who will love, cherish, and respect you.

I hope after reading these two books your eyes will be opened and they give you the strength to make a good, educated, safe, and sound decision and you know how to protect yourself. Enjoy. I hope my life will challenge the women of the world to fight back and take control.

Christi Golden-Clark

Songs With Special Meaning
1969-1974

1969

"A B C" by Jackson 5

"And When I Die" by Blood, Sweat & Tears

"Baby, I'm for Real" by The Originals

"Backfield in Motion" by Mel & Tim

"Bella Linda" by Grassroots

"Build Me up, Buttercup" by Foundations

"Can I Change My Mind?" by Tyrone Davis

"Crimson & Clover" by Tommy James & the Shondells

"Crystal Blue Persuasion" by Tommy James & the Shondells

"Dizzy" by Tommy Roe

"Don't Cry, Daddy" by Elvis Presley

"Easy to be Hard" by Three Dog Night

"Eli's Coming" by Three Dog Night

"Feeling Alright" by Joe Cocker

"Games People Play" by Joe South

"Get Ready" by Rare Earth

"Gimme, Gimme Good Lovin;" by Crazy Elephant

"Heaven Knows" by Grass Roots

"Hot Fun in the Summertime" by Sly & the Family Stone

"I Can't Get Next to You" by Temptations

"I Want You Back" by Jackson 5

"I'm Gonna Make You Mine" by Lou Christie

"I've Been Hurt" by Bill Deal & the Rhondels

"Love Land" by Charles Wright & the Watts 103rd Street Rhythm Band

"Marrakesh Express" by Crosby, Stills, Nash & Young

"My Baby Loves Lovin'" by White Plains

"My Whole World Ended (The Moment You Left Me)" by David Ruffin

"Na, Na, Hey, Hey, Kiss Him Good-by" by Steam

"Oh Me, Or My I'm A Fool For You Baby" by Lulu

"Oh What a Night" by Dells

"One" by Three Dog Night

"Only the Strong Survive" by Jerry Butler

"Someday We'll be Together" by Diana Ross

"Sugar, Sugar" by Archies

"Sweet Cherry Wine" by Tommy James & the Shondells

"That's the Way Love Is" by Marvin Gaye

"These Eyes" by Junior Walker & The All Stars

"This Magic Moment" by Jay & the Americans

"Up on Cripple Creek" by The Band

"Venus" by Shocking Blue

"What Does it Take (To Win Your Love)?" by Junior Walker & The All Stars

"What's the Use of Breaking Up?" by Jerry Butler

"Whole Lotta Love" by Led Zeppelin

1970

"Ball of Confusion (That's What the World Is Today)" by Temptations

"Band of Gold" by Freda Payne

"Didn't I (Blow Your Mind This Time)" by Delfonics

"Give Me Just a Little More Time" by Chairman of the Board

"Green-Eyed Lady" by Sugarloaf

"Hey There Lonely Girl" by Eddie Holman

"(I Know) I'm Losing You" by Rare Earth

"I Want You Back" by Jackson 5

"(If You Let Me Make Love To You Then) Why Can't I Touch You?" by Ronnie Dyson

"I'll Be There" by Jackson 5

"I'll Never Fall in Love Again" by Dionne Warwick

"It's a Shame" by Spinners

"Lay a Little Lovin' On Me" by Robin McNamara

"Love Grows (Where My Rosemary Goes)" by Edison Lighthouse

"Love on a Two-Way Street" by Moments

"Love or Let Me Be Lonely" by Friends of Distinction

"My Baby Loves Lovin'" by White Plains

"Reach Out and Touch (Somebody's Hand)" by Diana Ross

"Remember Me" by Diana Ross

"Signed, Sealed, Delivered I'm Yours" by Stevie Wonder

"Smile a Little Smile For Me" by Flying Machine

"Still Water (Love)" by Four Tops

"The Love You Save" by Jackson 5

"The Thrill Is Gone" by B.B. King

"(They Long to Be) Close to You" by Carpenters

"Tighter, Tighter" by Alive N Kickin'

"Turn Back the Hands of Time" by Tyrone Davis

"United We Stand" by Brotherhood of Man

"Vehicle" by Ides of March

"Walk A Mile In My Shoes" by Joe South

"War" by Edwin Starr

1971

"Bring the Boys Home" by Freda Payne

"Clean Up Woman" by Betty Wright

"Doesn't Somebody Want to Be Wanted" by Partridge Family
"How Can You Mend a Broken Heart?" by Bee Gees
"I Just Want to Celebrate" by Rare Earth
"If I Were Your Woman" by Gladys Knight & the Pips
"It's Too Late"/"I Feel the Earth Move" by Carole King
"I've Found Someone Of My Own" by Free Movement
"Just My Imagination (Running Away With Me)" by Temptations
"Liar" by Three Dog Night
"Lonely Days" by Bee Gees
"Love Her Madly" by The Doors
"Mr. Big Stuff" by Jean Knight
"Never Can Say Goodbye" by Jackson 5
"One Bad Apple" by Osmonds
"One Less Bell to Answer" by 5th Dimension
"Proud Mary" by Ike and Tina Turner
"She's a Lady" by Tom Jones
"She's Not Just Another Woman" by 8th Day
"Smiling Faces Sometimes" by Undisputed Truth
"Sooner or Later" by Grass Root
"Stairway To Heaven" by Led Zeppelin
"Sweet City Woman" by Stampeders
"Temptation Eyes" by Grass Roots
"Thin Line Between Love & Hate" by Persuaders
"Tired of Being Alone" by Al Green
"Treat Her Like a Lady" by Cornelius Brothers & Sister Rose
"Two Divided by Love" by Grass Roots
"Want Ads" by Honey Cone
"Won't Get Fooled Again" by The Who
"Woodstock" by Matthews Southern Comfort

1972

"Baby, Don't Get Hooked on Me" by Mac Davis

"Back Stabbers" by O'Jays

"Betcha by Golly, Wow" by Chi-Lites

"Clean Up Woman" by Betty Wright

"Daddy, Don't You Walk so Fast" by Wayne Newton

"Don't Say You Don't Remember" by Beverly Bremers

"Everybody Plays the Fool" by Main Ingredient

"Everything I Own" by Bread

"Go All the Way" by Raspberries

"Hurting Each Other" by Carpenters

"I Can See Clearly Now" by Johnny Nash

"I'll Take You There" by Staple Singers

"I'm Still in Love with You" by Al Green

"Lean on Me" by Bill Withers

"Let's Stay Together" by Al Green

"Long Cool Woman in a Black Dress" by Hollies

"Mother and Child Reunion" by Paul Simon

"Oh, Girl" by Chi Lites

"Papa Was a Rolling Stone" by Temptations

"Precious and Few" by Climax

"Starting all Over Again" by Mel & Tim

"Too Late to Turn Back Now" by Cornelius Brothers & Sister Rose

"The First Time Ever I Saw Your Face" by Roberta Flack

"Without You" by Harry Nilsson

"You Ought To Be With Me" by Al Green

1973

"Ain't No Woman (Like the One I've Got)" by Four Tops

"Break Up to Make Up" by Stylistics

"Could It Be I'm Falling In Love" by Spinners

"Drift Away" by Dobie Gray

"Free Ride" by Edgar Winter Group

"Half-Breed" by Cher

"Just Don't Want To Be Lonely" by Ronnie Dyson

"Let's Get it On" by Marvin Gaye

"Love Train" by O'Jays

"Neither One of Us (Wants to be the First to Say Goodbye)" by Gladys Knight & The Pips

"One of a Kind (Love Affair)" by Spinners

"Reelin' in the Years" by Steely Dan

"Right Place Wrong Time" by Dr. John

"Stir It Up" by Johnny Nash

"Stuck in the Middle with You" by Stealers Wheel

"We're an American Band" by Grand Funk Railroad

"Yesterday Once More" by Carpenters

"Your Mama Don't Dance" by Loggins and Messina

1974

"Band on the Run" by Paul McCartney and Wings

"Bennie and the Jets" by Elton John

"Best Thing That Ever Happened to Me" by Gladys Knight and the Pips

"Come and Get Your Love" by Redbone

"Don't You Worry 'bout a Thing" by Stevie Wonder

"For the Love of Money" by O'Jays

"Goodbye Yellow Brick Road" by Elton John

"Hello It's Me" by Todd Rundgren

"If You Love Me (Let Me Know)" by Olivia Newton-John

"(I've Been) Searchin' So Long" by Chicago

"Just Don't Want To Be Lonely" by Main Ingredient
"Lookin' for a Love" by Bobby Womack
"Mighty Love" by Spinners
"My Mistake (Was to Love You)" by Diana Ross and Marvin
    Gaye
"Never, Never Gonna Give You Up" by Barry White
"Nothing from Nothing" by Billy Preston
"Rock and Roll Heaven" by Righteous Brothers
"Rock the Boat" by Hues Corporation
"Seasons in the Sun" by Terry Jacks
"Show and Tell" by Al Wilson
"Takin' Care of Business" by Bachman-Turner Overdrive
"The Way We Were" by Barbara Streisand
"Then Came You" by Dionne Warwick & the Spinners
"Time in a Bottle" by Jim Croce
"Trying To Hold On To My Woman" by Lamont Dozier
"You Make Me Feel Brand New" by Stylistics

HONORING MY HEROES

William Elvis Rushing, Jr...

Age 87, passed away at home in Chugiak, AK on February 6, 2015. He was born September 2, 1927 in Dearborn, Michigan and most recently moved to Alaska from Holiday, Florida, some five years ago. Previously lived at Mack Lake/Mio, Michigan. Bill served in the United States Navy, WWII, His ashes were taken to Fort Richardson Military Cemetery JBER Alaska

Bill was a **Detroit Police Officer from 1949-1973 retiring as a detective/sergeant**.

He is survived by sister Joann (Jerry) Towner, brother John (Helen) Rushing, Daughter Linda F. Rushing (David), Son Larry W. Rushing (Jill), and 10 grandchildren.

He was preceded in death by wife Barbara, father William E. Rushing (Helen), mother Sarah Rushing and sister Dorothy Rushing.

He was 42 years old when he saved me from death's door by calling an ambulance and helping to apprehend my husband, Vic, who was the lone gunman. Though I was unconscious at the time, I was thanking God first and the cavalry second. He was one of the good guys. Thank you, Det/Sgt Rushing, for being there when I needed you the most and you never gave up on my behalf.

William Elvis Rushing, Jr.

Det/Sgt William Rushing, Jr.
Det/Sgt Robert Williams
TMU Emmett Armstrong
TMU Ralph Craig
Officer Curtis Bell
Officer James Brown

MY QUOTES TO REMEMBER

"Women, remember this: "There is a potential abuser for each one of us. Be aware of your surroundings and the harm he means to do." 11-6-18

"An abuser thinks he has control, but he is actually losing control, of his mind."   11-16-19

"Abuse can never end too soon." 11-16-19

"Abuse is not a victimless crime. Stop treating it as such." 11-16-19

"Abuse is never good. It is either bad or worse."   11-16-19

"Abuse is not a fairytale or fiction, but hardcore reality." 11-16-19

BIBLIOGRAPHY

Photos of the circular bed courtesy of James Leo Hemauer

Photo of the Grande Ballroom courtesy of Detroiturbex.com

Photo of the Eastown Theatre courtesy of Sean Doerr.

Copies of the Detroit Police reports courtesy of the Detroit Police Department

Copies of the Dearborn Police reports courtesy of the Dearborn Police Department

FAMOUS LAST WORDS

His last words: "If I can't have you, no one else can"

My last words: "Though the abuser was a nefarious man, the victim made good out of his evil deed. I am a survivor."